The Travels of Peter Kalm, Finnish-Swedish Naturalist, Through Colonial North America, 1748-1751

On the cover:

Illustration by Bernadette Wolf of mountain laurel, *Kalmia latifolia,* named by Linnaeus for Kalm.

Copy of a map drawn by Lewis Evans for Kalm in 1750. Kalm's journey from Raccoon to Cap aux Oyes in Canada is shown by a thick, broken line; his journey from Albany to Niagara by a dotted line. (Library of Congress)

The Travels of Peter Kalm, Finnish-Swedish Naturalist, Through Colonial North America, 1748-1751

Paula Ivaska Robbins

PURPLE MOUNTAIN PRESS
Fleischmanns, New York

The Travels of Peter Kalm,
Finnish-Swedish Naturalist,
Through Colonial North America, 1748-1751

First edition, 2007
Published by Purple Mountain Press, Lld.
P.O. Box 309, Fleischmanns, New York 12430-0309
845-254-4062, 845-254-4476 (fax), purple@catskill.net
http://www.catskill.net/purple

ISBN-13: 978-1-930098-80-0

Library of Congress Control Number: 2007927135

Manufactured in the United States of America on acid-free paper

Contents

PREFACE

PETER KALM IS NOT A FAMILIAR NAME to most people in the United States and Canada. Some of those who do recognize his name know him as a visitor to the British and French colonies in the mid-1700s who collected plants and animals for the Swedish naturalist Carl Linnaeus. More might recall his name because *Kalmia*, a spring-time flowering shrub commonly known as mountain laurel, is named for him. Few have read his *Travels into North America*, and fewer still the original Swedish version, *En resa til Norra America*, published in three volumes from 1753 to 1761. Until now, except for specialists in colonial American history, almost no one knew Kalm's insightful account of the cultural and political setting he found during his travels to the New World from 1748 until 1751. Happily, Peter Kalm is about to become much better known, thanks to Paula Robbins's biography.

The appearance of the first general-interest biography of Peter Kalm in English coincides with the 2007 celebration of Linnaeus's birth in 1707. The Linnaean tercentenary brings renewed attention to Linnaeus's key work, *Species plantarum*, published in 1753. It was in that two-volume book that Linnaeus summarized all the plants he knew, and in so doing, he established the modern system of botanical nomenclature. The importance of Kalm's contributions to Linnaeus's understanding of American plants is being underscored additionally by publication of a summary by the Linnaean Plant Name Typification Project at The Natural History Museum in London, started in 1981 in cooperation with the Linnean Society of London.

Kalm was not the first naturalist to visit America, but as a student of Linnaeus's, and one who provided his mentor with nearly 400 dried herbarium specimens, he was foremost in terms of the temperate North American flora. Before Kalm, such naturalists as John Banister, Mark Catesby and John Clayton gathered American plants, mainly in Virginia and the Carolinas. Linnaeus briefly saw some Catesby specimens while at the University of Oxford in 1736, but basically he knew both Banister and Catesby's plants from published illustrations. Only Clayton's dried herbarium specimens were available to Linnaeus prior to Kalm's visit.

By collecting from Pennsylvania northward, Kalm added considerably to Linnaeus's own collection of dried plant specimens.

Kalm played another role that was significant to the publication of *Species plantarum* in 1753, for it was Kalm's desire to publish his journal with correct scientific names of plants that spurred Linnaeus to complete his survey of all plants in the world. Depression, illness, and other duties had prevented him from finishing the task started in 1746. Taking up his manuscript again to add the numerous new species found by Kalm proved to be the impetus for Linnaeus's completion of the one book that would forever change systematic biology and the way the scientific world names all living things.

The life and times of Peter Kalm were challenging. In many respects he failed in the primary goal of his travels to introduce into Finland and Sweden American plants that would be a boon to the local economy. He was intimidated by Linnaeus (as were others, both students and fellow naturalists) so, as a result, he relied on his "Master" to name and describe his new discoveries. The "Prince of Botany," as Linnaeus called himself, would have expected nothing less. Perhaps, given Kalm's duties once back in Europe, this was for the best, as Linnaeus had the time and resources to do the work; Kalm did not. Perhaps too, had Kalm published his own results, the modern era of botanical nomenclature would have been delayed and Kalm's names would be little more than a minor curiosities in history. As events unfolded, the dried specimens gathered by Kalm would become a principal source of our modern understanding of the plants of northeastern North America.

Today, one can visit the Linnean Society at Burlington House in London and examine the actual Kalm specimens used by Linnaeus to name many of his American plants. For me, it is a bit humbling to touch a leaf or examine a flower collected by Kalm in the wilds of America, brought to Europe, and studied by Linnaeus. It is a reminder that most of my knowledge of American plants is based, to a considerable degree, on the efforts of others who lived generations ago in a time and under circumstances I hardly can comprehend. Now, in this book, one can gain a feeling for the man, Peter Kalm, and not just admire the surviving dried plant specimens he labored to bring to the Master.

JAMES L. REVEAL
PROFESSOR EMERITUS, UNIVERSITY OF MARYLAND
HONORARY CURATOR, THE NEW YORK BOTANICAL GARDEN

Introduction and Acknowledgments

ALTHOUGH I WAS BORN IN THE UNITED STATES, my parents were both born in Finland. I spoke Finnish before I learned English and was brought up to be proud of my Finnish heritage.

I first became aware of Peter Kalm at the annual Finnish-American festival, FinnFest, held each year in a different American city. In 2000, in celebration of the millennium, FinnFest was a joint Canadian-American effort and was held in Toronto. One of the sessions was presented by a Canadian-Finnish historian, Mauri A. Jalava, who spoke about Kalm. Afterward, I picked up a copy of his article, "Peter Kalm: First Contact (1749-1750)" in the *Journal of Finnish Studies*. Kalm was of particular interest to me because my second cousin, Ari Ivaska, is a professor of analytical chemistry at Åbo Akademi. Ari teaches at the newer university in the same place and with the same name as that to which Kalm returned from America in 1751 to become professor of economics and natural history. After the great fire of Turku, the original Åbo Akademi was moved to the new Russian capital, and the name was changed to the University of Helsinki.

Shortly before FinnFest 2000, I had retired and moved to Asheville, North Carolina, where I became a volunteer docent at the North Carolina Arboretum. Volunteers are treated well by the Arboretum staff, and I was able to attend many classes, improving my knowledge of horticulture and botany. I also learned about many of the noted botanists who had visited the Carolinas, including Philadelphia's John and William Bartram.

I had always been interested in American history and had written a historical novel, *Nights of Summer, Nights of Autumn,* about my Finnish grandmother, which necessitated a study of Finnish history. With all of these cross-sections of interest, a book about Kalm's travels in America seemed like an appropriate project.

I was surprised to learn that a biography of Kalm had never been written in English for an American audience, despite the fact that his journal is frequently quoted as a source in books about colonial history. Such a book would require a command of Swedish, English, Finnish and French as well as knowledge of the history of Finland-Sweden, the American colonies, and of botany—which may account for this surprising lack. Such a person is likely to be rare indeed. Without knowledge of Swedish, I could not claim to write a definitive biography of Kalm. However, because I had at least an amateur's background in botany, American and Swedish history, and a reading knowledge of English, Finnish, and French, I felt able to write about Kalm's central claim to fame: The journal of his travels in America.

Fortunately, Kalm's *Resa til Nord Amerka* and a number of his scientific articles on botanical topics had been translated into English. However, because of my lack of command of Swedish, I was unable to read *En Resa til Norra Amerika* in the original; nor could I translate any of Kalm's letters to Linnaeus, edited and published by J. M. Hulth in 1922; or to Bielke, edited by Carl Skottsberg and published in 1960; to Mennander, edited and published by Otto Hjelt in 1914, or any of the unpublished letters in old Swedish to the Royal Swedish Academy and other Swedish correspondents. Nor have I read Carl Skottsberg's 1951 biography of Kalm written for the Royal Swedish Academy of Sciences. Another gap is the 1977 edition of Kalm's account of his journey to the Swedish southwestern provinces of Västgötaland and Bohuslänk, edited by Claes Krantz and illustrated by Gunnar Brusewitz. Most of these books are only available in a Swedish or Finnish library and have long been out of print.

I have had some wonderful volunteer help, however. My Norwegian friend, Randi Nordmo, who is married to a Swedish executive of Volvo in North Carolina, kindly translated, with the help of her in-laws, Kalm's financial records of his American journey published by Bengt Hildebrand in 1956. Professor Roland Thorstensson, of Gustavus Adolphus College in Minnesota, was kind enough to read my early manuscript and Kalm's letters to Linnaeus, available on the Internet. In addition to providing the translation, he was able to recommend certain passages that would be useful to my work.

In the fall of 2003, I drove from Asheville to Teaneck, New Jersey, to attend my fiftieth high school reunion. On the way, I planned to spend a day in Philadelphia visiting Bartram's Garden, knowing that Kalm had spent much time there. I contacted Joel Fry, the curator, to set up an appointment, and he said that he would be happy to see me. Fry mentioned that he had just that past week attended an initial planning meeting at the American-Swedish Historical Museum in Philadelphia for their celebration of the tricentennial of the birth of Linnaeus in 2007. Kalm's name was mentioned several times. He suggested that I contact Richard Waldron, then the director of the museum. I did, and spent a delightful morning visiting with him. Because Kalm was the link between Linnaeus and Philadelphia, Waldron enthusiastically encouraged me to continue with my project. The next spring, I was invited to attend a two-day meeting funded by the National Endowment for the Humanities to plan for a traveling Linnaeus exhibition. There I met a number of Linnaeus experts, including Gina Douglas of the Linnaean Society of London, Annika Windahl Pontén, director of the Linnaeus Project at Uppsala University, and Karen Reeds, the guest curator of the Linnaeus Tricentennial Exhibition at the Museum, who have all been most helpful.

The following year, I was invited to give a paper at the museum for a celebration of Linnaeus's birthday. Karen Reeds provided a great many suggestions of sources about Linnaeus and Kalm and hosted an overnight stay at her home in Princeton, New Jersey. I also enjoyed the gracious hospitality of Phyllis Cole, professor of American Studies at Pennsylvania State University at Delaware County. Phyllis kindly drove me to see one of the earliest log cabins from New Sweden still standing in the Philadelphia area. She has been an unfailing supporter of my project, having herself been an independent scholar working outside a university to complete the highly-praised scholarly biography of Mary Moody Emerson.

In the fall of 2005, I received a generous travel grant from the Finlandia Foundation that enabled me to visit Uppsala, Sweden; Turku and Helsinki, Finland; and London. In Uppsala, I was a guest in a lovely bed and breakfast run for visiting scholars in the large and beautiful home of Elisabeth Kjellström. Annika Windahl Pontén was most gracious in pointing me to the appropriate people and places as well as entertaining me for dinner in her home. I spent a delightful two hours with Eva Björn, curator of the Linnémuseet, who gave me a personal tour of the museum. Mariette Manktelow, a botanist on the staff of Uppsala University, drove me to visit Linnaeus's farms at Hammarby and Sävja, as well as Sten Carl Bielke's estate at Lövsta. At Hammarby and Lövsta, we tramped around the grounds, identifying a number of plants that likely were the descendents of ones that had been planted in the eighteenth century by Linnaeus or by Kalm. Mariette also pointed out to me the routes of several of Linnaeus's botanical walks and Kalm's seven-mile walk from Lövsta to Uppsala. Malin Erickson, a landscape student at Uppsala University, shared with me her project researching how the gardens at Lövsta had been set up during the seven years that Kalm lived there from 1741 to 1748 by reading all of Kalm's and Bielke's correspondence during that period.

In Turku, I was provided gracious hospitality by my cousin, Ari Ivaska and his wife Outi, who also drove me to visit several sites frequented by Kalm in and around the city. I was able to see the inside of St. Mary's Church, where Kalm was memorialized by a plaque on the wall to the right of the altar.

Arno Kasvi and Matti Yli-Rekola of the Botanical Garden of Turku at Ruissalo drove me to see Kalm's summer garden, his "little America" at Seipsalo, Maanpää, on Hirvensalo Island. Arno Kasvi pointed out the eighteenth century buildings on the property where Kalm stayed and indicated plants that were likely descendants of those tended there by Kalm. Kasvi also followed up on my query regarding Kalm's place of burial by stopping at the central office of the Turku area churches to obtain the information that Kalm was buried at St. Mary's church, where he had been the vicar. My cousin's wife followed up with a phone call to Riikka Kaisti, of the church staff, who informed her that Kalm was probably buried beneath the floor of the church.

While in Turku, I attended the conference, "Thinking Through the Environment," sponsored jointly by Turku University and Åbo Akademi, where I gave a session on Kalm's reports on Native Americans. The conference director, Timo Myllyntaus, was most helpful in directing me to sources of Kalm information. At the conference, I met a doctoral candidate, Seija Niemi, who was later helpful in looking up the answers to several questions that I had about Kalm's family. She found the dates of birth of Margaretha Kalm's two children, one of whom was Peter Kalm's only son, Pehr Gabriel. I also met Anto Leikola, professor emeritus of history of science at the University of Helsinki, who delivered a most interesting talk on Kalm. Markku Löytönen, professor and vice-dean for research with the department of geography at the University of Helsinki, and the author of a children's book on Kalm, was another fellow participant in the conference. Professor Leikola and I later met in Helsinki, where he conducted an interesting tour of the University Museum.

In Helsinki, my cousin Pirkko Castrén and her husband, Lauri, provided gracious hospitality in their lovely old home on the shore in Espoo and chauffeured me to various places of interest. In the special collections at the University of Helsinki Library I was able to go through several of Kalm's original journals written in his tiny neat hand.

The high point of my brief stay in England was a day spent with Professor Emeritus William Mead of the department of geography at the University of London, with whom I followed Kalm's footsteps on his visit to the Chilterns, thanks to our chauffeur, William Willett. Bill Mead also provided a most delicious picnic lunch which we happily consumed amidst a flock of sheep with a lovely view of the Chiltern Hills. I also spent an afternoon at the Chelsea Physic Garden, where Kalm had spent much time. At the Linnean Society's offices I was able to see one of the dried specimens from Linnaeus's herbarium.

My research would have been impossible without the resources of the libraries of the University of North Carolina system and particularly the University of North Carolina at Asheville Library, which I have been able to use through my connection as a volunteer instructor at the North Carolina Center for Creative Retirement. I have also obtained copies of many manuscripts from Karen Reeds, Margaretha Talerman, and others at the American Swedish Historical Museum. The internet has been a wonderful resource, especially the Linnaean Correspondence and resource material about specific plants and their scientific names. Joel Fry, curator of Bartram's Garden, also directed me to several sources. I am also extremely grateful to the late Esther Larsen, who translated many of Kalm's articles on American topics in the *Transactions of the Swedish Royal Society.*

A number of people were willing to read and comment on the manuscript. I am particularly grateful to Karen Reeds and to Kalevi Ahonen of the Department of History of the University of Jyväskylä, who caught many of my errors. Professor Mead, who has been a strong supporter of the project, read an early version. Professor James Reveal read through the entire manuscript and also made many valuable suggestions; he was invaluable in pointing out botanical information that I had missed. Mike Winslow, staff scientist for the Lake Champlain Committee in Burlington, Vermont, provided useful information about Kalm's route to Canada and corrected some of the botanical names of plants mentioned by Kalm. Joel Fry also read and commented on chapters, as did Richard Waldron. Else-Marie Fänge sent me a copy of her late husband's introduction to *The Biology of Hagfishes*, describing Kalm's discovery in Grimstad, Norway of this unusual primitive vertebrate. Craig Williams of the New York State Archives and Margaretha Talerman of the American Swedish Historical Museum were very helpful in finding appropriate illustrations. I thank all of these people and more, who are unnamed, who made this book possible.

CHAPTER ONE
Linnaeus's Vision

HIS TYPICAL SCANDINAVIAN RETICENCE could not have kept the 33-year-old Peter Kalm from exclamations of joy when on September 14, 1748, he saw the banks of the Delaware River from the deck of the *Mary Gally*. His whole life had been a preparation for this moment. With delight he scanned, between the stands of fine oak, hickory and pine, "some farmhouses surrounded with grain fields, pastures well-stocked with cattle, and meadows covered with fine hay."[1]

Now he could finally begin the task assigned him so many, many months ago by the Royal Swedish Academy of Sciences and by his mentor, Carl Linné,[2] professor of medicine, natural history and botany at Uppsala University. (We know him by the Latin name he chose for himself, Carolus Linnaeus.) The great professor convinced fellow members of the academy to support Kalm, one of his favorite students, on a journey of exploration to North America. Linnaeus had helped to found the academy nearly ten years before, and his recommendation carried much weight.

In Sweden, the European Enlightenment had manifested itself in the early half of the eighteenth century with an emphasis on utility. Scientific and intellectual endeavors were to be directed to efforts that would be useful, and the natural scientists of the universities were to undertake investigations that would lead toward improvement of the economy. All things in nature, the Swedish Lutheran theologians declared, had been created by God for the benefit and use of man. They believed that their nation had vast hidden natural resources and opportunities for using them. All that was needed was for scientists to find them and direct their use. Once they did that, there would be no limits to the possible economic growth of Sweden.[3]

The goal of Kalm's journey to America was to describe the natural products of that part of the world and to find and introduce to Sweden such useful plants as might be expected to thrive in the harsh climate of Scandinavia. It was still believed that climate throughout the world was the same at equal levels of latitude, so that it would be easy to adapt plants found in the corresponding latitude of the French and English colonies of North America for cultivation in Sweden. Linnaeus presented to the royal court and to the Swedish Academy the prospect of "Lapland cinnamon groves, Baltic tea plantations, and Finnish wild rice paddies."[4]

In 1746, Linnaeus wrote to the Roayal Swedish Academy of Sciences to support Kalm's proposed journey to collect American plants. He explained that the discovery of suitable plants could foster national improvement in Sweden that would be based on peaceful botanical exploration, rather than on expansion of its territory through conquest.

In the mid-seventeenth century, Sweden had once considered herself one of the great powers of Europe.[5] However, because of losses in the Thirty Years' War, famines and the bubonic plague in the 1710s, and Russian invasions in 1719 and 1720, she found her powers greatly diminished.[6] She had lost all of her Baltic colonies except for Finland, Wismar, and Swedish Pomerania during the disastrous reign of King Charles XII.[7] "In 1721 she found herself at the mercy of Russia—and even, perhaps, of Denmark. It was painful to make the mental adjustment required by this new situation; to many it was impossible."[8] The leaders of the nation looked desperately for ways to restore Sweden's previous eminence.

They had looked with envy upon the other great powers of Europe, such as Spain and England, which had enriched themselves with the resources of the New World, from gold to cod to tobacco. By the eighteenth century, England, especially, was prospering because of the commerce from its colonies. The only hope of the Swedes seemed to be in the development of their country's natural resources, material and human, through the support of applied science and the growth of industry.[9]

In Scandinavia, hunger and famine were recurrent problems. Prior to 1800, the marriage, birth, and fertility rates rose and fell in Sweden according to the size of the harvest, and death rates rose dramatically whenever an early frost or other calamity destroyed a harvest.[10] An estimate made in the eighteenth century reported that there had been ten general famines in Europe in the tenth century, twenty-six in the eleventh, two in the twelfth, four in the fourteenth, seven in the fifteenth, thirteen in the sixteenth, eleven in the seventeenth, and sixteen in the eighteenth, in addition to the much greater number of local or regional famines.[11] Scandinavia, because of its short growing season and frequency of summer frosts, was particularly vulnerable. Scurvy was one of the ancient curses of northern Europe because of the lack of fresh fruits and vegetables.[12]

Northern Europeans were still dependent on the crops developed during the Neolithic Period, particularly wheat, barley, rye, and oats. The last three did better in the higher latitudes than wheat, but none of these grains produced a harvest that was as productive or as dependable as the Scandinavians needed to support a growing population, or to advance the complexity and richness of their cultures. Rye, especially, was likely to be affected by molds and fungus in cool, wet weather, and those who ate affected rye bread were likely to suffer from fungal poisoning, such as St. Anthony's Fire, and other disorders.[13]

If Sweden were to regain a prominent position among the nations of Europe, the causes of hunger and famine would have to be overcome. Perhaps plants could be found in other parts of the world that could grow in Scandinavia and add to the diet of the Swedish people.

The so-called Columbian Exchange—-of the life forms of the two biospheres, America and Europe—-altered and improved diets in Europe by introducing American food crops, such as maize, beans, peanuts, cocoa, sweet potatoes, and white potatoes.[14] The potato had been introduced to Sweden and Finland in the 1730s and slowly gained ground over the next two generations, until it would become one of the main crops in northern Europe by the beginning of the nineteenth century.[15] The potato harvest produced several times as much food per unit of land as any grain, including wheat, and could be cultivated in small plots and in a variety of soils and climates.[16] Could there be some other American plant that could grow as successfully in Sweden's harsh climate? If so, it might eliminate Sweden's cycles of famine resulting from crop failures.

Although Linnaeus's primary argument to the Swedish Academy for support of Kalm's journey to North America was the potential economic advantage to the nation, there was also another underlying purpose: to add to the accumulating knowledge about the natural world. Educated people in the eighteenth century had an insatiable curiosity about Nature, and they were eager to find and describe new and different plants and animals. For example, the 44-volume *Histoire Naturelle* of Georges-Louis Leclerc, Comte de Buffon, received more popular attention in France than the literary classics of Voltaire and Rousseau.[17]

In this period of the growth and development of scientific investigation, it was first necessary to discover the breadth and variety of the resources of the natural world and then to organize and categorize it. It was only after that was done that the underlying natural laws could be discovered, according to the empiricism of John Locke.[18]

Until the middle of the eighteenth century, botany was still considered a subdiscipline of medicine. Knowledge of plants and their medicinal properties had been accumulating for centuries, mostly recorded in Greek, Latin, and Arabic, the languages of learning. However, there was no recent adequate arrangement of that knowledge or systematic way to keep track of the names of newly discovered organisms. The problem was that there was no uniformity of names of plants and animals. Names varied according to location and many of the names consisted of long and cumbersome Latin descriptive terms or were based on traditional folk names.[19]

It was Linnaeus's systematic mind that brought order to the rapidly accumulating knowledge of strange plants that resulted from the expansion of European trade to many different parts of the world. Linnaeus grouped his species into genera, genera into artificial orders and classes. His classification system improved upon the previous schemes because it was based upon the sexuality of plants: the number and relative lengths of the stamens and pistils in the flowers. It was a simple system that could be easily learned and thus opened up the study of botany to anyone who wished to pursue it. Although some people considered the system "lewd and licentious" because of Linnaeus's colorful descriptions of flowery virgins and stamens as husbands, their objections were soon overruled.[20]

Linnaeus later defined and recorded the concept of the genus and developed the concept of varieties subordinate to species.[21] In *Species Plantarum*, published in 1753, Linnaeus established the system of binomial nomenclature, by which all plants (and later animals) were given names based on a single generic name and a specific epithet.[22] His scheme of nomenclature was accepted in all countries, and so enabled positive identification of a species anywhere, regardless of innumerable vernacular names. It was a giant leap forward that was crucial in the development of natural science. However, his artificial scheme of arranging plants into arbitrary orders and classes was largely rejected and within forty years was replaced by more "natural" schemes of classification.

LINNAEUS WAS BORN ON MAY 13, 1707, at Råshult in the parish of Stenbrohult in Småland, Sweden;[23] two years later, the family moved to Stenbrohult, where his father, Nils, became a parish pastor. Nils Linné was a gardener and amateur botanist and instilled his love of plants in his young son. Although his parents wanted him to study for the Lutheran ministry, it was clear that their son's interests lay in botany, and he was permitted to study medicine, which, at that time, included the study of medicinal herbs. He studied medicine and botany for a year at the university at Lund, and in 1728 transferred to Uppsala University, where he was soon mentored by several influential faculty members, including Anders Celsius, the inventor of the centigrade thermometer, and Olof Rudbeck the younger, who appointed him to a position as lecturer in the Botanical Garden while he was still a student.[24] In 1732, Linnaeus took a five-month trip to Lapland to collect the plants that he found there, resulting in the publication of *Flora Lapponica*, in which he described many hitherto unknown plants.

In 1735, he fell in love with Sara Lisa Moraea, the 18-year-old daughter of a wealthy physician, who would only consent to the marriage of his daughter if Linnaeus could demonstrate that he could support her with a thriving medical practice. Therefore, Linnaeus traveled to the Netherlands, where the most prestigious medical degrees could be obtained. There he rather quickly received the degree of doctor of medicine at the University of Hardevijk.

Netherlands was also a center of botanical knowledge. After obtaining his degree, Linnaeus traveled on to Leiden, where he became acquainted with several wealthy patrons who supported him financially in his research and writing on botanical subjects. One of Linnaeus's most important patrons there, Dr. Johan Fredrich Gronovius, paid for the publication of the work that made Linnaeus famous, *Systema Naturae*. In it, he described his sexual classification system of plants.

Gardening was a popular pursuit among Europeans of wealth, and they vied with each other to find and grow unusual plants. This appetite for growing exotic plants was whetted by the discoveries of various explorers in the Americas, Africa and Asia who brought back seeds of exotic plants. One of the leading Dutch scientists, Herman Boerhaave, wrote, "practically no captain, whether of a merchant ship or a man-of-war, left our harbours without special instructions to collect everywhere seeds, roots, cuttings, and shrubs and bring them back to Holland."[25]

Linnaeus moved next to Amsterdam, where he met Professor Johannes Burman, the superintendent of the botanical garden there, who supported Linnaeus while he helped Burman describe plants that he had obtained from Ceylon. In the autumn of 1735, a director of the Dutch East India Company, Georg Clifford, persuaded Linnaeus to supervise his botanical garden, adding new plants that Linnaeus obtained from other gardens in Holland. At Clifford's expense, Linnaeus spent July 1736 in England, where he met many of the members of the Royal Society of London, as well as the head of the Botanical Garden in Oxford, Professor Johannes Jacob Dillenius, and Phillip Miller, the director of the Society of Apothecaries' Physic Garden in Chelsea. At Chelsea, Linnaeus was allowed the run of the Physic Garden. Miller gave him many plants and dried specimens to take back with him to Holland.[26]

In October 1737, Linnaeus left Clifford's garden and spent six months again in Leiden with Professor Adriann van Royen and with the surgeon, Herman Boerhaave. He then went to Paris, where he visited Professor Anton de Jussieu, who showed him the gardens and herbaria of Paris. While there, Linnaeus was accepted as a correspondent by the French Royal Academy of Sciences.

Apparently, Linnaeus made an unfavorable first impression on the people whom he met because he tended to boast about himself. Soon, though, his listeners realized that his boasts were justified.[27] In the three years that Linnaeus spent in the Netherlands, he had published fourteen books or pamphlets.[28] Linnaeus's ability was so well recognized in all the cities of Europe that he received numerous offers of employment, but he chose, instead, to return to his native Sweden to marry Sara Lisa Moræa. The wedding finally took place in 1739 after Linnaeus had established himself as a physician specializing in the treatment of patients with venereal disease.[29]

During his visits to England and France, Linnaeus had been impressed by the usefulness of their scientific academies: the Royal Society of London, founded in 1660, and the French Royal Academy of Sciences, founded a few months later. In 1739, soon after his return to Sweden, Linnaeus was one of the six founders of the Swedish Royal Academy of Sciences.[30] The foundation of the Academy of Sci-

Right: Portrait of Carl Linné; Gustaf Lundberg, 1753. (Linnémuseet, Uppsala, Sweden)

Below: Gustavianum of Uppsala University. (Photo by the author)

Facing page, top: Linnaeus's garden plan. (Linnémuseet, Uppsala, Sweden)

Left column, top: Linnaeus's house in Uppsala. (Photo by the author)

Middle: Linnaeus's garden in Uppsala is still laid out according to his sexual system. (Photo by the author)

Bottom and right column: Linnaeus' farm at Hammarby, where he spent summers and where he showed plants from his collections to students. (Photos by the author)

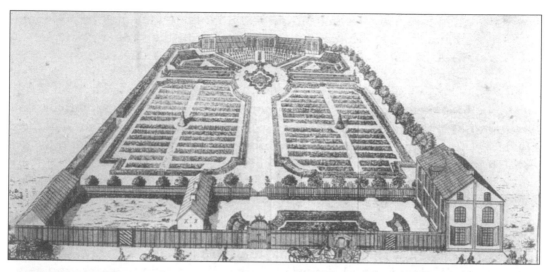

ences provided Sweden with an institution that facilitated the making and main-
tenance of contacts and the interchange of ideas with the similar academies in
other countries. In certain fields, Sweden could actually offer assistance to other
European nations, so that the transfer of knowledge was no longer only one
way.[31]

In May 1741, Linnaeus became professor of medicine at Uppsala, with respon-
sibility for botany and natural history as well as for care of the botanical garden.
He became a popular teacher; students thronged to the anatomical amphitheater
at the top of the Gustavianum building when he gave his public lectures. Botany
had not been a lecture subject for some time, and, in addition, Linnaeus was a
lively and interesting teacher who captivated his students.

Each year at the end of the spring semester, Linnaeus conducted "herbationes," walks through the countryside near the farm at Hammarby that he purchased in 1758, during which he pointed out plants along the way. They took
place every Wednesday and Saturday during the growing season, and large
groups of students followed along. Linnaeus had a number of set routes that he
chose according to the time of year and the interesting plants that were likely to
be seen along the way. As the group encountered a new plant, the Master would
give its name and anatomical description along with any folklore about the plant
and its uses. On the way back to the University, the students, and even some foreign visitors and ladies who came along, played music on trumpets and drums
and sang songs. At the end of the walk Linnaeus was thanked with a cheer, "Vivat
Linnaeus!"[32]

Linnaeus attracted many brilliant young men to his circle, some of whom
became what he termed his "apostles." He praised them lavishly and helped
them to find scholarships and positions. However, he demanded loyalty in
return. According to Sten Lindroth, "Linnaeus among his disciples was also a dic-
tator among his subjects, the ruler of slaves. Woe betide the young Linnaean who
did not swear by the writings of the master, who was not orthodox; the adepts
must be drilled in the true botanical faith."[33]

Linnaeus sent the best of his apostles on extensive voyages of discovery. With
his new means for identifying plants it would be possible to organize plants from
all over the world that they brought back to him. He helped to arrange and to
finance such journeys for nineteen of his students between 1745 and the year of
his death, 1778. Linnaeus's arguments were so convincing that he was able to gain
free passage for his apostles on ships sailing to foreign lands and funding from
various public and semi-public institutions, as well as private patrons.[34]

Two of Linnaeus's apostles, Daniel Carl Solander and Anders Sparrman,
accompanied Captain Cook on his circumnavigations of the world to such places
as Tahiti, New Zealand, and Australia—Solander on the first, and Sparrman on
the second. Carl Peter Thunberg visited Japan as a ship's surgeon for the Dutch

East India Company. Pehr Löfling explored in Spain and Spanish South America. Pehr Forsskål accompanied a Danish royal expedition through the Ottoman Empire and the Arabian Peninsula. Johan Petter Falck explored the Caucasus, Kazan and western Siberia. Five of the disciples, unfortunately, perished in their attempts, although one or two may have been ill before they left Sweden.[35] After his first disciple to go abroad died, leaving a grieving widow, Linnaeus insisted that all others had to be unmarried.

Peter Kalm was one of the lucky ones who survived.

CHAPTER TWO
The Perfect Candidate

IN CHOOSING APOSTLES to send abroad in search of new plants, Linnaeus preferred those of his students who were "young, penniless bachelors, sleeping as well on the hardest bench as on the softest bed." But, he continued, should they "find a little plant or moss, the longest road wouldn't be too long."[1] Before his students left for foreign shores, Linnaeus issued detailed orders and instructions as to what they were to accomplish. They seemed to have followed those orders faithfully. It was important, according to Linnaeus, to send a young man before it was too late. "Now is the time, another time he will be heavy-footed, lazy, and comfortable, and too fat to run like a hunting dog in the forests."[2]

Peter Kalm, one of the first of Linnaeus's apostles to journey abroad, was a perfect candidate, fulfilling all of the qualifications. Linnaeus wrote of him, "He has all the requirements one could wish for in one person for the carrying out of such a task, for he is strong in health, was brought up in poverty, is equally satisfied with bad as with good food, and has thus grown up able to stand whatever may befall; his keenness on plants, animals and stones is so great that he will run miles to get a single moss."[3]

According to a fellow apostle, Kalm was "tall and towering and with a manly and agreeable countenance."[4] He also possessed that special untranslatable Finnish characteristic called *sisu*, an ability to doggedly stick to a goal no matter how difficult the task.

Colonial New York official and amateur naturalist Cadwallader Colden commended Kalm's "zeal in the pursuit of knowledge" in a February, 1751 letter to Linnaeus, as Kalm was preparing to return to Sweden from America. On the return from his arduous trip to Niagara Falls, "Mr. Kalm was so industrious that I could not persuade him to stay above one night at my house in the Country tho' the fatigues he underwent seem'd to require his taking some ease & refreshment."

Further, wrote Colden, "Kalm has so much more knowledge in Botany & in natural history than any in this Country can pretend to & he has been so industrious & has undergon(e) such great difficulties in traveling through a great part of this vast Forest & risqued such dangers to his person from its savage inhabitants.[5]

PETER WAS BORN PETTER KALM ON MARCH 1, 1716, in Angermanland, then in the Swedish Province of Västerbotten, six weeks before the death of his father, Gabriel Kalm, who had been the parish minister at Närpiö (Närpes), in Ostrobothnia (Osterbotten), on the Finnish coast of the Gulf of Bothnia. The family fled to Sweden, as did many other members of the clergy and the Swedish-speaking upper classes, when Russian troops occupied Finland during the Great Northern War (1710-1721).

Finland had been a part of the Swedish kingdom for more than 400 years, and by the seventeenth century, Finland had become, not a subject province, but an integral part of the kingdom. Its inhabitants were "native Swedes" in the eyes of the law, possessing the same rights and privileges as were enjoyed by the inhabitants of the Swedish part of the kingdom. The governing and educated classes, like the Kalms, spoke Swedish, whereas the small farmers and landless laborers spoke Finnish. Men of this lower class were often forced to serve as conscripts in the Swedish military.

After the peace treaty of Uusikaupunki (Nystad) in 1721, the Russians withdrew, leaving much of the sparsely-populated countryside devastated and the Finnish-speaking population in dire poverty. The soldiers burned many properties, and fields had lain fallow for the duration of the fighting, nearly eight years. Widespread crop failures added to the misery of the people. Many of the menfolk had been killed in the war. Bread dough was stretched with ground bark to stave off hunger pangs. The population of Finland had declined from almost a half million to less than 300,000 people.[6]

After the war ended, Gabriel Kalm's widow, neé Catharina Ross, returned to Finland with her five-year-old son to live in a small dilapidated house that she owned in the village of Rökiö in the parish of Vöyri. They lived near Vaasa, where her father, Herman Ross, had been a merchant. The Ross family, its roots in Scotland, had immigrated to Finland in the 1620s.[7]

As a young man, Petter had to grow up quickly to assume the role of man of the house. His mother must have held up the education and accomplishments of his father and his grandfather as a goal that he must also attain. He learned the Lutheran catechism and the fear of a stern and righteous God. He must have learned early on to expect little in terms of material goods or luxuries and to work hard and to persevere against all odds.

Although Kalm grew up in poverty, his paternal uncle and cousin, both clergymen, financed his education. Throughout his youth and early manhood, he was the recipient of help from those more affluent and of higher station than he. Petter must have learned from his mother how to behave in such a way as to gain their approval. This knack was essential in this extremely hierarchical society in which one's success in life was determined by one's connections and birth, and not necessarily by merit. Men of obscure origins could rise to high positions, but they needed patrons and sponsors to do so. In that monarchical and rank-conscious age, patrons were often looking for bright young men, and when they found them, they were eager to bring them along. Patronizing inferiors and creating obligations was considered an important mark of an aristocrat.[8]

Kalm became a student at Finland's only university, Åbo Akademi in Åbo (later known by the Finnish name, Turku), in 1735. The university had been founded in 1640, primarily for the education of clergymen to serve the state-supported Lutheran religion of the Swedish kingdom. Because of the geographical separation of Finland from the Swedish mainland, it was not possible for many Finnish students to study in Sweden. The university became an oasis of new ideas in this remote and impoverished corner of northern Europe that was still primarily a backward area of small-scale subsistence farming, hunting, trapping and fishing. It was at Åbo Akademi that the idea of a Finnish fatherland and the sense of a separate Finnish nationality would first develop.[9]

The young man's family had certainly hoped that he would follow in his father's footsteps and study theology to become a Lutheran minister. However, in addition to his religious studies, Kalm also attended the lectures of several professors who had an interest in experimental natural sciences. Kalm learned to distinguish different rocks and minerals and to carefully record his observations of natural phenomena.[10]

Because of the young student's ability and keen interest, Professor Johan Browallius introduced Kalm to Baron Sten Carl Bielke, who had proposed Browallius' appointment to teach at Åbo Akademi. Bielke, only seven years older

The manor house at Lövsta, where Kalm lived and worked for seven years.
(Photo by the author)

than Kalm, was one of the founders of the Royal Swedish Academy of Sciences (along with Linnaeus), and shared his ideas about the importance of botanical exploration for economic growth. Bielke had been appointed an associate judge in the Court of Appeal in Turku (Åbo) in 1737, which required him to spend a large part of each year in Finland.[11] He kept his close connection with the members of the academy, however, and maintained a strong interest in botany.

In 1740, Bielke invited Kalm to live as supervisor of his estate, Lövsta, in Funbo parish, about seven miles from Uppsala, Sweden. This invitation was doubly fortunate for Kalm, because, in addition to providing a way to earn a living, it meant he could avoid conscription into another disastrous war with Russia, "The Lesser Wrath," that raged across Finland from 1740 to 1743.[12]

Bielke clearly saw the young Kalm as the sort of man needed to carry out the botanical explorations envisioned by the members of the Royal Academy and was determined to prepare him for that task. It was Bielke who suggested that he change his first name to Pehr, which he did soon after writing the first letter that we have from him to Linnaeus, dated 1742 and signed "Petter Kalm."[13] At his own expense, Bielke sent Kalm on expeditions to discover plants and animals.[14] Venturing into the sparsely occupied lands of forests, lakes, rivers and bogs in Finland and Sweden required many skills and a strong physical constitution. Kalm had to learn to use the Finnish *puukko* or sheath knife to cut his way through thick vegetation. He subsisted on whatever food was available and became inured to the attacks of swarms of gnats and mosquitoes—a foretaste of the mosquitoes, gnats and wood lice he would encounter in America.

On December 5, 1740, at Bielke's expense, Kalm became a student at the almost 300-year-old University of Uppsala, walking seven miles each way to attend lectures. His route took him through the flat fields of barley, rye and oats growing in the rich farmland district north of the city. On his return, he still had to tend to his duties on the estate.

Linnaeus became professor of medicine at Uppsala in the autumn of 1741, less than a year after Kalm began to study there. Kalm was already familiar with Linnaeus's writings, which he had read, along with other books on natural science and economics in Bielke's extensive library. Bielke encouraged Kalm to meet his friend. In a letter to Bielke, Kalm describes several unsuccessful attempts to meet Linnaeus at his home near the University, just a block away from the Fyris River and not far from the spires of the Uppsala Cathedral. Finally they met, and Kalm spoke in the most flattering terms of his desire to learn from the master. Linnaeus was immediately drawn to the young man. He offered to teach him privately in his demonstration room on the second floor of his house, along with the select private students who paid a fee.[15] Kalm also attended many of Linnaeus's public lectures.

Kalm concentrated on studies of botany in preparation for the travels that

The cathedral of Uppsala and university buildings. (Photo by the author)

Bielke envisioned for him. To learn as much as he could, he read many travel books and many of the botanical works of the leading European scientists.[16] Kalm received private instructions from Professor Anders Celsius on how to calculate latitude and other useful astronomical information. In 1742, Kalm traveled with his patron Bielke through Bohuslän, and in 1745 to Västergötland in Sweden, receiving advice beforehand from Linnaeus and Celsius. His account of those travels and the plants that were described, "Vestgötha och Bohuslän," was published in 1746. In 1743, Kalm visited the archipelago on both sides of Stockholm, in Roslagen and Södermanland. His findings were incorporated into Linnaeus's *Flora Svecia*, published in 1744. Kalm worked closely with Linnaeus, assisting him in the preparation of his publications and copying some of his unpublished works, which he sometimes shared with Bielke.[17]

In 1744, Kalm accompanied Bielke on a journey of exploration through Russia, to Moscow and to part of the Ukraine. In St. Petersburg, they met with Johann E. Siegesbeck, who had written an article in 1737 opposing Linnaeus's methods because of his reference to the sexuality of plants. Siegesbeck had written that such "loathsome harlotry as several males to one female would not have been permitted in the vegetable kingdom by the Creator." In payment for this remark, Linnaeus named a low, ill-smelling weed *Siegesbeckia*.[18]

At Lövsta, Kalm continued as supervisor of Bielke's estate and overseer of the expansion of his cultivated land.[19] Kalm lived at the estate from 1741 to 1747, and, under Bielke's supervision, he planted approximately 150 different plants, mostly grasses, but also herbs, trees and bushes and even ornamentals like tulips.[20] The farm was located in an area that in recent geologic time had been a bay that was an arm of the Gulf of Bothnia; the soil was hard clay that was still too wet and heavy to use for growing grain and was low in nutrients. Therefore, Bielke and Kalm used the land for grazing and to produce hay. They experimented on ways to improve the soil and to promote the growth of various grasses that might provide better fodder for farm animals. One of the routes of Linnaeus's "herbationes" was to Lövsta, where the master could point out the results of their experimentation.[21]

From the gardens of St. Petersburg and Moscow Kalm and Bielke had brought back the seeds of a number of Asiatic plants that might grow in Sweden, including clovers, licorice root, gentian, the larch, and the Siberian pine.[22] However, they realized that obtaining seeds was not enough; it was necessary to learn the conditions under which a particular plant grew in its native environment. At Lövsta, Kalm could oversee the cultivation of these plants and report on their growth to Bielke, who was often away in Stockholm or performing his judicial duties in Åbo.

From as early as 1741, Bielke, Linnaeus and Celsius were discussing possible journeys that Kalm could undertake. Under consideration were trips of exploration and collecting to Iceland, Siberia, Greenland, China and South Africa. In August 1744, Linnaeus first proposed North America. The goal was always to send Kalm to an area where he would be most likely to find plants that would serve a utilitarian purpose back home. There were thoughts of raising the wild rice of Canada in the many marshes and lakes of Sweden and Finland. Martin Triewald, one of the founders of the Royal Academy, had already experimented with growing mulberry trees for possible silk production in Sweden;[23] perhaps there was a hardy American species that could be found. Several desirable medicinal plants, native to America, were also mentioned.

It was finally decided, in the summer of 1745, that an expedition to North America would be the most profitable.[24] Financing had to be found for what would be a long and expensive journey. Linnaeus then went about the task of convincing his fellow members of the academy and others in authority that there were many American plants and animals that might be brought back to thrive and enrich the kingdom. The extensive list that he made up became the basis of Kalm's charge.[25]

Planning for Kalm's future continued from the spring of 1743 onward, including the question of whether he would sit for his final examinations at the university. (Passing the examinations was not essential for obtaining a position if, instead, one had the support of influential people.) Through the influence of Linnaeus, Kalm, although still a student, was elected a member of the Royal Swedish Academy of Sciences in 1745.[26] As part of the planning for the North American journey, the possibility arose of a professorship at Åbo Akademi, which would provide financial support. Count Carl Gustaf Tessin, the Chancellor of Åbo Akademi, proposed to King Gustavus III in 1746 that the professorship of poetry be discontinued and in its place a chair of economics be established. His rationale was that, with the aftermath of the two disastrous wars, efforts were needed to restore the economy of Finland.[27]

Kalm worked hard to present a convincing case for his appointment as professor at Åbo. He added to the list of North American plants that might grow in Sweden and Finland that Linnaeus had compiled, such plants as hemp, several species of pea, wild rosemary, and several plants used to dye fabrics—most of which were not actually native to America.[28]

Although the post at Åbo would provide the funds that would enable him to travel, Kalm wanted that particular position as well. He saw himself as a Finn and felt a loyalty to do what he could to improve his homeland. In a draft of a letter to Tessin, Kalm wrote, "Finland's prosperity and well-being in the future depends very much on this professorship . . . I make so bold as to affirm that the professor of economics will be responsible if people die of hunger in our country at a time when things are expensive."[29]

Even after his journey had commenced, Kalm wrote in a letter to Linnaeus of his desire to return to Åbo and to give whatever he had been able to collect to that academy. Apparently, there had been a possibility of a post at the University of Lund, where he might use his knowledge of botany for a professorship in medicine. He was adamant about his interest in economics and his "innate dislike of *Praxis medica.*"[30]

Kalm was eager to travel—to any of the destinations that his mentors offered. He agonized over the innumerable setbacks along the way and wrote to Bielke in 1746, "I am sure they could not find anyone so ardently desirous of going on the journey as I, who have done so much it might be realized rapidly, although I know better than any what troubles and dangers may befall, but these I have scorned."[31]

Finally, on September 12, 1747, the decision was made to send Kalm to North America on a proposal by Linnaeus to the Royal Academy. The money for the trip had been collected from a variety of sources, including the University at Uppsala and the Department of Manufactures of the Swedish Diet.[32] Just a month before his departure for America, Kalm was nominated as the first professor of economics and docent in natural history at Åbo Akademi.[33] His salary would also cover some of his expenses during the journey.

Kalm's task, the introduction of North American plants to Sweden and Finland, was defined in detail in an official directive by the academy and described later in a letter, in French, which Kalm sent to the Governor-General of Canada asking for permission to travel via Niagara before leaving that nation. He was to bring back seeds of the mulberry tree, chestnuts, nuts of all kinds, maize, Indian rice, bay myrtle from which candles are made, red and white cedar, any plant eaten by the natives, sassafras, sugar maples, chinquapins, potatoes, taho (*Peltandra virginica*), taki (*Orontium aquaticum*) and wild grapes. Whenever he found a tree or plant that is known for some particular use as a food or dye, or for its excellent wood, he was to take the seeds from the farthest north that he was able to find that tree or plant.[34]

In addition to collecting seeds and plants, Kalm was to collect information. Therefore, he needed basic instruments for measurement. Kalm took with him centigrade thermometers, a compass, and an astrolabe that had been supplied by the academy, as well as a microscope and surveying instruments.[35] He also took five of Linnaeus's books as well as other reference works, a number of which he

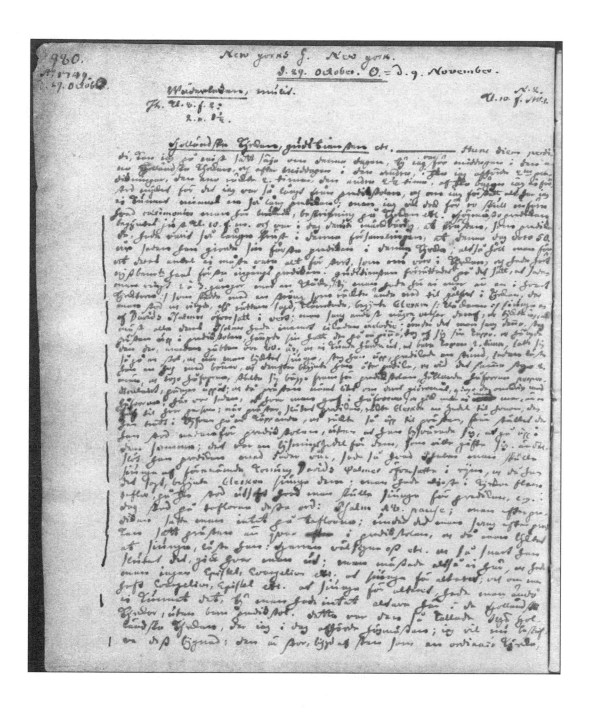

A page from Kalm's journal.
(The National Library of Finland, Helsinki University)

purchased while in London, "where they were both reasonable and easily available."[36]

During his journeys he usually carried ink powder, an inkhorn and pen, writing paper, coarse paper used for drying plants, and post paper, plus the octavo journals in which he kept notes in his neat, legible and tiny handwriting. Not a bit of space on each sheet of paper was wasted. He also carried a flintlock, scissors, tweezers, a spy glass, a clock, and a Swedish foot rule.[37] Alcohol was used to preserve fishes and insects in glass jars.

In an article he later wrote on lobelia as a cure for syphilis, Kalm described the procedure that he followed when encountering a new plant. "My method of traveling through forests and pathless areas does not permit me to carry many botany books. When I have paper in which to place my specimens, and paper on which to record my observations, together with pen and ink, I do not care to burden myself further." "I will, therefore, give a description of the plant in order that one may determine in a botanical library whether or not there is a previous description."[38] Kalm sent his dried specimens and detailed descriptions back to Linnaeus for identification and naming.

Kalm saw his task as not only to bring back American plants that might grow in Sweden, but, fortunately for posterity, to keep a detailed record of everything that he saw on his travels that related to nature and to man's use of nature's bounty. He wrote, "My only duty is to record as a matter of history what I have seen and heard. Thus, I have described the uses of some few herbs which, aside from satisfying botanical curiosity, were considered of no particular value. I often hear myself reproached when I gather plants: 'He who has nothing else to do must run to and fro and gather moss and more moss for what purpose?' I have found in my travels that the plant most neglected may prove to be most useful. I have learned that man at first may consider a plant or an insect as a mere curiosity, a nuisance, and a trifle in nature. However, when the uses of this new thing are understood, it cannot be too highly valued."[39]

Kalm knew that his charge when he returned to Åbo Akademi as professor of economics would be to instruct his students in mineralogy, botany, zoology, and chemistry and their application to economic activity in the country in agriculture, mining, manufacture and commerce.[40] Such a broad scope meant that he needed to keep detailed records of almost everything that he saw and heard. He had learned from Linnaeus and others how to make scientific observations and to record them methodically. Ironically, it was this detailed journal of his travels that he was to keep that made Kalm's journey important, rather than the seeds that he brought back.

Kalm was now ready and eager to embark on his long-awaited journey.

CHAPTER THREE
From Sweden to England
October 5, 1747–August 5, 1748

A RRANGING FOR SAFE PASSAGE through many foreign territories was not an easy business. Kalm describes his departure from Sweden in the following words:

> In the autumn of 1747, after His Majesty had granted me permission to leave my duties, and license to travel abroad on the errands of the Royal Swedish Academy of Sciences, and after his Majesty had not only given me his own Passport, but also had most graciously given orders to his Ministers at the French, Spanish, and English Courts, as well as those at the United Provinces in Holland, to obtain for me the Passports of these Powers, I commenced on 16th October [5 October] the voyage from Uppsala down to Götheborg.[1]

Kalm would be gone from Sweden for more than three and a half years, almost twice the two years that had originally been envisioned.[2]

Kalm chose as his traveling companion and assistant Baron Bielke's "dearest and most faithful servant," Lars Jungström.[3] He was trained in horticulture and became as adept as Kalm in the collection of plants and seeds. Often, he was sent off on his own to collect when Kalm was involved in other activities. They made a perfect team; never in the entire journal or in letters does Kalm mention any disagreements or disappointments with Jungström. Often, he voices concerns about Jungström's health and safety. He proved to be the perfect companion for Kalm, "indefatigable on journeys, and in the highest degree trustworthy."[4] Jungström was able to make up for Kalm's one deficit—-his lack of artistic ability to sketch the plants that he saw. Despite Kalm's satisfaction with Jungström, it was always clear that his role was that of servant, rather than an equal. When Kalm was entertained by various dignitaries during his journey, Jungström was relegated to dine in the servant's quarters.

It took almost two weeks for the pair to travel across Sweden to Gothenburg in an old carriage that Kalm had purchased; it required repair several times. A driver and horse had to be hired for each leg of the journey.[5] When they arrived in Gothenburg, Kalm found, to his dismay, that they would not br able to find passage on a ship from there until November 30. This was the first of countless delays that the impatient Kalm would face.

While in Gothenburg, Kalm visited several merchants who traded extensive-ly with England, providing such commodities as lumber and tar, pitch, turpentine and other products of pine trees used in ship-building, as well as pig iron from Swedish mines. As a result, they were able to refer him to a community of Anglo-Swedish merchants in London, to whom Kalm would be able to turn. There was even a recently built Church of Ulrika Eleanor, named after a Swedish queen, on the Thames side by the Port of London, which Kalm faithfully attended when he was in the city.[6] He also spent some time with Pastor Tobias Biörk, the chaplain to the Swedish congregation.[7]

Kalm and Jungström did not arrive in London until February 17 because of yet another delay. Adverse winds and severe storms forced them to stay for seven weeks in Grimstad, Norway, while their damaged ship was repaired.[8] Kalm used the time to study the plants, animals, agriculture and fishery of the surrounding area. One day in January a local fisherman, Pehr I Haven, brought Kalm a fish that he had never seen before, called *pihrål* by the local people; it seemed to him to be a kind of lamprey. It secreted enormous amounts of slime and was despised by the local fisherman because it devoured many of the fish that they had caught in their nets. Kalm described the fish to Linnaeus, who named it *Myxina glutinosa* and classified it among the worms. Modern evolutionary biologists have found *Myxine* to be an important and unique intermediate link between the lancelet and true vertebrates.[9]

As soon as he arrived in London, Kalm presented himself to Abraham Spald-ing, a Swedish merchant, to whom he had been directed by the Swedish Royal Academy of Sciences. Spalding gave him "every imaginable information, help, advice and explanations of various things; recommended me, partly himself, partly through his friends, to all the places I had occasion to visit, or where there was anything remarkable to see; lent me all the money I required for the whole of my foreign travels, and besides that, showed me manifold kindness."[10] Spalding also provided one of his own servants as a guide for Kalm in London.

The help of Spalding and others in the small Anglo-Swedish community was essential to Kalm. As a visitor from sparsely settled Scandinavia, Kalm occasion-ally was overwhelmed by the city and its drawbacks. He was much more com-fortable in the countryside or in the wilderness than in the hubbub of a large city. The sheer size of London was daunting to someone with little exposure to urban life, and travel was difficult. "The roads are full of travelers, on foot and on horse-back, in wagons and carts, who travel backwards and forwards, so that one often has, as it were, to steer through them,"[11] he wrote. The streets were muddy and clogged with manure and debris, often the carcasses of dead dogs or cats.[12] Later he complained that the roads were full of dust that filled the eyes, nose and mouth.[13]

Because the roads were so congested and often rutted, much travel was conducted by boat on the river Thames. Watermen were hired to ferry passengers from place to place. They had to zigzag in and out to avoid the myriad boats and ships of every size that plied the river. Much of the commerce of the city was carried out on the river, with colliers carrying everything from coal for fireplaces to manure from the thousands of horses. Collisions were frequent. Kalm wrote, "It is impossible to express the untold multitude of ships and vessels which sail up and down this river daily, especially in the summer time, when ships in some of the narrower places can hardly avoid running into each other, and often at the same time cause each other great damage."[14]

Kalm's initial frustration was his inability to speak English. Presumably, he had studied enough for a reading knowledge of the language, but he found spoken English so difficult to understand that at first he tried to communicate in Latin. But, as he wrote in a letter to Linnaeus three days after his arrival, although some of those he met knew how to write and speak in Latin, he could not understand them. Nor did they understand him, "even though we used Cicero's Latin when we spoke, and that's because they pronounce Latin much worse than do the Finns (my honorable countrymen) pronounce Swedish."[15]

Spalding made arrangements for Kalm and Jungström to lodge with a Madame Westfall for three and a half weeks. There he was able to obtain, in addition to firewood and laundry, tutoring from her four daughters to enable them to master the English language.[16] The daughters had, wrote Kalm in a letter to Linnaeus, "the innate quality of females of never being able to keep their mouths shut, but talk uninterruptedly, but they have promised to teach me, in two weeks, enough English to get along."[17]

Spalding may have advised Kalm that his rustic country attire was not appropriate for the sophistication of London, for Kalm paid a tailor to make four shirts and a pair of trousers for himself, as well as other clothing for Jungström. Later he purchased silver shoe buckles, and plain metal ones for everyday use or occasions where it might be necessary to avoid robbers. He also purchased a coat and additional shirts, and other clothing.[18]

Kalm soon learned that he would not be able to find passage on a ship to Philadelphia for some time. The conflicts between England and Spain in the nine-year War of Jenkins' Ear[19] made voyages across the Atlantic dangerous, so ships sailed closely together in convoys, and one was not prepared to sail for some time. Drifting icebergs in the stormy Atlantic in the early spring were also a challenge. Although the first ships left in May, Kalm had still not obtained the proper passport, so his departure was again delayed.[20] Disappointed at the delay—he would not arrive in America at the beginning of the spring growing season as he had planned—he nonetheless set about to make good use of his time in England.

In retrospect, Kalm's enforced delay in England was fortunate and probably led to the successful completion of his journey. England was, at this time, central in the study of natural history. It had renowned botanical gardens, and its extensive international commerce brought exotic specimens to the docks of London. Its circle of scientists associated with the Royal Society of London maintained numerous contacts with America. Several of its members were extremely knowledgeable about American plants as well as other aspects of life in the colonies, about which Kalm's advisors in Sweden had been unfamiliar.[21]

 After several weeks spent at the home of Madame Westfall improving his fluency in English, Kalm left London to stay in less expensive accommodations in the countryside and to avoid the unhealthy air of the city. Jungström was badly affected by the smoke-filled air, and Kalm was concerned about his servant's health. He wrote to Linnaeus, "As Master can understand, that worried me greatly since I didn't want to lose him. I was also convinced that even if I had had gold to offer, I could not have procured his match in terms of loyalty and everything one loves in a servant and travel companion."[22]

Kalm attributed the prevalence of lung disease in London to the coal smoke from the many fireplaces. He repeatedly complained of the smoky haze that lay over the city. He reported that he was unaware of a huge fire that had burned down more than a 100 houses in the city until he read about it later in the newspaper, since its smoke was just mingled with the accustomed fog and soot.[23] He, too, often suffered from a cough, which disappeared when he was out of the city for two days.[24]

Spalding referred Kalm to Richard Warner, who lived in Woodford, Essex, ten miles from the city. Warner kept extensive gardens and a greenhouse. While he stayed in Woodford, Kalm learned a great deal about English gardening from Warner and obtained seeds from him that he sent back to Linnaeus and Bielke.[25]

In late March, with the voyage to America still not imminent, Kalm and Jungström went to Little Gaddesden in Hertfordshire at the request of Bielke and at his expense. They traveled by stagecoach from London and stayed for a month at the Robin Hood Inn.[26] Their goal was to see John Ellis, the author of *Agriculture Improved* and *Farmer's Instructor*. Ellis had a great reputation for his writings on agriculture and rural economy and for inventing agricultural implements. Linnaeus and Bielke had read his books. In addition, Hertfordshire was considered the most advanced agricultural area in England. It was thought that Kalm could learn a great deal to bring back to his students in Finland.

As he wandered about the rolling Hertfordshire countryside, he could see that the woodlands were retained on top of the hills, grasses were grown on the upper slopes, and the valley bottoms were preserved for arable fields. On his walks, Kalm often stopped to converse with farmers whom he met in the area. He paid for punch, beer, cider and tobacco for them at local pubs as they sat and chatted.[27] He could relate to them directly because of his experience on Bielke's farm at Lövsta and must have pumped them for their ideas on how to improve the soil and increase crop yields.

Above: Little Gaddesden Church, Hertfordshire, near the home of agricultural writer John Ellis.

Above, right. Kalm and Jungström stayed for a month at the Robin Hood Inn, now a nursing home.

Right: The quarry near Toternhoe in Bedfordshire where Kalm observed rock strata and fossils.

Below: The rolling Hertfordshire countryside.

(Photos by the author)

Kalm spent several days in the company of Ellis at his farm near the Little Gaddesden Church, which dates from the thirteenth century. He became increasingly skeptical of Ellis's work because he felt that his writing had not been informed by his own experimentation and practice.[28] He indignantly reported that he had learned more about English rural economy from the farmers in Little Gaddesden than he had from Ellis.[29] Kalm was clearly dismayed to realize that someone whom he had been led to believe was an expert was in reality a sham.

Kalm also visited a quarry near Toternhoe in Bedfordshire where stone for buildings was quarried. He was interested in the methods and tools used by the quarrymen and also the fossils found in some of the stone. He raised several questions as to how the rock formations had been formed. This curiosity about geo-

Peter Collinson, influential Quaker merchant and member of the Royal Society of London, who served as the go-between for many naturalists in Europe and America, especially John Bartram of Philadelphia.

(Hunt Institute for Botanical Documentation, Carnegie Mellon University, Pittsburgh)

logical formations would be expressed many times during Kalm's journey. He constantly tried to fit what he saw before him on the land with his orthodox biblical explanations of the creation and the flood.

On April 21, 1748, after Kalm's return to London, Spalding introduced him to John Ellicott, a Fellow of the Royal Society of London and one of the best clockmakers in London. Just before he left London, Kalm purchased a fine silver watch from Ellicott.[30] Kalm went with Ellicott to a coffee house to meet Peter Collinson, a wealthy Quaker merchant, naturalist, and antiquary who was a leading member of the Royal Society. Like many of the members of the Society, Collinson was not a practicing scientist, although he did write some scientific papers that were well-received.

Collinson took Kalm to the Society's meeting, which took place every Thursday afternoon at five o'clock. Collinson was an important contact for Kalm because Collinson had been, for more than fifteen years, the prime promoter in

England of the sciences in the American colonies, especially in Philadelphia. It was he who had put the Philadelphia botanist and fellow Quaker, John Bartram, in contact with Linnaeus, whom Collinson had met during Linnaeus's visit to England in 1736.[31] Collinson was a gifted amateur botanist, an avid gardner and a collector of plants. Bartram regularly supplied Collinson with American specimens. Collinson introduced some 180 new species of plants, trees, and shrubs to England, according to Lewis Weston Dillwyn's 1843 *Hortus Collinsonianus*.[32]

Collinson had been a long-time friend of Benjamin Franklin, dating from Franklin's first stay in London. Collinson was also responsible for arousing Franklin's interest in electrical experiments and was soon to bring him to the attention of the Royal Society.[33] A vital factor in stimulating Franklin to conduct his famous experiments in electricity had been the gift of books and electrical apparatus from Collinson in 1745.[34] Collinson had also provided, in 1747, a long glass tube for generating static electricity that Franklin used in his experiments.[35]

Not only was Collinson in contact with men of science in the colonies, but he corresponded as well with many eminent British and European scientists. His role as go-between was made possible because of his successful business as a merchant importing and exporting high-quality woolens and other fabrics. His far-flung trade brought him into contact with the British colonies in North America as well as many other quarters of the world. His warehouses became a clearing house from which specimens and communications received from America were redirected to Linnaeus in Sweden, Dillenius at Oxford, Gronovius at Leyden and other members of the European botanical circle. Because of Collinson's wealth and position, he had access to men at the highest levels of government and business in England and on the continent. He counted among his friends several of the nobility.[36] "Scientific circles, especially those of the New World, would have been far less tightly knit together without the pen and the generous assistance of Peter Collinson."[37]

In this era when botany and zoology were in their early stages as scientific studies, focusing on the gathering of data and classifying it, communication between collectors was crucial. There were few journals devoted to the natural sciences, and the only other publications were the transactions of the academies. As a result, correspondence between naturalists was essential, and they spent much time writing letters to each other. National boundaries did not impede the flow of information, nor did the class distinctions that otherwise were so carefully observed. Even in times of war, naturalists from opposing sides would exchange letters and specimens.[38]

At the conclusion of the April 21 meeting of the Royal Society, Collinson introduced Kalm to Dr. Cromwell Mortimer, secretary of the Royal Society. Kalm also attended the Royal Society meetings on May 19 as a guest of Dr. Mortimer and on May 26 as a guest of Joseph Warner.[39]

Statue of Sir Hans Sloane in the Apothecaries' Garden in Chelsea.

Plaque at the entrance to the Apothecaries' Garden.

(Photos by the author)

On April 22, after his first visit to the Royal Society, Kalm was taken by Warner to Westminster Abbey, to both houses of Parliament, to St. James Park, and to the Royal Palace. They went also, by boat up the Thames to the Physic Garden at Chelsea, founded by the Society of Apothecaries in 1673 as a place for apprentices to learn to grow medicinal plants and to study uses for the plants. It had been established on four acres of leased land in Chelsea beside the River Thames so that the Apothecaries could also have there a boathouse for the gaily painted barge they used during royal pageants and for their plant-collecting expeditions. The site was south-facing, had free-draining soil and was also away from the coal smoke of London.

Over the years, the Society had encountered difficulty in raising enough money to support the garden and its greenhouse, and its members were unable to purchase the land, which had been offered to them. Finally, Sir Hans Sloane, a successful physician who later became President of the College of Physicians and of the Royal Society, purchased the Manor of Chelsea in 1712. He deeded the Garden, which was near his own, in perpetuity to the Apothecaries in 1722 for a yearly payment of five pounds, to "enable the Society to support the charge thereof, for the manifestation of the power, wisdom and glory of God in the works of Creation," and to show how "useful plants" may be distinguished from "those that are hurtful."[40] Sloane stipulated that every year, for forty years, fifty specimens of plants should be sent to the Royal Society; ensuring that a wide variety of plants would be grown in the Garden.

At the Apothecaries' Garden, Kalm met Phillip Miller, employed by the Society as the gardener, whom Linnaeus had also met in 1736. This gifted botanist had written the popular two-volume *Gardener's Dictionary* in 1731, which ran through eight editions during Miller's lifetime, and which Kalm purchased.[41] Kalm expressed his admiration for Miller, as a practical gardener and theoretician. Miller's father had been a nurseryman who had taught his son much practical knowledge. This early training was followed by extensive travel throughout England and then to Flanders and Holland to observe the practice of horticulture and agriculture wherever Miller went.[42] He had been the first to notice how insects are instrumental in fertilizing flowers.[43]

During Miller's tenure, the Apothecaries' Garden in Chelsea became the most famous English botanical garden, performing valuable services in botany and pharmacy.[44] It was said to rival the botanical gardens of Paris and Leiden, especially in its quantity of American plants. The garden included a glass house or orangerie that was heated in the wintertime to maintain those plants that were not winter-hardy[45].

Kalm was delighted with Chelsea and stayed there in lodgings for two weeks.[46] Here there were many orchards or vegetable market-gardens among the beautiful houses. He was impressed by the number of tree nurseries and marveled that someone who had purchased a new estate or was starting a new garden was able to purchase small trees and shrubs already shaped and clipped and could thus quickly landscape their property without waiting for years for seeds to grow.[47] In Chelsea, he also observed the use of broken bottle necks for forcing asparagus, which grew through them and thus matured faster.[48]

Kalm returned several times to Chelsea. On May 18, he and Phillip Miller went to pay their respects to the ninety-four-year-old Sir Hans Sloane, who in his youth had accompanied the Duke of Albemarle when he became Governor of Jamaica.[49] Sloane had collected some 800 specimens of plants on the island. Sloane heartily approved of Kalm's mission in North America, and Kalm obviously thought of the old man as a role model.[50] On two occasions, April 28 and May 26, Kalm went with others to see Sloane's museum, which housed an extensive collection of antiquities, stones, specimens of animals, birds, insects, dried plants, and other curiosities as well as an extensive library. Kalm was so fascinated that he made a complete copy of Sloane's catalog in his diary.[51]

On April 22, Kalm visited the home of Dr. Mortimer, whom he had met the previous evening, and there met George Edwards, the ornithologist and author of *A Natural History of Uncommon Birds*.[52] He again visited Mortimer on May 18, and they discussed a number of subjects, including cartography.[53]

On April 29, Kalm was taken sight-seeing again by Warner to the top of the tower of St. Paul's Church, which provided "a matchless view on all sides if only the air had got to be clear, but the thick coal smoke, which on all sides hung over the town, cut off the view in several places."[54] From the tower he counted sixty churches.[55] Kalm also visited the tomb and monument to the revered Isaac Newton, which he found impressive.[56]

On the morning of May 4, Kalm went to the home of Archibald Campbell, third Duke of Argyll, another of the many wealthy and well-connected English gentlemen who had a passion for gardening. He spent most of the rest of the day at the home of Dr. John Mitchell, the first person with first-hand knowledge of American plants and animals with whom he had an opportunity to converse at length.[57]

Mitchell was born to a family that had lived in Virginia for several generations. He grew up there, studied medicine in Scotland, and returned to Virginia to practice.[58] Mitchell was interested in scientific pursuits and had taken time from his practice to collect plants, some of which he sent to Collinson; ten of these were new genera.[59] He also studied various other topics, writing a description of the opossum and his theories on the pigmentation of the skin of "Negroes."[60] Mitchell also corresponded with the Philadelphia naturalist, John Bartram. In 1744, Mitchell had traveled to Philadelphia, where he visited with Bartram as well as with Benjamin Franklin and James Logan, who were also to become important American contacts for Kalm.[61]

Unfortunately, Mitchell suffered from recurring bouts of malaria that made him too ill to continue his medical practice. As a result, he left Virginia and moved to London in 1747.[62] There, he became acquainted with many of the scientists in the Royal Society and became a Fellow at the end of the next year.[63] Among those with whom he corresponded on scientific subjects was Linnaeus, who named the partridge berry, *Mitchella repens*, after him.[64]

Mitchell had also published a paper about the plants of Virginia. Presumably, he and Kalm discussed Linnaeus's methodology, with which Mitchell was in agreement.[65] In their conversation, Mitchell recommended the excellence of American pork, which he said was well-flavored because the swine were fed with maize and in the fall were allowed to roam through oak forests to eat acorns.[66] Kalm and Mitchell also discussed the use of silk grass, *Yucca filamentosis*, in place of flax and hemp to make cloth.[67] Kalm had earlier made a study of grasses and their use as fodder for livestock, so he was particularly interested in querying Mitchell about American grasses. Mitchell told him that perennial grasses were rare in tidewater Virginia when he lived there, and that the grasses often turned brown rather than staying green as they did in Europe.[68]

Later in May, Kalm went on a botanizing expedition to Dulwich in Surrey to look for rare plants with Mitchell, Sir William Watson (who the next year would read Benjamin Franklin's paper on lightning to the Royal Society), and George

Graham, the clockmaker.[69] In July, Kalm again met with Mitchell to deliver a letter from Linnaeus sent in his care. It included an essay on the manufacture of potash, a subject on which Mitchell was completing his own investigation.[70]

On May 23, Kalm spent an afternoon at the home of Mark Catesby, author of *The Natural History of Florida, Carolina and the Bahama Islands.*[71] Collinson had introduced the two men to each other at the first meeting of the Royal Society that Kalm had attended on April 21. Catesby had been to America twice. His first visit (1711-1719) was to accompany his sister, who married a physician immigrating to Williamsburg. As a boy, Catesby evidenced a passion for the study of nature and had been tutored by the renowned naturalist John Ray, who happened to live nearby. During his stay in Virginia, Catesby was befriended by some of the most influential men of the colony and began collecting botanical specimens, which he took back to England. As a result, he attracted the attention of a number of wealthy English patrons who wished to grow American plants.[72]

Catesby returned to England for a time and then spent about three years in the Carolinas and Georgia (1722-1725), based in Charles Town, South Carolina. His stay was sponsored by a dozen patrons, including Sir Hans Sloane and Peter Collinson, for whom he collected many previously unknown specimens of flora and fauna. They shared their plants with other collectors, so that Catesby's collections made an impact upon some of the principal European naturalists of the time. He had also supplied some of the curios in Sloane's museum. Catesby kept notes of his observations on the topography, geology, climate, agriculture, and the Indians of the area and drew figures of birds, plants, animals and fishes.[73] Catesby was careful to observe plants at different seasons, to measure their growth and their requirements for soil, water and sun. He also commented on the medicinal uses of various plants and the value of the wood of American trees in building and in carpentry.[74]

Catesby had returned to London in 1726. He spent the next two decades writing and illustrating his book on American flora and fauna, learning the art of etching on copper plates to do so. During this time, Catesby supported himself by working as a nurseryman in several gardens that contained large collections of American plants and was thereby able to observe their requirements and growth. In 1733 he was elected to membership in the Royal Society.[75]

Kalm praised Catesby's *Natural History,* saying that "in this work he has incomparably well represented with lifelike colours, the rarest trees, plants, animals, birds, fishes, snakes, frogs, lizards, painted toads, and insects, which are there found." Although he recognized their value, Kalm complained of the high cost of the two volumes of Catesby's work which were "therefore not for a poor man to buy."[76]

Kalm and Catesby must have spent time discussing several of the theories then debated in European scientific circles. For example, Catesby, whose best work was in ornithology, delivered the first accurate account of bird migration to a meeting of the Royal Society.[77] He was also able to lay to rest the widespread belief, shared by Linnaeus, that starlings hibernate in the mud of ponds in the winter.

Catesby also questioned the belief of Linnaeus and many others of the day that climatic conditions on the earth were roughly equivalent to latitudes, that is, that the climate on one side of the globe would be similar to that on the other in the same latitude. This belief, of course, underlay the decision of Linnaeus to send Kalm to America to the latitudes corresponding with those of Sweden.[78] Catesby noted that other factors, such as the quality of the soil, made a difference in the size of plants.[79] Kalm was later to examine the validity of this theory during his American travels, although he was temperamentally unlikely to challenge his mentor and thus the rationale for his journey.

On May 29, Kalm visited the Duke of Argyll at his country home, garden and orangery on Hounslow Heath near London.[80] Kalm was so accustomed to the notion that those of high rank would live in elegant and expensive mansions that he expressed surprise that Argyll's home was so unpretentious. The Duke's property, called Whitton, had a collection of various trees from all over the world, including many North American pines. The original soil had been barren and had required many years of enriching; Kalm was impressed by the transformation the Duke had accomplished.[81] Kalm especially noted the cedars of Lebanon, which he thought might be able to survive in the heaths and sandy tracts of Sweden and Finland.[82] The Duke grew a number of North American bayberry bushes, *Myrica cerifera*; Kalm learned that the berries were used to make candles.[83]

The delightful day in the garden ended with a moonlight cruise down the Thames to London with Mitchell, Argyll and the Duke's other guests, probably in his colorfully painted private boat, rowed by two uniformed watermen.[84] How far Kalm had come in just three months from his initial inability to communicate in English to now hobnobbing with nobility and men of learning!

On June 3, Kalm again visited the home of Dr. Cromwell Mortimer, secretary of the Royal Society of London, and there met Henry Baker, another of the Fellows of the Society interested in North American botany.[85]

On June 10, Kalm was able to visit Collinson at Peckham, about three miles from London in Surrey. Here Collinson kept a beautiful little garden, where he amused himself, when he could get away from the responsibilities of his business, with planting and arranging his living collection of plants. Many of them were American specimens that were able to survive outdoors in the English climate. Kalm marveled that this small garden probably had more different kinds of rare trees and plants than any other in England.[86] Curiously, Collinson's flower beds were bordered with the leg bones of horses. Collinson demonstrated to Kalm his method of planting mistletoe berries into tree bark and for seeding cranberries,

Vaccinium palustris. He also recommended siting a garden so that it receives morning sun.[87]

Kalm noted that the elm was the most popular tree in England, both in London, where it was able to survive the coal smoke, and in the villages, where they were planted in rows on both sides of the road, providing shade and creating an attractive alee. Collinson had an elm in his garden that was pruned so as to form the roof of a summer house. A horse chestnut was similarly treated to provide shelter over a garden bench.[88]

On May 31, Kalm went to Vauxhall Gardens, "to see vanity and the spoiled English youth."[89] Vauxhall was only open in the summer; its twelve acres of formal gardens were laid out with various paths and pavilions, as well as shady nooks.

Kalm also visited Ranelagh House in Chelsea, a large pleasure garden where people could sit and drink and listen to music. It featured a large Rotunda, 555 feet in circumference, covered with a roof so that it could be used year-round. An orchestra played in the middle, surrounded by elaborately decorated alcoves and boxes, with tables for eight people. There was sufficient room for the fashionable to promenade back and forth. Kalm reported with distaste that there were many such places in and outside London, where people with nothing better to do killed time for hours in the afternoons and evenings.[90] He expressed his concern over such indulgence, that would lead them to "nothing else than to waste their youth and lead them to dissipation, idleness and *libertinage*. Everything has its measure. Here they are accustomed to vanity, ostentation, *inutilité*, *bagatelles*, to waste precious time, to fall by degrees into weakness and indolence and to fight shy of work."

The puritanical Kalm disapproved of the English custom of spending time sitting and conversing in a pub over a glass of ale or brandy. "It only occurred to me, a foreigner, how folk, who commonly are so self-seeking, could spend often a great part of the day in this way." He concluded that "the ease with which a man could in every case have his food, if only he was somewhat industrious, seem to have conduced to this result." However, he scolded, "It is not to be wondered at then, if a great many labourers and others, however large the daily wages and profits they can make, can, for all that, scarcely collect more than what goes from hand to mouth."[91]

Kalm also disapproved of the books that the English seemed to prefer to read. As he wrote in a letter to Linnaeus, "With respect to the nation's taste for literature, little books of comedies, tragedies, novels, etc. seem to be preferred, that is, books that entertain and amuse."[92]

Kalm was always interested in the religious practices of the countries he visited and attended many different worship services during his journey. He visited a meetinghouse of the Society of Friends in London and was much impressed by the Quakers, whose lifestyle appealed to his own strait-laced and hard-working ethic. "This people is a very praiseworthy body, because they are commonly more temperate and sober-minded, more peaceable, more charitable, and betake themselves more to guarding against all resentment, and outwardly sinful life," than many of the Presbyterians or Anglicans.[93]

Kalm was among the many travelers to Great Britain over the centuries to notice that the British kept their rooms chilly.[94] He marveled that English cottages were colder than those in Sweden, despite the fact that an English farmer, laborer or peasant seemed to burn more wood in a year than would a comparable Swede, even though the winters were milder and shorter. He attributed this to the fact that Englishmen were ignorant of the use of a damper. As a result, "here all the warmth goes freely up the chimney; windows, doors, roof, floor, etc., are not stopped or made tight, but the wind and cold get freely to play through them."[95]

Kalm was entranced with the beauty and orderliness of the cultivated English landscape. This was a milieu that he could understand and enjoy. He repeatedly expressed his admiration for the area around London, "Round about this place the country is full of gardens, orchards and market-gardens, both for pleasure and use, and it can indeed be said that the country here is everywhere nothing but a garden and pleasance."[96] Like most men of his times, he believed that the taming of "Nature" and the use of "God's gifts" for the benefit of mankind was one of the highest forms of endeavor. Not for another century or more would the idea of the value of the preservation of wilderness be expressed.

Kalm marveled at the lushness of the enclosed meadows or pastures outside of London in its suburbs, which he attributed to the generous use of manure. The owners charged for the privilege of keeping cows for milk, cattle awaiting slaughter, or horses in the meadows. In addition, dung collected in the streets of London was piled into large heaps, transported by barge or cart, and then spread on the fields in September and October.[97] Such piles of composting manure and other refuse, covered with straw litter, were seen throughout England.[98] Fruits and vegetables were fertilized with night soil from London brought back by farmers in the carts that they had used to bring their produce to market.[99] Kalm reported that a number of plants that grew both in England and Sweden were much more luxuriant and larger in England, which, he said, "all seems to be a sign of the soil, and its richness hereabouts, partly natural, partly from long continued manuring and turning over."[100] He was convinced of the necessity to constantly improve the soil and was always scornful of farmers who neglected their lands.

In his journal, Kalm frequently described the various means used in England and America to enclose gardens, fields, and pastures, including earth berms, stone walls, wooden fences, and hedges of various plants such as hawthorn. His concern highlights the problem of preventing animals from entering fields and destroying crops that plagued farmers until the invention of barbed wire in the late nineteenth century.

In addition, land in Finland and Sweden was usually divided into small strips, which was inefficient because the arable land of a farmer was divided into many different parcels, which might be far from each other. Common pasture and woodland was also a part of the Swedish system. Kalm was certainly aware of this problem. The strip system was then under investigation by the Swedish government and eventually led to the passage of legislation in 1757 that resulted in a general re-parceling and compacting of land holdings throughout Sweden and Finland.[101] During his visit to England he wrote in his diary, "Today we had plenty of proof of the harm and inconvenience that it is for a farmer to have all his property lying in strips with those of his neighbours and what an advantage it is to have a unitary property of his own, which can be arranged and managed according to his own good sense."[102]

Kalm always reported on the role of women wherever he traveled. He called England "a paradise for ladies and women." Although common servant girls had to work, "the mistresses and their daughters are in particular those who enjoy perfect freedom from work. To us in Sweden, where the wife, no less than the husband, is obliged in every way to bestir herself and keep her wits about her, to help to win the bare necessaries of life, an English wife would not seem to be particularly well-suited."[103] He complained of the indolence of the women he saw at Ranelagh House, "Married ladies and Mistresses of Establishments, and the young girls become in many ways altered and ruined, and lose all pleasure in household duties."[104]

When he was in Little Gaddesden, he found "that the greater number of the English women in this district trouble themselves very little about such domestic duties as in other countries form a great part of the occupations of women, but that they had laid most of the burden of that on to the men. I saw, however, in some places some part of the women afford proof that they are not wanting in ability for various things, if only the custom of the country had not freed this sex from such." He saw women employed in making straw hats that they later sold.[105]

In dress and appearance, he compared English women favorably with those in Sweden. Kalm also begrudgingly praised English women for their cooking, their concern for cleanliness and their ability at needlework. With a baker in every village, they need not do any baking, and since cloth was readily available, no weaving or spinning were necessary. Their sole occupation was cooking, washing dishes, washing and starching linen clothes, knitting stockings or sewing linen wear. "Here," he wrote in his diary, "there is an abundance of money and of everything that is needed to liberate them from the manifold cares. In many places they do not even brew their drinks, but buy them from the ale house."[106]

Kalm began negotiations for a place on board a ship bound for America early in May. He spent much time going back and forth on the wherries, the long, light rowboats that carried passengers from London to Gravesend, where ocean-going vessels were boarded, to inquire about various ships sailing to America and when they would leave.[107] He had several meetings with Captain Lawson of the *Mary Gally*, bound for Philadelphia, until final arrangements were made. Meanwhile, he and Jungström found lodgings in Fleet Street for a month in late June and most of July.

Before he left England, Kalm purchased Del'Isle's map of North America, several pairs of spectacles (to compensate for his near-sightedness), and a new brown suit and overcoat. Various purchases were made of items that would be useful in their collections of flora and fauna in America: boxes for insects, a drawing box and a dozen brushes, as well as lots of various kinds of paper, and French and English dictionaries. Jungström, too, had been outfitted with new clothes as well as the *New Testament* in French and *The Book of Common Prayer* in English so that he might learn French and improve his English. It was also necessary for them to bring onboard their own bedding.[108]

ALTHOUGH HE HAD USED HIS TIME IN ENGLAND WELL and learned much that was valuable for his mission, Kalm must have been relieved and excited when, on August 5, 1748, he and Jungström were finally aboard a ship bound for North America.

CHAPTER FOUR
Why Philadelphia?

KALM CHOSE PHILADELPHIA as his first destination in America rather than other ports, such as Boston or Québec, for many reasons: It was the location of Sweden's former colony; merchant ships sailed regularly between London and Philadelphia; and because in Philadelphia there were several men known to Linnaeus and to Kalm's informants in England, to whom Kalm could bring letters of introduction.

At that time, there were no contacts among Linnaeus's circle of men interested in natural history in the other cities. Because the primary purpose of Kalm's visit was to acquaint himself with the plants of the New World and to bring back specimens of those that might profitably grow in Sweden, it was important for him to find the most knowledgeable person to advise him. John Bartram was the obvious choice.

Bartram, now considered one of America's first great naturalists, was born in 1699. His grandfather, Richard Bartram, settled near Darby, Pennsylvania in 1682, arriving along with William Penn from Derbyshire, England, where he had been persecuted for his Quaker beliefs. He had two sons, John and Isaac. John's third son, William, also a member of the Society of Friends, had two sons, the eldest of whom was the botanist who befriended Peter Kalm. John Bartram's mother died in childbirth when he was only two years old, and his father, who had left him and his brother with their grandmother to move to North Carolina, was killed by Tuscarora Indians there when John was twelve.[1]

Bartram had only a rudimentary education. He had an interest in medicine and was known as someone who helped to tend the sick among his neighbors. His first wife died young, but left him a son. In 1729, John married Ann Mendenhall, who bore him nine children, including his now more-famous son, William, who was only ten years old at the time of Kalm's visit.

Bartram's long-standing interest in botany was explained in a letter he wrote to Peter Collinson on May 1, 1764, "I had allways since 10 years ould A great inclination to plants, & knowed all that I once observed by sight though not thair proper names having no person or books to instruct me."[2]

In his *Letters from an American Farmer*, J. Hector St. John de Crèvecoeur described a visit of several days made by a supposed Russian gentleman to Bartram's farm. In response to a query by the Russian, Bartram described how he first became interested in the study of botany: "One day I was very busy in holding my plough (for thee seest that I am but a ploughman) and being weary I ran under the shade of a tree to repose myself. I cast my eyes on a daisy, I plucked it mechanically and viewed it with more curiosity than common country farmers are wont to do; and observed therein very many distinct parts, some perpendicular, some horizontal. What a shame, said my mind . . . that thee shouldest have employed so many years in tilling the earth and destroying so many flowers and plants, without being acquainted with their structures and their uses! This seeming inspiration suddenly awakened my curiosity, for these were not thoughts to which I had been accustomed."[3]

Apparently, Bartram's "inclination to plants" had attracted the notice of the wealthy Quaker, James Logan, for many years the Proprietary Agent for the Penn family and one of the most important men in Philadelphia business and government. Logan, born in Ireland of Scottish parents, had come to Pennsylvania in 1699 as William Penn's secretary and became secretary of the province and clerk of its council. In addition to holding important government offices, he became immensely wealthy through trade with the Indians and speculation in land.[4]

Logan was an enthusiastic amateur botanist, and his researches supplied the final proof in the long-vexing question of the sexuality of plants.[5] Logan conducted an experiment with maize in the summer of 1727 that clearly demonstrated the sexual theory of plant propagation. He did further experiments with other plants and in 1735 sent his observations in a letter to Peter Collinson, which was read at a meeting of the Royal Society of London. The letter was printed in their *Philosophical Transactions* and later appeared, in Latin, in Leyden through the efforts of the Dutch botanist, Frederick Gronovius. In 1736, Collinson sent to Logan printer's sheets of Linnaeus's *Systema Naturae*, in which he had systematically arranged "all the productions of nature in classes," based on their sexual organs. Soon Linnaeus himself began a correspondence with Logan in Latin. In appreciation of his work, Linnaeus named a genus for Logan.[6]

Logan, an ardent book collector, was a man of brilliance and wide knowledge. On several occasions when he was in England on behalf of William Penn and his family, Logan spent long hours in London's bookshops selecting books to bring home. When he returned to Pennsylvania, he sent frequent orders to Europe for the latest books as well as those that were old and rare. He developed what was considered the finest private library in the middle colonies and certainly the best in its holdings of works of science.[7] Logan was generous in showing his collection and lending volumes to a number of promising young men.[8]

John Bartram was among the recipients of Logan's generosity. Logan lent him several botanical works and encouraged him in his study, tutoring him in Latin so that he could read them. They also looked together through Logan's microscope at the stamens and pistils of several flowers. Later, Logan recommended Bartram to Linnaeus, "If God grants him life, and if his narrow circumstances do not hinder, you may look for great things from him."[9]

At the urging of Logan and other friends, including Joseph Breintnall, the secretary of the Library Company of Philadelphia,[10] Bartram sent specimens of some of the plants that he had collected along with his written observations to Peter Collinson in London. This initial contact led to a correspondence of nearly fifty years, from the time Bartram was about thirty-five years of age until his death.

Collinson introduced Bartram to the work of such eminent European botanists as Linnaeus, Dillenius and Gronovius, with whom Bartram corresponded from 1743 to 1755, receiving copies of their books. Collinson also sent some of Bartram's previously undocumented dried specimens to these famous botanists so that the plants could be named and the information returned to Bartram.

Collinson was eager to obtain information about American plants and specimens that he could grow in his own garden. He gave Bartram instructions on how to collect and dry plants to be sent to England. He also described a method for keeping live plants fresh for several days on a journey by tying the moistened root ball into an ox bladder.[11] The two men exchanged seeds, roots and cuttings. Collinson also introduced Bartram to Dr. John Fothergill and other wealthy English plant collectors who became his patrons. Over the years, Bartram sent seeds to more than 100 customers in England, Europe and America.[12]

With earnings from his sales to these men, Bartram was able to make extensive journeys of exploration to collect specimens of plants, insects, birds, reptiles and fossils. He also noted the conditions under which the plants grew, including the soil and surrounding rock formations. During his lifetime, Bartram traveled as far as Lakes Ontario and George; to the sources of the Hudson, Delaware, Schuylkill, Susquehanna, Allegheny and St. Juan Rivers; and he collected extensively in the Carolinas and northern Florida. William Bartram wrote of his father, "Neither dangers nor difficulties impeded or confined his researches after objects in natural history."[13]

Sometime between 1738 and 1742, Bartram drew a map of the east coast of the American colonies from New York to the Carolinas to orient Collinson to descriptions that Bartram sent him in his letters. The map identifies the major rivers, portraying them all as flowing from west to east, as well as the mountain ranges. Political boundaries between colonies or the location of cities, other than Philadelphia, were not identified.[14]

Despite his correspondence with the great scientists of England and Europe, Bartram lacked the education, time, and probably interest, to write systematic studies of natural history. He was a collector and would send his annual shipment of seeds and specimens to England and then wait expectantly until one of the experts could classify them and report his findings. He did not always agree with the classification assigned because he knew the plants better than anyone else.[15]

In a letter to Linnaeus, Kalm wrote of Bartram, "when you talk with the man and listen to him, you find out that he has been a very keen observer; he is everything: farmer, carpenter, turner, shoemaker, mason, gardener, clergyman, lumberjack and who knows what else. Quite a head on that man!"[16]

After he returned from America, Kalm wrote admiringly, but not uncritically of Bartram. "He has acquired a great knowledge of natural philosophy and history, and seems to be born with a peculiar genius for these sciences. . . . We owe to him the knowledge of many rare plants which he first found and which were never known before. He has shown great judgment and an attention which lets nothing escape unnoticed."[17]

Kalm agreed with the later assessments by Cadwallader Colden and Alexander Garden, the most capable botanists in America at the time. They agreed too that, although Bartram was a wonderful observer and collector of nature, his knowledge of the principles of botany was limited.[18] Kalm faulted Bartram for not taking the time to write down his observations or to preserve "the great knowledge which he has acquired in natural philosophy and history, especially in regard to North America."[19]

Kalm expressed his gratitude to Bartram, writing, "I, also, owe him much, for he possessed that great quality of communicating everything he knew. . . . I should never forgive myself if I were to omit the name of a discoverer and claim that as my contribution which I had learned from another person."[20]

PHILADELPHIA WAS A WISE CHOICE AS KALM'S DESTINATION for reasons in addition to the presence of such men as Bartram and Logan, already known to Linnaeus and other European botanists. By the time of his visit, Philadelphia, because of its flourishing trade and because it was an important destination for immigrants, had become the second most populous city of the British overseas empire.

The Delaware River was wide and deep enough so that the largest ships could simply anchor next to the city's docks. The only drawback was that the river usually froze for a month or more in the winter, preventing ships from arriving, in contrast to the ports of Boston or New York, which remained open all winter.

Kalm was impressed by the natural advantages of Philadelphia. As one who had developed a long-time habit of weather observation, he thought the city's temperate climate was a definite advantage, as was the ample supply of good fresh water from easily dug wells.[21]

Kalm noted that, although the city carried on an extensive trade with many parts of the world, especially the West Indies, all of it was required to be conveyed in ships flying the English flag. In addition, almost all manufactured goods had to be procured from England, despite the fact that Kalm encountered "excellent masters in all trades and many things . . . made here fully as well in England. Yet no manufactures, especially for making fine wool cloth, are established."[22]

Kalm pointed out conditions which we know were soon to lead to conflicts between the colonies and the mother country: "But all the money which is gotten in these several countries, must immediately be sent to England in payment for goods from thence, and yet those sums are not sufficient to pay all the debts."[23] He warned, "it is much to be feared that the trade of Philadelphia and of all the English colonies will rather decrease than increase in case no provision is made to prevent it."[24]

Kalm, coming from mercantilist Europe, marveled at the rapidity with which Philadelphia had grown from a wilderness village to "such grandeur and perfection without any powerful monarch contributing to it, either by punishing the wicked or by giving great supplies of money." He attributed its growth to the city's "fine appearance, good regulations, agreeable location, natural advantages, and trade. . . . It has not been necessary to force people to come and settle here; on the contrary, foreigners of different languages have left their country, houses, property and relations and ventured over wide and stormy seas in order to come hither."[25]

The fairly continuous economic prosperity of Philadelphia permitted the development of a vigorous cultural life and a high level of literacy. By 1742, there were eight print shops, two newspapers and five bookshops to serve the reading public of the city.[26]

Kalm admired the broad paved streets and fine architecture of Philadelphia. He noted that a flagstone sidewalk fronted the buildings, and posts separated them from the roadway to keep pedestrians safe. He described with approval the custom of gentlemen walking on the outside nearest the street so that ladies were protected from the splatter of dirt from the roadway.[27]

Philadelphia, because of its acceptance of different religious beliefs and tolerance of new ideas, had become a port of entry of secular and humanistic Enlightenment ideas from Europe. Although founded by Quakers, the Friends, by 1750, numbered only eight hundred families, or about twenty-five percent of the city's population. In Philadelphia, there was widespread toleration for all sects or for those who had no religious affiliation. Many in the city, like Benjamin Franklin, believed in the moral value of churches and supported them and attended worship services without being deeply religious.[28]

Kalm was immediately impressed by the number of different churches to be found in Philadelphia, "for God is served in various ways in this country."[29] It must have been a surprise for Kalm—who had studied to be a Lutheran minister in a country in which the state church was all encompassing and powerful—to adjust to the diversity of religions that were not only tolerated but allowed to flourish. "Everyone who acknowledges God to be the Creator, preserver and ruler of all things, and teaches or undertakes nothing against the state or against the common peace, is at liberty to settle, stay and carry on his trade here, be his religious principles ever so strange."[30]

Kalm provided a long description of the various church buildings early in his journal. They included an English established church, a Swedish church, a German Lutheran church, the old Presbyterian church, the Old German Reformed (Calvinist) church, the new Reformed church, the Roman Catholic church, the Moravian or Zinzendorfian Brethren church and the Anabaptist church. In addition, the Quakers had two meeting houses.[31]

The New Presbyterian Church was built in 1750 by the "New-lights," followers of George Whitefield,[32] who had preached to thousands in the streets because the established churches were closed to him. Beginning what historians have termed the "Great Awakening," Whitefield appealed to people from the middle and lower classes, many of whom belonged to no church. In this era of renewed interest in religion, Whitefield expressed contempt for formalism and the pretensions of orthodox faiths and advocated a social gospel.[33]

Kalm made a point of attending various churches in many of the cities that he visited during his travels and described the buildings and their worship services in great detail. He reported that Christmas Day was celebrated with the most solemnity in the Roman Catholic Church in Philadelphia, where there was also excellent music. The Catholics had the only working organ in the city, and the priest, a Jesuit, played the violin, while others played other instruments and sang. Protestants in the English, Swedish and German churches treated Christmas much like an ordinary Sunday, whereas the Quakers did not celebrate Christmas at all.[34]

Kalm also documented several disputes between adherents of different clergymen and described the marriage practices of the various churches. Catholic priests were not permitted to conduct marriage ceremonies in Pennsylvania. In addition, "No clergyman is allowed to marry a Negro with one of European extraction, lest he must pay a penalty of one hundred pounds, according to the laws of Pennsylvania."[35]

Kalm reported that "It was a custom in Philadelphia among the English to express good wishes to a newly married couple by paying them a personal visit during the first week or first month of their married life." The guests were served wine or tea and given a piece of wedding cake to take home with them.[36]

Kalm was impressed by the freedom enjoyed by the inhabitants of Philadelphia. He marveled that each citizen was "so well secured by the laws, both as to person and property, and enjoys such liberties that a citizen here may, in a manner, be said to live in his house like a king. It would be difficult to find anyone who could wish for and obtain greater freedom."[37]

Kalm reported that, "The town is now well filled with inhabitants of many nations, who in regard to their country, religion and trade are very different from each other."[38] Among the other immigrants who sailed with Kalm aboard the *Mary Gally* had been a group of Germans whose passage was to be paid by Pennsylvania farmers to whom they became indentured for a period of years.[39]

No American colonial city, and few in contemporary Europe, could boast the galaxy of intellectual and civic leaders produced by Philadelphia at the time of Kalm's visit. Such men included, in addition to John Bartram and James Logan, the Rev. David Muhlenberg, who found almost 1400 species of plants in nearby Lancaster County; Thomas Godfrey, who invented a new and improved mariner's

Benjamin Franklin portrait, London, 1777 steel engraving. (North Wind Picture Archives)

quadrant; and Charles Thomson, a classical and biblical scholar who was an expert in Indian languages.[40]

Most important of all was Benjamin Franklin. Franklin was at the peak of his powers and involved in a myriad of projects. He had become sufficiently successful in his printing business that he was in the process of winding up his affairs and turning over the print shop to a partner. He was deciding to devote the remainder of his life to public service. During this period he was the leader in organizing the Philadelphia Hospital; the academy, which eventually became the University of Pennsylvania, and an insurance company. He became involved in local politics, accepting membership in the Philadelphia Common Council, became an alderman, and agreed to be elected to the assembly. According to biographer Edmund Morgan, "Despite his best efforts to keep himself in the background he had become the best-known and most popular man in Philadelphia and, indeed, a tribune of the people."[41]

In addition to all of these activities, Franklin had spent much of his time in the years 1747-49 in carrying out experiments on the conduction of electricity, including his famous experiment with a kite during a thunderstorm. He established some of the terminology still used to describe electrical phenomena.[42] He became the most well-known American in Europe because of his scientific findings. In addition to conducting crucial experiments that helped to explain electricity, he was able to invent a most practical application, the lightning rod.

Philadelphia had the first subscription library in America, the Library Company of Philadelphia, incorporated in 1731, which Franklin had organized.[43] The library was open for borrowing to all of the subscribers who contributed to the cost of purchasing books. During his stay, Kalm was permitted, as an honored guest, to borrow books from this fine collection, most of them in English and many written in French and Latin.[44] In appreciation for this favor, Kalm presented his copy of Linnaeus's *Fauna Svecia* to the Library Company, an acquisition noted in 1749 by Logan.

Philadelphia, thus, was the ideal choice of an initial destination for Kalm in North America, for there he could find information and advice from men known to his master and to his informants in England.

CHAPTER FIVE

Arrival in Philadelphia
September 15—November 10, 1748

THE WEATHER throughout Kalm's voyage from England to Philadelphia was unusually calm, and the trip was uneventful, except for a brief grounding on a sandbar off the coast of Maryland. Always eager to learn more about his surroundings, Kalm queried the captain about the winds of the Atlantic and the sailors about the birds and fish that he saw. During the remarkably short forty-one days at sea, Kalm spent his time profitably noting details of the various sea weeds, crabs, shrimp, jellyfish (including the Portuguese man-of-war), porpoises, whales, and dolphins, flying fish, bonitos and birds, including petrels, puffins, gulls, and terns. Kalm also remarked on what he called "night-time sparks of fire," which were probably phosphorescent marine flagellate protozoans.[1]

As the *Mary Gally* sailed up the Delaware, Kalm stood on the deck and noted with approval the fine stands of oak, hickory and pine that covered both shores. He was told that some English ship captains spent the winter in Philadelphia supervising the construction of a new ship in which to go to sea the following spring. The English were suffering the loss of many merchant ships to French and Spanish privateers.[2] Kalm reported that more shipbuilding took place in New England because oak grown in a more northerly climate was more durable. He felt that the oak grown in Sweden was of better quality than that of any of the American oaks.[3]

The *Mary Gally* docked at Philadelphia at ten o'clock on the morning of September 15, 1748. Kalm saw a variety of kinds and sizes of vessels docked the length of almost two miles of wooden wharves along the Delaware River waterfront.[4] As soon as the ship arrived, many people who expected mail from England hurried on board to collect their letters; mail that remained was left for pickup in a local coffee shop.[5]

Kalm immediately inquired for directions to the home of Benjamin Franklin to whom he had been recommended by Dr. John Mitchell, and, in the following letter, Peter Collinson.

Friend Franklin   London, June 14, 1748.
The Bearer Mr. Kalm is an Ingenious Man and comes over on purpose to Improve himself in all Natural Inquiries. He is a Sweed per Nation and is as I am informed

Imployed by the Academy of Upsal to make Observations on the Parts of the World. I recommend Him to thy Favour and Notice—-by Him I send the first Vol. of the Voyage to Discover NorWest passage. I hope the pacquett &c. sent under the Care of Hunt & Greenlease is come safe to Hand. I am thy sincere friend, P. Collinson.[6]

Franklin must have introduced Kalm to two Swedes living in Philadelphia, Jacob Bengtson and Gustavus Hesselius, a portrait painter who had emigrated from Sweden to Philadelphia in 1712 and who had painted a portrait of James Logan. On the afternoon of Kalm's arrival, the two Swedes gave him a walking tour of their city and its surrounding fields. Kalm was amazed at what he saw and dismayed at the realization of how much he had to learn.

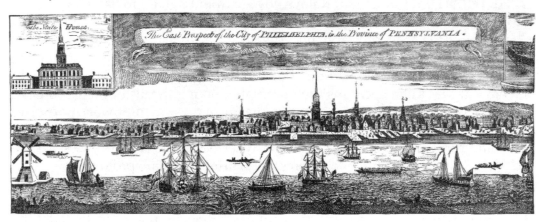

Philadelphia from the harbor, 1750s woodcut.
(North Wind Picture Archives)

"Whenever I looked on the ground, I found everywhere such plants as I had never seen before. When I saw a tree I was forced to stop and ask its name of my companions. The first plant which struck my eyes was an *Andropogon*, or a kind of grass, and grass is a part of botany I always delight in. I was seized with a great uneasiness at the thought of learning so many new and unknown parts of natural history. At first I only considered the plants, without venturing a more accurate examination."[7]

Franklin had offered lodging to Kalm at his own home, but the offer was not accepted.[8] Kalm may have felt that his activities would have been curtailed by the comings and goings of the busy Franklin household. Instead, Kalm found lodging with a Quaker grocer, Mistress Durburow, who provided him and Jungström with "a room, candles, beds, attendance and three meals a day," with an extra charge for wood, washing and wine.[9]

It was only three days after his arrival in Philadelphia and after he had rented a horse that Kalm went with Hesselius to meet John Bartram at his farm.

Unfortunately, Bartram was not at home; instead, Kalm stopped at the homes of several Swedes who lived in the area.[10] One of these was a fine two-story house built of stone and surrounded by a large orchard, belonging to Anders Rambo. Here Kalm and Jungström stayed overnight.[11] They were kept awake by the loud croaking of frogs, locusts, and grasshoppers from the nearby marshes and brooks.

Every farm that they passed had an orchard full of apple and peach trees. Kalm was astounded to learn that many of the orchards they passed on their way back to Philadelphia were so full of fruit that their owners were not the least concerned that passersby might pick and eat from them, and that excess was even fed to the swine. He marveled that "the country people in Sweden and Finland guarded their turnips more carefully than the people here do the most exquisite fruits."[12]

Gustavus Hesselius, self-portrait. (The Historical Society of Pennsylvania Collection, Atwater Kent Museum of Philadelphia)

Bartram House and Upper Garden, Bartram's Garden, May 2002. (Photograph by Joel T. Fry, courtesy of The John Bartram Association, Bartram's Garden, Philadelphia)

Kalm and Jungström were finally able to meet John Bartram at his farm on September 25, ten days after their arrival. Twenty years before Kalm's visit, in 1728, Bartram had acquired the initial 102 acres of his farm on the west bank of the Schuylkill River, at Kingsessing, near Gray's Ferry, now within the city limits of Philadelphia and preserved as a city park. This tract had been part of a plantation of New Sweden known as Aronameck, and Bartram acquired it from the heirs of the Swedish owners.[13]

The only structure that had been on the land when Bartram purchased his farm was the stone house of Swedish settler, Peter Yocum, dating from 1684. When Bartram began the construction of his house in 1730, he incorporated the earlier building as the kitchen on the first floor, and a bedroom on the second. The house was originally one room deep, two-and-a-half stories with a gable roof, and built of coursed ashlar, split and laid by Bartram's own hand. At the time of Kalm's visit, the later additions to the house that we now see had not been built.

In front of his house, Bartram had established a botanical and kitchen garden facing southeast, extending six or eight acres sloping toward the riverfront. It contained an extensive collection of most of the then-known universe of North American plants that Bartram had collected for his European patrons.[14] This was exactly the reference collection that Kalm needed in order to quickly learn what he had to know.

Kalm immediately began to tap into Bartram's vast store of knowledge and was full of questions that Bartram patiently answered. He may even have become somewhat exasperated with Kalm's curiosity, for he took advantage of his credulity by telling him the following story, which Kalm, who seemed to lack a sense of humor, faithfully recorded. "Mr. Bartram told me that when a bear catches a cow he kills her in the following manner: he bites a hole into the hide and blows with all his power into it till the animal swells excessively and dies, for the air expands greatly between the flesh and the hide."[15]

Kalm and Jungström went again to see Bartram three days later and delivered a letter to him from Linnaeus. Bartram replied, "I received thy kind letter by the hands of our Curious friend Mr Kalm whome I have had ye pleasure to converse with; & whom I value not onely for thy sake but for his own ingenuity."[16] Kalm apparently stayed for several days, following Bartram around his farm and peppering him with more questions. It must have been a tight squeeze to find sleeping room for Kalm and Jungström along with the Bartram family and slaves in the small house.

Linnaeus's original thought had been to send Kalm to New England as well as to Canada.[17] As late as September 29, 1748, in a letter written from Philadelphia, Kalm was debating whether he should go by road or by ship to New England, and he expected to spend the coming winter in Boston. Optimistically, he anticipated being able to go from there to Canada in the early summer and to be ready to return to England by the end of the summer.[18]

He was undoubtedly told that, given the lack of roads, travel by water up the Hudson Valley and Lake Champlain was the only feasible route to Canada. In addition, because of the recurrent conflicts between the British colonies and those of France, it would have been almost impossible to go from New England, where the hostilities had been greatest, to Canada. There was ongoing conflict between the French and British in the area from Boston north to the mouth of the St. Lawrence River, as settlers from New England encroached farther north toward Micmaq Indian and French Acadian enclaves.[19]

It must have been as a result of Bartram's advice that Kalm decided to spend the winter in Pennsylvania, New Jersey and New York. It was with some degree of trepidation that he wrote Linnaeus of his change in plans on October 14. He emphasized that "All my friends and public gazettes warned me against traveling to Canada this year for the wild Indians that the French had agitated either killed or plundered or captured all those whom they met in the border region, even if people had twenty passports or twelve drums to show that they had peaceful intentions."[20]

Linnaeus and the members of the Swedish Royal Academy of Sciences were dismayed at Kalm's deviation from his initial instructions when they learned of this plan. They firmly believed that it was essential for Kalm to travel north to regions in the same latitude as Sweden.[21]

It was just as well that Kalm avoided New England, as he would probably have been less successful there in his search for native plants and for their uses by Native Americans. By the mid-eighteenth century, he would have found that much of the land had been converted to use for agriculture and for livestock, and that there were few Indians left. The mindset of the Puritans who settled New England had been to introduce English plants and agricultural methods to the new world as quickly as possible. Despite the story that American children learn about the first Thanksgiving and how the Pilgrims learned from the Wampanoag Indian, Squanto, how to plant corn, the truth was that they had little interest in adopting the practices of the Native Americans or in using unfamiliar plants, except for the cultivation of maize. Kalm was able to learn much more from the descendents of the early settlers of New France and New Netherlands, who continued to have intimate interactions with native populations and had greater respect for their knowledge.[22]

On October 7, Kalm crossed the Delaware on a ferry, for which he paid fourpence, to go to New Jersey, where he spent the day, returning in the evening. On October 10, he went with Peter Cock, a wealthy Swede with whom he became quite friendly, to his home about nine miles north of Philadelphia and stayed there overnight. Here Cock ran a paper mill on a small brook, where he manufactured "coarser sorts of paper."[23] Cock apparently owned slaves, one of whom showed Kalm a ground hog that he had killed.[24]

Kalm seemed to accept the fact of slavery in America. He often noted expenditures of tips to both servants and slaves. In his account books, the slaves were always referred to as, for example, "for Mr. Cuyler's negro."[25] Many of the other men who befriended him owned black slaves, including Bartram and Hesselius.[26]

Kalm described the history of black slavery in the English colonies and the laws governing slavery, especially against intermarriage between blacks and whites. He also noted, "A man who kills his Negro is, legally, punishable by death, but there is no instance here of a white man ever having been executed for this crime."[27] He reported that slaves in the North American colonies were treated more mildly and fed better than those in the West Indies. He explained that some masters, especially Quakers, set their slaves free, but "free Negroes become very lazy and indolent afterwards."[28]

Kalm repeated the belief that blacks were not able to withstand cold as well as Europeans and reported that they frequently suffered from frostbite. He also noted that their color did not lighten after living for several generations in a cold climate. He observed that, although there were severe penalties against intermarriage, he saw children "of a mixed complexion."[29]

Kalm did not express any particular disapproval of slavery except to note that it was "greatly to be pitied that the masters of these Negroes in most of the English colonies take little care of their spiritual welfare, and let them live on in their pagan darkness." He reasoned that white masters might find it "shameful to have a spiritual brother or sister among so despicable a people; partly by thinking that they would not be able to keep their Negroes so subjected afterwards; and partly through fear of the Negroes growing too proud on seeing themselves upon a level with their masters in religious matters."[30]

Kalm also discussed other kinds of servants in Pennsylvania. He divided free persons into two groups: those who worked for wages and those who were indentured. The former were paid an annual wage and also provided with food. They were free to leave whenever they wished, but if they left before the year of their contract expired, they would forfeit their wages.[31]

Indentured servants were usually those too poor to pay their passage from Europe. They arranged with the ship's captain to be sold into service upon their arrival in America. The farmer or tradesman who bought their service would then pay for their passage in return for a certain number of years of servitude, during which he would provide them with food, lodging and clothing. Parents would often sell their children into service for a number of years in exchange for a certain sum of money. Some Germans who had been able to pay for their passage still became indentured for a time in order to learn English and develop skills and knowledge that would eventually help them to make their own living.[32]

Kalm tried to spend as much time as possible in the field before the onset of winter weather. On October 12, he noted that he and Jungström had been on the banks of the Schuylkill, presumably at Bartram's suggestion, to gather seeds and collect plants. They purchased paper to make cones to hold the seeds, sand to keep the seeds dry, boxes for shipment and a trunk to hold the boxes.[33] On the twenty-fifth and twenty-sixth, he spent the day packing up all of the seeds that he had gathered so that they could be sent aboard a ship leaving for England. Packing required careful work to make sure that they arrived in good condition. He may have received instruction from Bartram, who had worked out successful shipping methods during his long dealings with Collinson and his friends.

Kalm enjoyed the taste of persimmons, but not until after the fruit had been touched by frost. Hesselius, as a practical joke, offered one to Jungström before the frost had removed its bitterness.[34] The poor man found his mouth so puckered up with the acidity that he could hardly speak, and he was unwilling to taste the fruit again during their stay in North America.

Kalm decided to purchase a horse rather than having frequently to rent one, so the expenditure was made on October 15, along with purchase of fodder, shoeing of the horse and a saddle and bridle.[35] Alas, several months later he discovered that the mare was pregnant and had to be exchanged for another.[36]

On October 27, when the season for seed and plant collection had mostly passed, but before wintry weather would make travel difficult, Kalm set out for New York City, accompanied by Peter Cock. No mention of Jungström was made; perhaps he was left behind to continue collecting. The purpose of the journey was primarily to obtain information on the safest route to take to Canada the following spring.[37]

Kalm and Cock traveled north along the Delaware, crossing by ferry to Trenton, New Jersey, where they spent the night of October 27. The town, consisting of about 100 houses, served primarily as a way station for travelers and goods between Philadelphia and New York. At Trenton, goods were loaded from boats onto wagons for the journey across the state to New Brunswick. This area was well populated and extensively cultivated, with spacious orchards full of peach and apple trees, heavy with ripe fruit. Kalm noted that every farmhouse had a cider press for apple juice. Hard cider was a beverage of choice throughout the northern colonies.

Most of the inhabitants were descendants of the Dutch and Germans, who built their barns in a style prevalent in their home country. In each of the towns that Kalm passed through, he described the nature of construction of the homes and the materials used. Much of the next day and night, October 28, was spent in Princeton because of a heavy rain storm. Kalm and Cock arrived at about noon the next day in New Brunswick, about thirty miles from Trenton and sixty from Philadelphia. A ferry took them across the Raritan River, and they continued their journey on a road through Woodbridge to Elizabethtown, where they spent the next night. Kalm approved of the town's two fine churches, one Presbyterian and the other Church of England, and the many gardens and orchards. On October 30,

the pair were ferried across the river to Staten Island, which they crossed by horseback to embark on the ferry for Manhattan Island.[38]

There Kalm met with Cadwallader Colden, to whom he had sent a letter, along with one from Linnaeus and some pamphlets, which were forwarded to Colden by Franklin.[39]

Colden, trained as a physician in Edinburgh, first came from Scotland in 1710 to Philadelphia. There he became a friend of Franklin and of James Logan, a fellow Scot.[40] Like them, he had broad interests and excelled in many fields, ranging from science to politics. In 1715, Colden returned to Scotland to marry, and while there he submitted a paper on a medical subject that was read to the Royal Society. After his return to Philadelphia, he visited

Cadwallader Colden. (Edmund Bailey O'Callaghan, *O'Callaghan's Documentary History of the State of New York*)

New York City, 1750. (New York State Library)

New York and was persuaded to stay there by Governor Robert Hunter, a Fellow of the Royal Society. In 1720, Colden was appointed Surveyor General of the Province of New York.[41] He was thus one of the most knowledgeable persons on the geography of the Hudson Valley.

Colden had studied botany, then considered part of the medical curriculum, at Edinburgh and later, after reading *Genera Plantarum,* mastered the Linnaean system of plant classification, the first person in America to do so. He carried on a correspondence with Collinson and with Gronovius in the Netherlands as well as with Linnaeus, and had sent them some specimens of American plants. Gronovius was so impressed by the collection that he drew up a catalog of the flora found in the vicinity of Coldengham, Colden's country estate near New-burgh, New York, about sixty miles north of Manhattan. The catalog, *Plantae Cold-enghamiae,* drew praise from Linnaeus. John Bartram had made a visit to Colden in 1742, and the two men also corresponded and exchanged plant specimens for many years.[42]

Colden sent a letter to Linnaeus in February 1749, informing him that he had met Kalm and saying that he hoped to see him again on his way to Canada. He assured Linnaeus that he would help Kalm, "if I can be of any use to him in making his voyage more convenient or safe for him."[43]

While in New York, Kalm was also able to obtain advice on his journey to Canada from James Alexander, a Scotch-born lawyer and politician who was knowledgeable in astronomy and mathematics and who corresponded with many European scientists. Alexander was the surveyor general of New Jersey and had also held that post in New York. Alexander was one of the early members of the American Philosophical Society, which had been proposed in 1743 by Franklin in his pamphlet, *A Proposal for Promoting Useful Knowledge among the British Plantations in America,* based on an idea that had been discussed by him with Bartram and Colden.[44] Their role is shown in the priority given botanical research and related mineralogical matters in the organization's announced purposes.[45] The American Philosophical Society was organized the following year according to Franklin's proposals and based in Philadelphia. However, the outbreak of King George's War ended the project, not revived for many years.[46]

Kalm was surprised to learn that, in addition to eight different Christian sects, each with their own house of worship, there was a community of Jews in New York. They enjoyed "all the privileges common to the other inhabitants of this town and province," Kalm reported, including a synagogue and ownership of shops, farms and ships.[47] Kalm attended the synagogue, noting that the women sat in galleries, while the men sat below.

Kalm noted the lack of good drinking water in New York, a condition that was not remedied until a century later. He was impressed with the excellence of New York harbor, its shelter on three sides and the fact that its salt water did not normally freeze. He noted that New York's commerce was more extensive than that of its closest rivals, Boston and Philadelphia.

Kalm was especially interested in the economy of the colonies and how it benefited the mother country. He described the triangular trade between Boston, England and the West Indies. Boston sent fish, tar, pitch and lumber to England in return for manufactured goods. Fish, butter, cheese, horses, cattle and lumber were traded to the West Indies in return for sugar, molasses and rum.[48] He marveled at the advantage to England of its control over colonial commerce. "England, and especially London, profits immensely by its trade with the American colonies; for not only New York but likewise all the other English towns on the continent import so many articles from England that all their specie, together with the goods which they get in other countries must all go to Old England to pay their accounts there, for which they are, however, insufficient. Hence it appears how much a well regulated colony contributes to the increase and welfare of its mother country."[49]

Kalm may have later been influenced by conversations with Franklin regarding the role of American trade in the British Empire. In 1750, Franklin published a small treatise in response to Parliament's passage of the Iron Act, prohibiting the growth of iron manufacturing in America in order to benefit English producers. Franklin pointed out the economic opportunity in America that led to a greatly expanded population. He thought it unnecessary and unwise to restrain American manufacturing and to discourage economic opportunity and growth within the Empire.[50]

Kalm described the government of New York at great length. His comparison with that of Pennsylvania was unfavorable. He said that one of the reasons why New York was more sparsely populated was that Germans who had migrated there were badly treated and thus moved to Pennsylvania, where they found a welcome.[51]

In Manhattan, Kalm greatly enjoyed eating the oysters that were harvested in great quantities in the area for local consumption and were also exported to the West Indies. They were peddled from push carts on the streets of the city and usually fried in butter and then eaten in a sandwich with soft wheat bread.[52]

Kalm spent from November 1 to 3 in New York, arriving back in Philadelphia on November 5. The next day, he went to visit Bartram, presumably to report on his visit to Colden. There he met a visitor from Carolina, who described the methods used there to obtain tar from the pitch pines that grow in the low country. They also discussed the method for growing rice in South Carolina. Kalm again paid a visit to Bartram on November 18. They discussed the slate used for roofs in the area. Bartram also described a cave that he had explored in which he found stalactites.[53]

In a letter to Collinson, dated October 29, Franklin wrote that Kalm had been out of town a great deal since his arrival a month before, in the countryside botanizing and visiting New York, but planned to spend the winter in Philadelphia. He added that "no Service I can do him shall be wanting; but hitherto we have but little Acquaintance."[54] It was not until almost two weeks later, on November 10, that Kalm dined with Franklin.[55] Several times after that, Franklin reported to James Logan that he had called on Kalm, but never found him at his lodgings.[56] Kalm's single-mindedness to get about his long-delayed tasks made him forgetful of some of the social niceties that would have created a better impression on such important people as Logan and Franklin. He had no time for socializing while the weather was still good.

During his visits with Franklin, Kalm learned a great deal about New England fisheries and the habits of herring and cod that Franklin recalled from his Boston childhood. They also discussed moose and the fire-resistant nature of asbestos, a sample of which Franklin gave him. Franklin also suggested that, rather than obtaining their salt from the West Indies, as was their practice, the people of Pennsylvania might make good salt of sea water, as was done in New England. Franklin also told Kalm of his observations of ants and experiments with them, suggesting that they had some means of communicating with each other to indicate where food might be found.[57]

As winter approached, there was no longer much that could be done to collect seeds and to learn new plants. Kalm had to wait now until spring arrived and he could embark on his planned journey.

CHAPTER SIX
New Sweden
November 20, 1748—May 19, 1749

THE SHORES OF THE DELAWARE RIVER had been the site of Sweden's only attempt to establish a colony in the new world. Kalm met a number of the descendents of Swedish colonists; he was eager to learn more about the settlement and why it had failed.

IN THE EARLY SEVENTEENTH CENTURY, Dutch, German and Scottish traders, who saw opportunities for economic advance, came to Sweden with goods from the outside world along with new ideas.[1] One of Kalm's maternal ancestors, from Scotland, had been among them, and settled in Finland. Connections were especially strong between Sweden and the Netherlands, and many Swedes, including Linnaeus, went there to further their education and to learn from what was then one of the most successful entrepreneurial nations in Europe. Several Dutchmen played an important part in the formation of the New Sweden Company in 1637, hoping to duplicate the success of the Dutch West India Company and the British Hudson's Bay Company in North America. Half of the funds for the initial enterprise came from Dutch members, and there had been encouragement for the project from a disgruntled member of the Dutch West India Company, Samuel Blommaert, who felt that there had been mismanagement in New Amsterdam. Pieter Minwe (Minuit), who had been appointed governor of New Netherland by the Dutch West India Company in 1624 and purchased Manhattan Island from the Indians for the fabled $24 worth of trinkets, led the first Swedish expedition. He had been recalled by the Dutch West India Company and was smarting from what he perceived as unfair treatment.[2]

Minuit knew the Dutch claimed the territory bordering the Delaware River but that they had not sent settlers there. It was protected by only a few sparsely-guarded forts used as trading posts. He led two ships, the *Calmare Nyckel* and the *Fogel Grip*, manned by Dutch and Swedish sailors but flying the blue-and-yellow Swedish flag, up the Delaware in March 1638. An armored war party of Swedish soldiers landed on a rocky point off Delaware Bay next to a stream called the Minquas Kill, now the site of Wilmington, Delaware.[3]

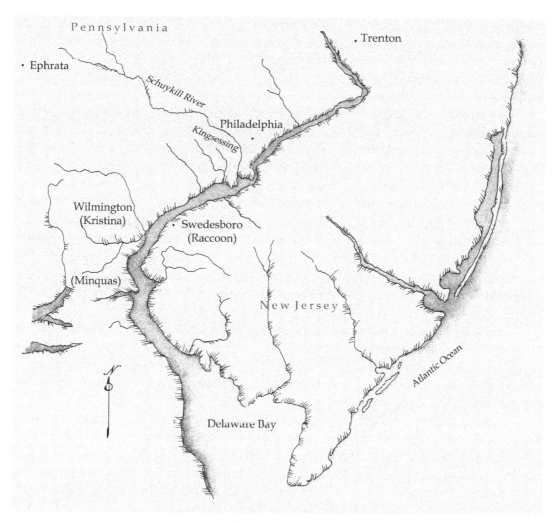

New Sweden.
(Map by Bernadette Wolf)

Minuit set up a trading post there that they called Fort Christina, in honor of Sweden's twelve-year-old queen.[4] Minuit also negotiated a purchase from the Lenape Indian chiefs similar to the one he had made of Manhattan. The land extended 40 miles along the west side of the Delaware River below Kristina Creek and about 27 miles north to the Schuylkill River. This purchase was not carried out so much as a matter of fairness to the native inhabitants but as a way to establish the legality of the Swedish settlement against the prior claims of the Dutch. Later purchases would extend the territory to the falls of Trenton and the east side of the Delaware.[5]

The Lenape were Algonquian-speakers and lived in small villages or family clusters spread throughout the area. They subsisted mostly by hunting and gathering, as well as by growing corn, beans and squash. The Lenape sachems did not really understand the concept of ownership of land. They had actually "sold" their land and granted sovereign authority to three of the different competing colonial powers during the 1630s.[6]

Several Swedish fortifications were erected near the land in Kingsessing that Bartram later purchased for his farm. At Kingsessing, Minuit set up another trading post on the west side of the Delaware at the entrance to the Schuylkill, where the Minquas Indians, an Iroquoian-speaking tribe to the north and west, could bring their furs for trading.[7] When the Swedes had merchandise to sell in exchange for the beaver and other pelts, they charged less than did the competing Dutch and English, so relations with the Indians were generally good.[8]

The initial ships returned to Sweden, leaving a small contingent of twenty-five men to establish a colony in the wilderness. Minuit died in a storm off the island of St. Christopher, where the *Calmare Nyckel* stopped on its return voyage.[9] The first round of Swedish settlers was augmented by a small group of Dutch from Utrecht who came in 1640.[10]

The New Sweden Company had difficulty in obtaining willing emigrants for subsequent expeditions and had to rely on people who were not necessarily the most qualified for such a venture. Some of the settlers had been men who had run afoul of the law: poachers, persons guilty of breaking forest ordinances, military deserters and debtors.[11]

Another source was displaced farmers, many of them ethnic Finns. From 1580 to 1650 between 12,000 and 13,000 settlers from Finland had moved to central and western Sweden to begin cultivating new lands.[12] They were farmers who used the cut-and-burn method of clearing, and then moved on in a few years after the soil had become exhausted.[13] At first, Sweden encouraged this practice because it opened up remote areas of forest to cultivation. Eventually, however, it was recognized that this method was wasteful, and strict laws with harsh penalties were passed against this practice.[14] It may also have begun to interfere with the expansion of Sweden's successful copper and iron mining industries, which required large amounts of wood for charcoal to fuel the smelters.[15] Therefore, farming in these regions was discouraged, and the Finnish settlers and some of their fellow Swedes in these provinces were left with no place to go. As a result of the increasing restrictions placed upon them by the forest ordinances, about half of the later inhabitants of New Sweden were thus displaced ethnic Finns, who had come from the provinces in Sweden in which they had pioneered.[16] The Finnish settlers attended the Swedish church, but spoke Finnish among themselves. Most of them settled around the community athat was later called Penn's Neck.[17]

These colonists had lived close to the land in Sweden, augmenting their simple farming with hunting and gathering, not dissimilar to the ways of Native

Americans, with whom they got along reasonably well. In the early years, they purchased much of their corn from the Indians, who taught them their methods of planting.

The majority of the houses in New Sweden were built by Finns because of their traditional skill in woodworking and use of wood in making so many of the implements of daily use.[18] It was these settlers who brought with them their unique method of home building—the log cabin. This type of dwelling dated from the medieval period in Norway, Sweden and Finland and had perhaps been brought back there from Russia by the Vikings. It was soon adopted by many other American colonists because it was fast and economical; the use of horizontally laid notched logs eliminated the need for nails.[19]

The Finns also brought with them the practice of the sauna. The settlers of New Sweden ordinarily bathed on Saturday night in preparation for the Sabbath. According to Joseph J. Kelley Jr., who wrote about life in colonial Philadelphia, they thus set a precedence, which became an American tradition.[20]

The Swedish government was distracted by other matters more important, and thus supported the colony only sporadically. Despite frequent requests for more settlers, more supplies, and more goods for Indian trade, ships from the mother country arrived infrequently. During the seventeen years after the initial landing at Wilmington, twelve more ships left Sweden for the Delaware Valley, of which eleven, carrying some 600 Swedes and Finns, reached their destination.[21] New Sweden was poorly funded, lacking both human and material resources. Many emigrants perished during the long voyage or were lost at sea. Others returned to Sweden on the ships that brought new settlers, although those who were released prisoners were not permitted to return.[22] The colonists were not as successful in trading for furs with the Indians as they might have been because they did not have regular supplies of items from Sweden with which to trade. Neither were they successful in producing such cash crops as tobacco, which grows better in a more southerly climate. They had to purchase much of their necessary supplies, including livestock, from New Amsterdam and from New England.[23]

After Minuit died, the next governor was Peter Hollander Ridder. He was succeeded in 1643 by the 400-pound Governor Johan Printz, who maintained generally good relations with the Indians. He had been discharged as an officer in the Thirty Years' War and, in an attempt to restore his reputation, tried to impose military discipline on the colonists.[24] Some of them, discouraged by the lack of support from Sweden, the increasing encroachment of the Dutch, and failure of some of the grain crop in the summer of 1652, revolted against the large governor. The leader of the dissent was tried and executed by Printz's order.[25] Printz finally returned to Sweden in 1653; the lack of success in the colony was only partially his fault.[26] He was replaced as director of New Sweden in 1654 by Johan Rising.[27]

Relations with New Amsterdam were relatively peaceful until Peter Stuyvestant became governor and initiated a more aggressive policy against New Sweden. In the summer of 1655, he sailed up the Delaware heading a flotilla of seven gunboats carrying three hundred soldiers. The ships anchored on the western shore of the river between the two Swedish forts. Stuyvesant sent a contingent of soldiers to occupy the road connecting them and also sent an ensign named Dirck Smith, accompanied by a drummer, to one of the forts carrying a demand for unconditional surrender. After some brief discussion in a mixture of languages, the Swedes realized that, with their limited numbers, they had no choice but to comply.[28]

At the time of the Dutch takeover, 130 families—no more than 550 people—lived in New Sweden.[29] Fortunately, Governor Stuyvesant permitted the colonists to govern themselves as a "Swedish Nation," with their own court, militia, and religion. The early Finns and Swedes made a significant contribution to the future of the region in several respects. Despite their limited numbers, writes Kelley, "the first courts, houses, civil government and farms were introduced by them, and while these had little influence on the eventual development of Philadelphia under the English, they shaped the attitudes of a sizable group of early citizens."[30]

Surprisingly, Stuyvesant also allowed the Swedes to continue their trade with the local Indians.[31] The trading rights may have been maintained because the local Maquas and Susquehannocks preferred to continue their long-cultivated trading relationship with the Swedes. They had actually fomented an attack on New Amsterdam in retaliation for Stuyvesant's dismantling of New Sweden.[32]

It was only nine years later that the Dutch flag was replaced by that of the English, who had taken New Netherland in 1664. Quakers had begun to settle the Delaware Valley as early as 1675.[33] In 1681, King Charles granted William Penn a proprietary colony of all the land west of the Delaware between forty and forty-three degrees north latitude. The Swedes and Finns were soon joined by the many Quakers who came from England with Penn, and they gradually became assimilated into the English-speaking community. The remaining colonists of Sweden were required to be naturalized as English subjects.

From October 3 to 5, some two weeks after his arrival in Philadelphia, Kalm journeyed to Wilmington, Delaware, the initial settlement of New Sweden. On the way, he crossed a bridge and had to pay a toll of two pence for himself and his horse.[34] He found the town quite attractive, with many stone houses built with open places between them to permit a pleasant view of the Delaware River. Kalm described a fortification that had been built that summer on the site of a similar one built earlier by the Swedes. Its purpose was to guard against the possible attack by French and Spanish privateers. During the construction, he reported with interest, some iron tools and an old Swedish coins were found from the earlier redoubt. The new structure consisted of planks with a rampart on the outside next to a powder magazine in a vault built of bricks. Kalm wryly noted that the fear of attack had overcome many of the local Quakers' scruples regarding participation in a defensive war.[35]

Kalm attended the Swedish church a half-mile east of Wilmington while he was there. Although, after 1655 the Swedish Kingdom had no role in the governance of what had been New Sweden, the established Swedish Lutheran Church did continue to maintain a relationship with its far-flung parishioners and supplied clergy, Swedish bibles, hymnals and other religious books for several congregations over the next century.[36]

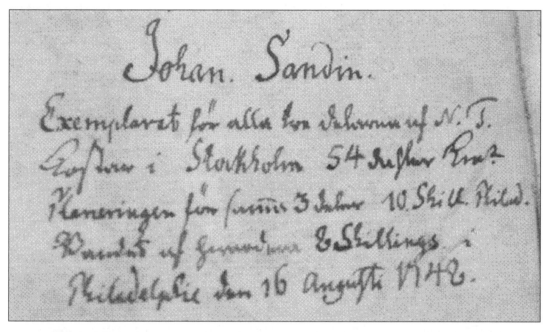

The inscription by the Reverend Johan Sandin on the cover of a dissertation on *Sponsalia plantarum* **by Linnaeus's student, Johan Gustav Wahlboom.** (American Swedish Historical Museum, Philadelphia, Pennsylvania)

One of these clergymen was the Reverend Johan Sandin, who had been sent to America in April 1748 to serve as rector of the Swedish congregations at Raccoon (now Swedesboro), and of Penn's Neck, New Jersey. Sandin brought with him a dissertation of Johan Gustav Wahlboom, a student of Linnaeus, on *Sponsalia plantarum*, which, on his arrival in Philadelphia, Sandin delivered to Franklin, who then forwarded it to Logan.[37] During the summer, Sandin collected some native plants to send to Linnaeus.[38] Six months after he arrived in Raccoon, Sandin became ill "with the fever and ague, which was followed by other disorders."[39] He may have been infected with malaria, which was endemic in the area, and he died in October. Sandin and Kalm must have known each other as students at Uppsala University and during Linnaeus's *herbationes*.

On November 20, after his trip to New York and when the autumn weather was so far advanced that the time for collecting seeds and plants had passed, Kalm went with Jungström to Raccoon to see his old friend and to visit the Swedish settlement there. After a ferry ride across the Delaware, they journeyed for most of the remainder of the day across the level countryside, where the sandy soil supported many pines and firs as well as the mountain laurel, *Kalmia latifolia*, later named by Linnaeus for Kalm.[40]

Kalm refers to *Kalmia* as "the spoon tree," so named by the Swedes because the Indians used its wood to make spoons and trowels. He notes that the English called it "laurel" because of the resemblance of its leaves to *Laurocerasus*. He admired the beauty of the plants, "They have the quality of preserving their fine green leaves throughout the winter, so that when all other trees have lost their ornaments, and stand quite naked, these adorn the woods with their green foliage. About the month of May they begin to flower in these parts, and then their beauty rivals that of most of the known trees in nature."[41]

However, he pointed out that the leaves of *Kalmia* are toxic to many animals. He also noted that the wood of *Kalmia* "has a very suitable hardness and fineness. The joiners and turners here use it in all kinds of work which requires the best wood; they use chiefly the root because it is yellowish."[42]

Much to Kalm's disappointment and sorrow, when he arrived in Raccoon, he was told of Sandin's recent death, leaving a widow with a newborn baby girl. He was greatly concerned for their welfare. He was probably aware that Sandin had not wanted to take this post so far away from home and had suffered financial loss because of having to sell property in Sweden in order to finance the journey. Like Kalm, the Sandins had been forced to spend time in England awaiting passage to Philadelphia, which ate away their savings and forced them into debt. Now that her husband had died, poor Mrs. Sandin could only hope that the Swedish Church might alot her the salary that would have been paid her husband for the next year or two so that she might return home.[43]

Kalm apparently decided that he would stay for the rest of the winter as a paying guest in Mrs. Sandin's home.[44] In addition to providing assistance to her, Kalm would also be able to save on rent in Philadelphia for himself and for Jungström. He was always careful to husband his own limited funds as much as possible.

Another advantage of this arrangement was that Kalm could serve the needs of the local congregation, left without a pastor because of Sandin's death. He took on the role of pastor to the Swedish Church in Raccoon and preached nearly every Sunday and also delivered funeral sermons. According to Sandin's successor, the

Reverend Israel Acrelius, the congregation "took him for a regular Minister."[45] Kalm had, after all, initially studied to become a Lutheran minister to follow in the footsteps of his father, uncle and cousin in Finland.

Of course, as a stranger in a foreign country still unsure of his command of English, it must have been a real pleasure to be able to converse in his own language and to worship in a church whose ritual was familiar. He was more comfortable in gaining information from the Swedish colonists about the plants and animals with which they were familiar than he might have been from English speakers. The Finnish farmers were the kind of people he had grown up with.

Kalm returned to Philadelphia on December 3, probably to collect his belongings from the home of Mistress Durburow. He and Jungström, though, continued to lodge with her during their many visits to Philadelphia over the next five months.[46] He returned to Raccoon again on December 7.

On December 11, Kalm journeyed to Penn's Neck and across the Delaware to Wilmington, returning to Raccoon on the thirteenth. This trip may have been to confer with the pastor of the Swedish church there to obtain his approval of Kalm's ministry and seek his advice and assistance. Kalm apparently stayed in Raccoon for the remainder of December and January, when the ice on the Delaware prevented the ferries from crossing. He made a brief visit to Philadelphia on February 10, returning on the twelfth.[47]

Kalm disapproved of the fact that Christmas was no longer observed in New Sweden as it was in the old country. The Swedes followed the practice of the English churches and especially the Quakers, for whom Christmas was at that time not an important holiday.[48]

In January, Kalm noted that the temperature in New Sweden was as cold (22° C) as it was likely to get in old Sweden, despite the fact that it was so much farther south. He was appalled that "the rooms here are without any shutters, the cracks in the walls without moss, and since sometimes there is no fireplace or chimney in the room, the winters here must be very disagreeable to one who is used to our warm Swedish winter rooms."

"Some days of this month the room in which I lodged was such that I could not write two lines before the ink froze on my pen. When I did not write I could not leave the ink-stand on the table, but was forced to put it upon the hearth or into my pocket."[49] Fortunately, he reported that the cold usually did not last long.

Kalm was naturally curious about the history of the New Sweden settlement and the reasons for its failure. He spent a great deal of time during that first winter researching the records of the remaining Swedish churches and interviewing elderly Swedish men to learn what they knew about the early days of the colony.[50]

Kalm reported an interview with a man descended from a family that had been in New Sweden at the time of its surrender to the Dutch. He said that the residents of New Sweden had been satisfied to surrender to Dutch rule because they had had so little help from Sweden, and they had chafed under the harsh rule of Governor Printz, who treated them like slaves.[51]

According to Kalm, William Penn had persuaded the three Svenson brothers, the Swedish owners of the land on which Philadelphia was to be built, to give up their property in exchange for land farther away.[52] Several of the old Swedes whom Kalm met implied that Penn had defrauded the Swedish colonists to obtain some of their land. The Pennsylvania cartographer Lewis Evans, with whom Kalm conferred, agreed with them in their disapproval of the Penn family. He characterized Penn's son, Thomas, as "one of the meanest and stingiest of men," who, through various pretexts had taken back lands that had been deeded to various Philadelphia residents.[53]

After seeing the prosperity of the descendants of New Sweden, Kalm believed that Sweden had made a mistake in allowing the settlement to slip out of its grasp. Upon his return to Finland, he proposed an unrealistic plan that Sweden should obtain a new colony by purchasing one of the Spanish colonies in South America. This proposal was made in a letter to Count Henning Adolf Gyllenborg, leader of the estate of Nobility in the Swedish Riksdag, in the spring of 1752. Kalm also inspired one of his students to write a thesis in 1754 entitled "Thoughts on the advantage that might have been obtained by our dear fatherland from the colony once known as New Sweden." The thesis proposed that Sweden's lack of some resources might be supplemented by a colony in a southern climate.[54]

Kalm had stayed the first night of his visit to Raccoon with a Swede named Rambo. His grandfather had been one of the first settlers and was one of the interpreters who knew the "Delaware Jargon."[55] Trade and the exchange of information were facilitated by use of this pidgin dialect of the Lenapes' Unami language.[56]

During his first visit, Kalm also stayed for several days at the home of Eric Ragnilsson, a deacon of the Swedish church. There Kalm interviewed Åke Helm, a man of 70, whose father had come to New Sweden with Governor Printz. Helm explained the lack of native grasses in the area by saying that there were now more cattle than could be supported by the available grass land. Therefore, the native annual grasses were eaten before they could produce seed, although grasses previously had grown thick and to a height of two feet.[57]

On March 27, Kalm interviewed an old Swede named Nils Gustafson who was 91, and the son of one of the original settlers in New Sweden. Gustafson explained that the Swedes had brought horses, cows, oxen, sheep, hogs, geese and ducks with them. The hogs, especially, had propagated a great deal because they had been allowed to roam free in the woods, where there was plenty for them to eat. The cattle, too, in the early days had found much grass and became fatter than they were at the time of Kalm's visit. Additional cattle were purchased from New England and New York.[58] Kalm disapproved of the fact that the cattle were not stabled but were allowed to stay outdoors all winter, where they suffered from the cold.

The Swedes had also brought seeds of wheat, rye, barley and oats, but bought corn from the Indians. They also grew cabbage, kale, rutabagas and turnips. Their beverage was beer brewed from barley; they learned to make cider and drink tea, coffee, and chocolate only when the English arrived. The early settlers made clothing from animal skins and wove linen from flax that they had grown.

Bayberries (*Myrica cerifera*), which grew abundantly in wet soil near the sea, had formerly been used extensively by the settlers in New Sweden to make candles. However, they found that gathering berries was too much trouble, so they preferred to use the tallow of animals if they could afford it.[59]

Several of the Swedish elders agreed that there had always been enough to eat in New Sweden and that the settlers had never had to face the kinds of famines that frequently occurred in the old country. Kalm attributed this abundance to the many different kinds of grain sown and two crops annually. He was also told that the early settlers associated a great deal with the local Lenape Indians and learned to live much like them.[60]

Kalm often reported on how the colonists used foods or methods of preparation unfamiliar to his European readers. Pumpkins and squashes were vegetables that the American colonists had learned to cultivate and prepare from the Indians. Pumpkin was often boiled, then mashed and mixed with milk or with cornmeal and then eaten as a porridge or a pancake.[61]

Kalm described the methods used by the colonists to dry apples and pears for winter use. In the Philadelphia area, okra, *Hibiscus esculentus,* a native of the West Indies, was planted and used in soups. The colonists also used red peppers as a spice. Wine was made by ladies, according to Kalm, using such fruits as white and red currants, strawberries, blackberries, wild grapes, raspberries and cherries.[62] Brandy was made from peaches and apples as well as from persimmons. Buckwheat was used to make flour for pancakes, which were commonly eaten for breakfast in Philadelphia and in other English colonies.[63]

Kalm was intrigued by a machine a German had made to grate cabbage for sauerkraut.[64] He provided a recipe for apple dumplings, which he found to be good.[65]

In early spring, Swedish and English settlers cooked new sprouts and leaves of dock, *Rumex crispus,* lamb's quarters, *Chenopodium album,* and poke, *Phytolacca americana,* and prepared them as they would spinach, often accompanied with vinegar, along with meat.[66]

Because of the fear of fires and the lack of proper stones on the New Jersey side of the Delaware for building fireplaces, most of the cooking ovens were built of clay. They were placed separately in the yard a short distance from the house, covered by a little roof of boards.[67]

On April 14, Kalm visited a sawmill in Chester; on the twenty-sixth, he went again to Penn's Neck, perhaps to preach there, and on May 2, he went to Salem. This was a trading town near the Delaware River located close to swamps and low-lying meadows. He noted that cases of "intermittent fevers" were frequent there. On May 5, Kalm went to the village of Rapaapo, whose inhabitants still spoke only Swedish.[68]

By early April, Kalm began to look for spring flowers. He traveled about the area surrounding Raccoon looking for plants and noting their time of flowering and leafing, which was important if he were to properly describe them. During the winter, he had been told about the medicinal and agricultural uses of many American plants with which he had been unfamiliar before his arrival, and he needed to be able to identify and describe them accurately.[69] It was not until May 19 that Kalm left Raccoon for his journey northward. He explained the lateness of his start by his need to learn about the many plants, the so-called spring ephemerals, that can only be seen in the spring and that were not evident when he arrived the previous fall.

CHAPTER SEVEN
The Journey to Canada
May 19—July 6, 1749

KALM WAS AMAZINGLY FORTUNATE in the timing of his journey to Canada. For thirty-eight of the seventy-four years between 1689 and 1763, England was at war with either France or Spain, or both, for territory in North America. Hostilities in the late spring and early summer of 1749 would have made travel along his proposed route impossible.[1] As Kalm arrived in Philadelphia, King George's War (called the War of the Austrian Succession in Europe) was just ending. The peace made Kalm's 225-mile journey northward up the Hudson from Albany to Montréal possible. The Peace of Aix-la-Chapelle had also been proclaimed in the British colonies and honored by the French in Canada months before Kalm would see the formal proclamation of peace in Montréal.[2]

Although the fighting in North America had gone against the French—New Englanders successfully captured the strategically vital French fort at Louisbourg on Cape Breton Island—the English had not fared as well in Europe, so the peace treaty restored the American territories to the status quo.[3] Fighting was to begin again formally in 1754, three years after Kalm's return to Europe, in what was known as the French and Indian War in America and the Seven Years' War in Canada and Europe.

Kalm's Swedish citizenship was also a distinct advantage for him because Sweden was a neutral party to the French and English disputes, and he was welcomed by both sides. His welcome in the English colonies was an unofficial one from private citizens who honored the letters of recommendation that Kalm brought with him from their European correspondents. However, in French Canada, Kalm was accorded many favors as a guest of the French government and was treated as a visiting dignitary, with all of his expenses paid.

The hospitality that Kalm received as an honored guest in Canada was repayment of a scientific favor that had been accorded the French crown by that of Sweden. One of the great scientific questions of the early eighteenth century regarded the exact shape of the earth and consisted of a debate between the followers of Descartes and those of Newton. Was the earth shaped like a squashed orange, as the Newtonians believed? Or was it elongated at the poles and pulled in at the equator—the view of the Cartesians? It was agreed that the only way the debate could be resolved would be to send one team of scientists to the equator and one to an area above the Arctic Circle and to compare their findings. In 1736-7, French scientists, sponsored by Louis XV and the Royal Academy of Sciences and led by Pierre Louis Moreau de Maupertuis, journeyed to Lapland, where they stayed above the Arctic Circle for almost six months in very difficult circumstances while making astronomical observations. They were greatly aided by the Swedish government, which financed their costs while they were in Sweden. Three French academicians and a priest were joined by the Swedish astronomer, Anders Celsius, one of Kalm's mentors. They were able to determine that the earth is considerably flattened towards the poles, thus confirming Newton's theory.[4] Support of Kalm's visit to Canada was thus seen by the French crown as an opportunity to reciprocate Sweden's hospitality in another scientific endeavor.[5]

In the conflicts between the English and the French for control of the constantly shifting frontiers along the territory bordering the St. Lawrence River, Lake Champlain, the Hudson River, lakes Ontario and Erie and the Ohio River, Native Americans played a crucial role. The Five Nations of the Iroquois (Mohawks, Senecas, Cayugas, Onondagas, and Oneidas, and later the Tuscaroras) were the major allies of the British. The *Hotinonshonni*, as they called themselves, were an umbrella confederation that at one time or another sheltered descendants of at least thirty-nine other Native American groups. Many of the tribes had been decimated by the scourge of smallpox that had been introduced by Europeans and had been driven from their traditional hunting grounds by the settlers who cut down the forests to grow crops and support livestock. The remnants of various dispossessed Indian tribes that had formerly lived in coastal areas east of the Appalachians found refuge in Iroquois territory.[6]

Indians often comprised the bulk of the warriors in colonial raiding parties, with only a few British or colonial soldiers in charge. After the defeat of the British at Fort Duquesne, George Washington wrote of the Indians, "They are much more serviceable than twice their number of white men. If they return to their nation, no words can tell how much they will be missed."[7]

The English saw the Iroquois as a defensive buffer for their settlements. As Governor George Thomas of Pennsylvania wrote in 1744:

> These Indians by their situation are a Frontier to some of (the English colonies), and from thence, if Friends, are Capable of Defending their Settlements; If enemies, of making Cruel Ravages upon them; If Neuters, they may deny the French a Passage through their Country, and give us timely Notice of their Designs. These are but some of the Motives for cultivating a good Understanding with them . . . This has been the Method of New York and Pennsylvania, and will not put you to so much Expence in Twenty Years as the carrying on a War against them will do in One.[8]

The Iroquois confederation was thus in a position to play off the French against the British. Because they understood the need to secure Iroquois agreement and cooperation, the British realized that they had to follow the practice of the French and bow to the demands of Indian culture. This required them to take part in days of feasting, speeches and exchange of gifts before agreements could be made. Even then, the colonists had to wait for the emergence of a consensus among the representatives of the various tribes involved.[9] Kalm, who often expressed skepticism regarding the inefficiencies of democratic government, noted, "The sachems of the Indians have commonly no greater authority over their subjects than constables in a meeting of the inhabitants of a parish, and hardly that much."[10]

The Iroquois Confederation was governed by a constitution, the "Great Law of Peace," establishing a Great Council of fifty male leaders, each representing one of the female-led clans of the alliance's nations. According to historian Charles C. Mann, who has pointed out that Iroquois governance may have provided an important model to the American colonists as they drew up their own constitutions with limited powers, the jurisdiction of the Iroquois Confederation's council was a limited one. They could deal only with the relations between the entire Confederation and outside groups, such as the colonial governments. Each of the individual Indian nations governed its own internal affairs. Any important decision had to be submitted to a kind of referendum in which both men and women were consulted.[11]

Kalm, with his neutral stance, was able to view the English strategy more clearly than did most of the American colonists. He noted that, during the skirmishes between the English and the French, the English colonies, because they were largely self-governing with deliberative assemblies that held the purse strings, did not work in concert against the French, who, in contrast, maintained tight central control through the Governor-General of Canada.

> [I]t is to be observed that each English colony in North America is independent of the other, and that each has its own laws and coinage, and may be looked upon in several lights as a state by itself. Hence it happens that in time of war things go on very slowly and irregularly here; for not only the opinion of one province is sometimes directly opposite to that of another, but frequently the views of the governor and those of the assembly of the same province are quite different; so that it is easy to see that, while the people are quarrelling about the best and cheapest manner of carrying on the war, an enemy has it in his power to take one place after another."[12]

Some colonies, especially those in New England, suffered from enemy attack and continued skirmishes with the French and their Indian allies in Nova Scotia even during the interval between declared wars.[13] Other colonists actually carried on trade with the French. For example, the Dutch in Albany remained neutral, trading for silver and pewter goods that the Indians had stolen from inhabitants of New England whom they had murdered.[14]

Kalm's comments are extremely prescient.

> The French in Canada, who are but an unimportant body in comparison with the English in America, have by this position of affairs been able to obtain great advantage in times of war; for if we judge from the number and power of the English, it would seem very easy for them to get the better of the French in America.
>
> It is however of great advantage to the crown of England that the North American colonies are near a country, under the government of the French, like Canada. There is reason to believe that the king never was earnest in his attempts to expel the French from their possessions there; though it might have been done with little difficulty. For the English colonies in this part of the world have increased so much in their number of inhabitants, and in their riches, that they almost vie with Old England. Now in order to keep up the authority and trade of their mother country and to answer several other purposes they are forbidden to establish new manufactures, which would turn to the disadvantage of the British commerce. They are not allowed to dig for any gold or silver, unless they send it to England immediately; they have not the liberty of trading with any parts that do not belong to the British dominion, excepting a few places; nor are foreigners allowed to trade with the English colonies of North America. These and some other restrictions occasion the inhabitants of the English colonies to grow less tender for their mother country.
>
> I have been told by Englishmen, and not only by such as were born in America but also by those who came from Europe, that the English colonies in North America, in the space of thirty or fifty years, would be able to form a state by themselves entirely independent of old England. But as the whole country which lies along the seashore is unguarded, and on the land side is harassed by the French, these dangerous neighbors in times of war are sufficient to prevent the connection of the colonies with their mother country from being broken off. The English government has therefore sufficient reason to consider means of keeping the colonies in due submission."[15]

Kalm gave much thought to the likelihood that the colonies would soon become wealthy and populous enough to break away from England. Ten years after his return to Finland, one of Kalm's students, Sven Gowinius, wrote a thesis based largely on information provided by Kalm in which he questioned whether the colonies might become powerful enough to separate from England and establish their own kingdom.[16]

Gowinius wrote in 1763 regarding the British colonies, "When these countries become stronger, and more heavily populated, might they not separate from England, and set up a kingdom of their own. Particularly if England restricts their right to manufacture? Professor Kalm has told me that he noticed a great hate between the colonies and their motherland when he was there. Freedom to manufacture goods was much curtailed. He often heard it said openly that in 20 or 30 years, they could become a separate kingdom and have their own king."[17]

Kalm's observations regarding the squabbles between the colonies regarding preparations for war would apply as well to the future new nation in its ongoing attempts to balance federalism with states' rights.

UNTIL THE TIME OF KALM'S VISIT, the disputed territory between the English and French colonies was largely uncharted by Europeans and remained a "no-man's land" with only a few trails known to Indian raiding parties from either side. By the middle of the eighteenth century, the French were at a definite advantage in terms of geographic knowledge of the interior of the eastern North American continent because of their control of the two largest and longest rivers: the St. Lawrence and the Mississippi. They provided the routes by which many French explorers had been able to penetrate and describe the interior of the continent. The English, on the other hand, were confined to a narrow strip of settlements along the Atlantic seaboard by the barrier of the Appalachian Mountains and by the fact that the warlike Seneca tribe of the Iroquois federation guarded the Native American hunting grounds beyond the mountains. It was simply too dangerous for mapmakers to venture into their territory. Because of the competition between the French and the English, map makers from one side did not compare notes with those on the other.[18]

The most important item that Kalm needed to enable him to accomplish the task set for him by the Swedish Royal Academy of Sciences was a map that would indicate the route that he could take from the English colonies of Pennsylvania and New York to New France. Another of Kalm's lucky breaks was the fact that Lewis Evans, a Philadelphia cartographer, had completed a map of Pennsylvania, New Jersey, and New York in March 1749, just in time for Kalm's departure. It was the first time that so much of the middle British colonies had been mapped in such detail.[19]

Evans was a friend of Franklin and had made for him two excellent diagrams of his Franklin stove, which aided in its marketing.[20] He had accompanied John Bartram and Conrad Weiser on their trip to Onondaga and Oswego , but Osego was in the colony of New York when the first fort was built there in 1743, documented by Bartram in a travel journal.[21] Evans was able to accumulate considerable data for his map during the journey.[22] Two years later, he traveled with a Pennsylvania delegation to Albany to negotiate a treaty with the Iroquois.

Evans also obtained valuable information from Cadwallader Colden. In 1726, Colden, while serving in his official capacity as surveyor general of the New York Colony, and on various boundary commissions, had made a map of the manorial holdings along the Hudson River, which had not changed substantially in twenty-five years.[23]

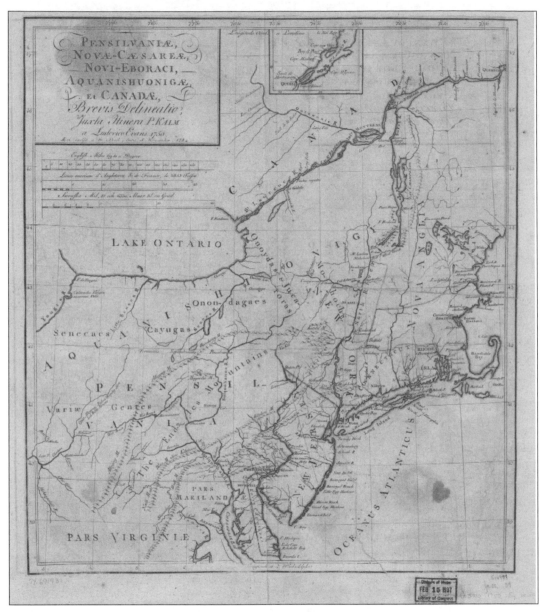

**Copy of map drawn by Lewis Evans for Kalm in 1750. Kalm's journey
from Raccoon to Cap aux Oyes in Canada is shown by a thick, broken line;
his journey from Albany to Niagara by a dotted line.**

(Library of Congress)

    Kalm spent much time in the company of Evans in the fall and winters of
1748-1749 and 1749-1750, and he frequently mentions Evans's name in reports of
weather or geographical phenomena. Evans prepared a map specifically for
Kalm's trip to Canada in 1749.[24]

ON MAY 19, 1750, KALM LEFT RACCOON FOR PHILADELPHIA, presumably to make final preparations for his trip north and probably to consult once again with Evans. He wrote a letter to the Royal Swedish Academy of Sciences on May 28, outlining his plan, optimistically hoping to be able to return to Sweden in the autumn or in the following spring to sow the seeds he had collected.[25]

Kalm dined with Franklin on May 30 and was served a dish of yams, a vegetable new to him, which he found tasty.[26] Kalm was very adventuresome when presented with new foods or methods of preparation and was always eager to experiment.

The next day he and Jungström left Philadelphia and sailed up the river, stopping at Burlington, and arrived at Trenton, New Jersey, early on the morning of June 1. The next day they traveled by wagon to New Brunswick through fields sown with wheat, rye, corn, oats, buckwheat, hemp and flax, and they saw many wild flowers in bloom in the woods. The air was perfumed with the scent of magnolia blossoms from the trees growing in swamps that they passed.[27]

On June 3, in pleasant weather, they boarded a boat bound for New York that sailed down the Raritan River and around Staten Island. In New York he was able to purchase wild strawberries from a street vendor. They spent a week in the city making final preparations, even purchasing fabric for the tailor to make their summer clothing.[28] Kalm conferred again with Cadwallader Colden.

With the aid of the incoming tide, Kalm and Jungström boarded a boat on June 11 that sailed up the Hudson, through the majestic Highlands, past the current site of West Point. At first, the sloop was able to make use of its sails to propel them, but when the wind died down, the sailors were forced to use oars. When the tide turned and the wind blew against them, they stopped for a time on shore, where Kalm saw *Kalmia latifolia* in full blossom and sassafras, chestnut and tulip poplar trees. On June 12, they were propelled by the tide, and later the wind, past the village of Rhinebeck. "This little town is not visible from the riverside."[29]

They arrived in Albany at eight o'clock on the morning of June 13, having sailed all night with a favorable wind. Albany's location, at a point where the Hudson was still deep enough for large vessels, was an advantage. The merchants of the city sent lumber, wheat, flour, and dried peas to New York City. The city was also the main collection point for furs from Oswego, the trading town on Lake Ontario to which Indians from the interior brought their furs. Kalm reported with disdain that the merchants of Albany sold brandy to them, which often enabled them to cheat drunken Indians on the price of the cloth and metal goods which they obtained in exchange for furs.[30]

Kalm had an unfavorable view of the inhabitants of Albany and the area north of the town; they were mostly descendants of Dutch colonists and still spoke that language. Kalm was charged what he considered exorbitant prices for goods that he purchased there. He reported great animosity between the Dutch settlers of Albany and the people of the other English colonies.[31]

**Colonel William Johnson (1715-1774);
John Wollaston (1736-1767); ca. 1750-52;
oil on canvas, ht. 30 1/16 in., w. 25 in.**
(Albany Institute of History and Art,
Albany, New York, gift of Laura Munsell
Tremaine in memory of her father,
Joel Munsell, 1922.)

Kalm observed that many of the Dutch in Albany were quite wealthy, owning extensive estates in the countryside that often included lumber mills. Kalm found that one reason for their wealth was their frugal style of living. He complained of their lack of hospitality, noting that they were stingy with food and seldom offered guests a drink of punch. But he commended their womenfolk, "The women are perfectly well acquainted with economy; they rise early, go to sleep very late, and are almost superstitiously clean in regard to the floor, which is frequently scoured several times in the week."[32]

The Dutch in Albany ate a breakfast that consisted of tea sweetened with sugar and accompanied by bread and butter and radishes and sometimes a slice of cheese. The noontime meal was one similar to that of other Europeans, with meat and vegetables. Supper usually consisted of cornmeal porridge with milk or buttermilk sweetened with syrup or sugar and accompanied by bread and butter with cheese and any meat leftover from dinner.[33] Neither pudding nor pie, "the Englishman's perpetual dish," was served.[34] A visitor to a home in the Albany area was offered tea with a bowl of cracked nuts (walnuts, butternuts and hickories) and a plate of large sweet apples.[35] On his return from Canada, Kalm was able to first enjoy an interesting dish prepared by his landlady in Albany. Made from thinly sliced cabbage, oil, vinegar and melted butter, the Dutch called it *cole slaw*.[36]

Kalm had been advised by Colden to consult with Colonel William Johnson regarding the route he should follow to Montréal.[37] Johnson was an Irish émigré who had become a prominent fur trader and landowner, an adopted Mohawk, colonel of the frontier militia, and the most influential intermediary in New York with the Iroquois. Colden had written a letter on May 27 (old style) to Johnson, introducing Kalm. "He comes strongly recommended to me by the King of Sweeden's Physicean & other friends in Europe & therefore what civility you shew him will be an obligation on me."[38] He strongly urged Johnson to "give him any assistance he wants & he wants no other but that of advice in what manner to travel to Canada most conveniently & with the least danger whether by Oswego or Crownpoint."[39]

Kalm's party left Albany on June 21, having procured the services of two guides, recommended by Johnson, at five pounds each,[40] who were to accompany them as far as Crown Point, or Fort St. Frédéric, the first French outpost. The guides started out in a canoe, while Kalm and Jungström walked along the shore on a road, so that they would have a better opportunity to investigate the countryside and the farms that they passed. They stayed the first night in a countryman's cottage. The next day they arrived at the Cohoes Falls, where the Mohawk River empties into the Hudson. Lewis Evans had calculated the height and breadth of the falls, and Kalm agreed that his calculation seemed accurate.[41]

Beyond the Mohawk, the road ended and they were obliged to continue their journey in a canoe. Large canoes, such as the one they used, were not easy to procure, as Kalm had to pay a man to travel 40 miles away to find a suitable one.[42] They were made by hollowing out a tree trunk, usually a cedar, chestnut, white oak, white pine or tulip poplar. The red (*Juniperus virginiana*) or white (*Thuja occidentalist*) cedars were preferred because they lasted the longest, often as long as twenty years, and floated lightly upon the water. The largest canoes would hold

Cohoes Falls.
(New York State Library)

as many as six people. Kalm warned that the passengers had to be careful to avoid tipping over in a strong wind because the canoes had no keel.[43] Passengers sat on the bottom of the canoe, while it was propelled by someone standing at each end guiding the canoe with a short paddle.

Another kind of boat in use along the Hudson was called a *battoe*. It was made of boards of white pine, with a flat bottom and points at both ends. It was employed chiefly to carry goods, and it had seats and was rowed like a rowboat.[44]

Kalm stayed the next night, June 23, about ten miles north of Albany in an area in which many farms had been destroyed by Indians loyal to the French during the recent skirmishes. Their owners were just beginning to return to cultivate their lands, having fled to Albany during the war. The travelers lodged one night in a farmer's barn; his house and other buildings had been burnt.

Kalm had bargained with several Indians to guide them to the French fort, but they chose instead to accompany an Englishman who offered them more money, so he and Jungström had to proceed with just the two guides from Albany. They passed the site of Fort Saratoga, which the English had burned the previous year, because they were unable to defend it against attacks by the French and Indians. They spent the night in a little hut of boards that had been erected by the people who had recently returned to the area.[45]

Travel was difficult; they encountered numerous rapids and several waterfalls, which required portages. Kalm described several large kettle holes that had been carved out by small stones and pebbles driven by the force of the water. Finally, one of the falls was so large that they were unable to get over it with the heavy canoe. Therefore, they were forced to leave the canoe and carry their baggage almost fifty miles through forests that were seldom frequented except by Indians. They were plagued with mosquitoes, gnats and wood lice at night and by heat during the day. Their sleep was disturbed by fear of poisonous snakes and possible Indian raids as well as the sound of trees cracking with the weight of thousands of passenger pigeons that roosted in them at night. Several times they had to cut down tall trees to use as a bridge across streams. They were able to find an old path leading to Fort Nicholson on the eastern shore of the Hudson where a wooden fort had stood formerly.[46]

In a letter to Linnaeus, Kalm vividly described the rigors of his journey, explaining that "it is not as easy to travel here as it is in Sweden or Russia."

> In the woods the grass reaches up to under one's arms, the trees are entwined by thorny *Smilacibus*.[47] If one wants to move forward, one sometimes has to crawl on all fours. And the poisonous green snake is often resting in the trees. It bites those who come near him right in the face, and many have died of its bites.[48] And on the ground you are never safe from the rattlesnake, one of the most poisonous snakes in the world. I must admit that I haven't always been calm when I have had to crawl on all four under the bushes, groping my way forward, and the multitude of *Grylli* and *Cicadae*, with all their noise, have prevented me from hearing the snake's rattling that is warning one not to come too near."[49]

They finally arrived on June 27 at Fort Anne. Here they stayed for two days in weather that was stiflingly hot while they constructed a new boat of elm and hickory bark with ribs of hickory branches. Kalm described in detail the process that was used.[5] It required finding a large elm whose bark could be stripped off in a large enough piece to accommodate four men and their goods. This stop also allowed one of the guides, who had become ill, to recover.

When the canoe was completed, it was paddled by the guides while Kalm and Jungström walked along the shore. Care had to be

Native American building a birchbark canoe.
(North Wind Picture Archives)

taken to prevent protruding rocks or branches from puncturing the bark. The canoe encountered many hazards, with trees across the river and, later on, several beaver dams. Eventually the river became deeper and swifter, and the two were again able to return to the canoe.[51]

About three miles from Fort Anne they passed a place where they knew that Indians had camped the night before, as their fire was yet smoldering. Toward evening they were met by six French soldiers on their way to Saratoga accompanying three Englishmen who were being exchanged. They told of a party of French Indians who had been on their way to revenge a killing by the English of one of their brothers. They guessed that they were the men who had camped at the site that Kalm and his party had passed only hours before. Only by chance had they avoided being mistaken for Englishmen and killed by the Indians. Despite the entreaties of the French soldiers to return with them to Saratoga to avoid encountering the Indians, Kalm was determined to continue on to Fort St. Frédéric rather than having to retrace his steps. He could ill-afford to lose another week or two of the precious summertime in Canada that such a detour would have taken.[52]

After leaving the French soldiers, on June 30, the party proceeded on foot because during the war the French had clogged the channel of the river with trees to prevent the English from attacking Canada. However, after walking about six miles, they came to the place where the French soldiers told them they left their boats, and the party took one that had been offered, and again paddled down the river, which was now broader. Alas, after rowing some time they discovered that the river was flowing in "the wrong direction,"[53] so they had to retrace their twelve-mile route, paddling late into the night. That night they were so afraid of being found by the Indian war party that they did not dare to light a fire.[54]

The countryside through which they rowed the next day was bleak and forbidding, with swampy banks flanked by high steep mountains. At breakfast they ate the last of their provisions. Despite a strong north wind, they rowed as fast as they could. Finally, at about six o'clock they arrived at a point of land about 12 miles from Fort St. Frédéric, where the river widens into a spacious bay.[55] Here they slept from exhaustion, despite the remonstrances of their empty stomachs.[56]

Kalm thanked the grace of God that they had encountered the French soldiers who left them their canoe. Without it, they would have had great difficulty in

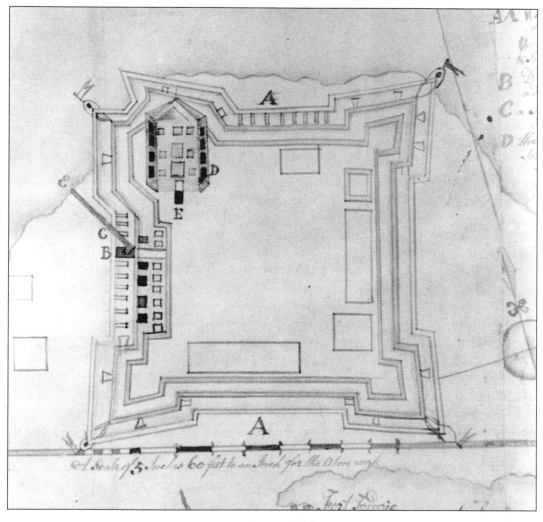

Fort St. Frédéric.
(New York State Library)

crossing the bay in any makeshift bark boat that they would have been able to construct. They had no firearms with them, so they would have had to subsist on the frogs and water snakes which abounded in the area. They set out in the moonlight before dawn the next morning. The wind had not yet begun to blow, and by eight o'clock on July 2 they arrived at Fort St. Frédéric.[57]

Three days later, from the window of the fort, they saw the party of Indians—six Ottawas, Nipissings, and Abenakis—that they had so fortunately avoided, now sailing past the fort. Displayed at the prow of their boat was a bloody scalp that they had taken from an English colonist. One of them had put on the dead man's clothing, and when they got on shore not far from the fort, they stuck the pole in the ground and danced around the scalp. They had crept up on the farmer while he was working in his fields near the Connecticut River in Charlestown, New Hampshire. A nine-year-old boy, whom Kalm had assumed was his son, was taken by the Indians with the intent of raising him and eventually marrying him to a woman in their tribe.[58] This adoption was typical of the Indian custom of "mourning war," in which the families of warriors killed in raids could only properly mourn them by replacing them with captives taken from the enemies' community.[59] The French governor, seeking the release of prisoners from New England, later took the boy and sent him back to his family. The boy was Enos Stevens, the son of Captain Phineas Stevens, emissary to New France.[60]

Fort St. Frédéric, with its thick black limestone walls and forty mounted cannon, was a physical reminder of the French assertion that the boundary of their territory began at Crown Point at the narrows of Lake Champlain. It was from this fort that many raiding parties had terrorized the frontiers of New Hampshire, Massachusetts, Connecticut and New York.[61]

Despite the fact that there were far fewer French in Canada than the English in their colonies (the population of the colony of New York alone outnumbered that of New France by three to two), Kalm found the French militarily much stronger.[62] He later learned that their soldiers were well-paid and well-cared for. He admired the hospital for sick soldiers in Montréal, where they received most of their medical care without charge. The French forts were well-built and well-supplied, whereas those of the English were poorly constructed and maintained. As a neutral observer, Kalm's estimate of the relative strength of the French and British forces was probably an accurate one.

Kalm and his party came upon one of the English forts that had been burned, apparently by colonists on the English side. When asked why they would burn down their own fort, "They replied that it was done to have another opportunity to extract money from the government; for the latter would appropriate a large sum for the rebuilding of the fort, the biggest proportion of which would perhaps reach the pockets of a few of the promoting authorities, who would then again erect only a wretched fort."[63]

Kalm surmised that many of the wealthy original Dutch settlers of the Hudson Valley, who had no love for the English, had found the replacement of the forts another profitable way to add to their income. It seemed clear to Kalm that New France had won King George's War and that the countryside between Fort St. Frédéric and the Hudson could rightly be claimed by Canada.[64]

Montréal, Canada, seen from the St. Lawrence River, 1760 woodcut.
(North Wind Picture Archives)

CHAPTER EIGHT
The Honored Guest in Canada
July 2—October 25, 1749

A S SOON AS KALM ARRIVED IN FRENCH TERRITORY, bedraggled, hungry and covered with insect bites from his month-long journey through New Jersey, New York and the wilderness, he was transformed into an important visiting dignitary, accorded many privileges. No longer was he the student and beneficiary of patronage that he had to beg for, as in Sweden, or a curious foreign traveler on a tight budget, as had been the case in Philadelphia and New York.

He reacted with great pleasure to his preferential treatment from the French officials:

> The governor of the fort, M. Lusignan, a man of learning and of great politeness, heaped kindness upon us, and treated us with as much civility as if we had been his relations. I had the honor of eating at his table during my stay here, and my servant was allowed to eat with his. We had our rooms, etc. to ourselves (at a time when travelers often had to share a bed with strangers), and at our departure the governor supplied us with ample provisions for our journey to Fort Saint Jean.[1]

Kalm and Jungström stayed for more than two weeks at Fort St. Frédéric, recuperating from their harrowing journey and exploring the nearby countryside. On July 16, he noted seeing wild rice (*Zizania aquatica*) "in mud and in most rapid parts of brooks" in full bloom.[2] It was one of the plants that he had been instructed to investigate for its potential transplantation to Sweden.

They left by boat,[3] under sail northward on July 20, and arrived at Fort St. John on the western shore of the mouth of Lake Champlain on July 21.[4] There they found horses and two casks of wine sent especially for them by the governor-general of Canada. In addition, they received a letter stating that Kalm "had been particularly recommended by the French court"[5] and that the commander should supply him with everything he wanted to forward his journey."

They left Fort St. John on July 23 en route to La Prairie de la Madeleine on the east side of the St. Lawrence River opposite Montréal. As they neared the village, they emerged from the forest into a well-tended farmland with fields cultivated mostly with grains, especially summer wheat. Kalm was impressed, writing that this countryside was "one of the finest of North America that I had hitherto seen."[6]

**Roland-Michael Barrin,
Comte de la Galissonnière,
Governor-General of Canada.**
(Library and Archives of Canada)

On July 24, Kalm and Jungström crossed the St. Lawrence in a bateau that took them to Montréal. As the first Swedes to come to Montréal, they were met by a curious crowd and taken to meet the soon-to-be governor, Longueuil, who, Kalm wrote, "loaded me with greater favors than I could expect or even imagine, both during that stay and on my return from Québec."[7]

Kalm stayed in Montréal with the family of a merchant, René de Couagne, to whom he had been given a letter of recommendation by William Johnson.[8] They treated him as almost a member of the family and refused any payment for his food and lodging.[9]

On July 27, Kalm took part in the celebration of the peace of Aix-la-Chapelle of October 18, 1748, which formally ended King George's War between France and England. The festivities included fireworks and artillery salutes, and a supper with the governor at which the guests "drank merrily far into the night."[10]

In Montréal, Kalm made his usual observations of temperature and weather, particularly the length of winter and the greatest degree of cold. He was favorably impressed by the location and climate of the city and by the many fine buildings that he saw. Near Montréal, Kalm had found wild plum trees growing in great abundance and laden with tasty fruit.[11] The American cranberries that grew in the area were very similar to those in Sweden, although he reported that the fruits were larger and very abundant.[12]

On August 2, Kalm and Jungström, accompanied by an officer, departed from Montréal in a bateau that sailed down the St. Lawrence en route to Québec. The farmhouses along the banks were spaced apart, forming an extended village all along the river. All the cultivated lands were along the banks, not extending far inland except when they encircled a town, and then only for a distance of less than twenty miles. After spending the night in a farmhouse on the shore of Rivière de Loup, they proceeded the next day to Trois Rivières, a little market town.

There, while his companions rested, the indefatigable Kalm went on horseback to view a nearby iron works, which he found similar to those he had seen in Sweden.

On August 5, they arrived in Québec, where Kalm was housed for the first nights in an apartment specially prepared for him in the palace of the Vice-Governor-General of Canada, Roland-Michael Barrin, Comte de la Galissonnière. Later la Galissonnière found for Kalm and Jungström a pleasant lodging in the home of Madame La Jus, whose son had been a surgeon in the Swedish Navy at Karlskrona in 1742. As an honored guest in Québec, Kalm needed to keep up appearances. He paid for two pairs of silk stockings, powder and pomade, and several times for the services of the peruke maker who arranged his hair, all of which he charged to the Swedish Royal Academy.[13] However, many other items of clothing and other necessities, such as a leather valise and two crystal goblets, were paid for by the French government.[14]

Almost every day that he was in Québec, Kalm dined with la Galissonnière, whom he admired tremendously. "He has a surprising knowledge in all branches of science, and especially in natural history, in which he is so well versed that when he began to speak with me about it I imagined I saw our great Linné under a new form. He told me several ways of employing natural history to the purposes of politics, the science of government, and to make a country powerful in order to weaken its envious neighbors."[15]

Kalm was impressed by the French and with his experiences in French Canada. He compared the government's official interest in the advancement of the natural sciences with that of the English colonies. For the French, it was a matter of national policy enforced by an edict that had been written by la Galissonnière. Officers at all French forts were requested to send specimens of seeds, roots and of minerals, and each official was instructed in the proper manner of collection and observation. In contrast, Kalm wrote disparagingly of the acquisitiveness of the English colonists, "I found that the people of distinction had here [French Canada] in general a much greater taste for natural history and other learning than in the English colonies, where it was everybody's sole care and employment to scrape a fortune together, and where the sciences were held in universal contempt."[16]

Québec was the only port in French Canada used by ocean-going vessels. All of the fur traders came to Québec in September or October to sell their pelts for shipment to France. All trade was closely regulated. Only ships from France were permitted to enter the St. Lawrence, not even those from French possessions in the West Indies. Only salt that was imported from France was used, although it had been possible to make salt from sea water in Canada. In those days before refrigeration, salt was an essential commodity used to preserve foods.[17]

Kalm was much impressed by the importance of religion in the lives of the

French in Canada and the faithfulness of their observances. They were said to be more devout than the people of the mother country. He noted the many roadside shrines with an "image of our Savior, the Cross, or of the Holy Virgin with the Child in her arms."[18] Each morning at the start of their travels, the French would read a prayer in Latin. Kalm commented from his Protestant perspective that "it was both strange and amusing to see and hear how eagerly the women and soldiers said their prayers in Latin and did not themselves understand a word of what they said. It all seems to be a ceremony."[19]

In Québec, Kalm noted the presence of seven or eight churches in addition to the Cathedral, as well as the buildings housing the Recollet clergy, the College of the Jesuits, the Bishop's House, and the convent of the Ursuline Nuns. As a special favor, he was permitted to visit the nunnery, where men were usually prohibited. He was shown the small cells of the nuns, furnished only with a bed, desk, and a chair or two. No heat was provided to their rooms in the wintertime except from a stove in the hallway. During the day, the nuns did fine needlework and made silk flowers. Their lives were confined to the nunnery, the surrounding garden and the hospital, where they attended the sick.

About fifty nuns lived in the convent; most were more than forty years of age, since few Canadian women joined a convent unless they were of an age at which "she had small hopes of ever getting a husband."[20] Kalm reported, "All agree here that the men are much less numerous in Canada than the women, for the men die on their voyages" or are killed in battles.[21]

Kalm was also invited to visit the Jesuit College, and he dined with the twenty men then in residence in a magnificent stone building which he likened to the new royal palace in Stockholm. The Jesuits, like the nuns, kept a fine garden planted with fruit trees and vegetables for use in the kitchen. He reported that "They dine very well, and their dishes are as numerous as at the greatest feasts."[22]

Kalm was favorably impressed, too, with the Jesuits whom he met, despite whatever he may have learned against them from Colden and from his friends in Philadelphia, who, like Bartram, were suspicious of these "popish missionaries."[23]

> The Jesuits are usually very learned, studious and civil and agreeable in company. In their whole deportment there is something pleasing. It is no wonder therefore that they captivate the mind of people. They seldom speak of religious matters, and if it happens they generally avoid disputes. They are very ready to do anyone a service, and when they see that their assistance is wanted they hardly give one time to speak of it, falling to work immediately to bring about what is required of them. Their conversation is very entertaining and learned, so that one cannot be tired of their company.[24]

Kalm explained that most of the Jesuits were missionaries scattered over the country, where their goal was to convert the Indians to Christianity and to see that they did not revert to pagan ways. The Jesuits lived among the Indians and followed them on their hunts. "The Jesuits undergo all these hardships both for the sake of converting the Indians and also for political reasons. The Jesuits are of great use to their king, for they are frequently able to persuade the Indians to break their treaty with the English, to make war upon them, to bring their furs to the French and not to permit the English to come amongst them. They are here held a most cunning set of people, who generally succeed in their undertakings and surpass all others in acuteness of understanding."[25]

Kalm was puzzled by the fasting of the Catholics, finding that they seemed to eat better and more varied dishes on fast days than on the other days of the week, despite abstaining from meat. Kalm approved, however, of avoiding over-consumption of meat, "which is injurious to health, fattens the body too much, and makes it inadaptable for many things."[26]

He found that among the French, "people of quality" generally ate very well. They ate three meals a day, beginning with a light breakfast of chocolate or coffee and bread. Some of the men started their day with a dram of brandy. Dinner exactly at noon consisted of several courses. The table was set with a plate of delftware, napkin, silver spoon and fork; both ladies and gentlemen had their own knives. Kalm noted, again in contrast, that a napkin was seldom used by the English colonists. "The meal begins with a soup with a good deal of bread in it. Then follow fresh meats of various kinds, boiled and roasted, poultry, or game, fricassees, ragouts, etc.," accompanied by salads of different kinds. Red claret, spruce beer, and water were drunk. Butter was seldom served. After the main course was finished, the table was cleared, and a dessert course of fruits, nuts, and cheese was served, followed by black coffee. A similar meal was served again at seven or eight o'clock in the evening. Neither puddings nor punch, so common in the English colonies, were served in Canada.[27] Both colonies used much less sugar than did the Swedes, Kalm reported. Most of the French were fond of milk, which was boiled and eaten with bits of wheat bread and sweetened with sugar.[28]

In Canada, Kalm found that the French colonists ate the early shoots of milkweed (*Asclepia syriaca*) like asparagus, despite the fact that its sap is somewhat toxic, causing dermatitis. He also said that they boiled the flowers of the plant to make sugar. The poor collected the ripe pods and used the wool as a substitute for feather beds.[29] The leaves of gale, or sweet willow (*Myrica gale*) were used by the French to season broth; woolen yarn was dyed yellow with the seeds of this plant.[30]

Tobacco was universally used by the French; every farmer planted a small plot. It was smoked in a pipe or taken in the form of snuff. In the area around Montréal, the tobacco was mixed with the crushed inner bark of the red Cornelian cherry (*Cornus sanguinea*) to make it less strong.[31]

In addition to collecting plants, the Swedish Academy had requested Kalm to bring back "wild oxen, big-bodied but short-legged; they have a rather fine and long shaggy hair, useful for spinning, but it doesn't mill." They falsely believed that "the Colonies there have found ways to tame this kind of creature, employ them for everyday haulage and use their milk as food."[32] This was a request that Kalm was unable to fulfill. He found that attempts to tame young buffalo calves in Québec had been unsuccessful, although he had some hope that it still might be possible to find animals in Illinois that could be tamed.[33]

From Québec, Kalm wrote the following letter to John Bartram, indicating that he was sending Jungström back to Philadelphia.

Because I have an opportunity of writing to you, sir, I would have the honour to tell you, that I now have come here to Québec. I do now send my servant-man from me to Philadelphia, to gather there seeds of all trees and herbs he can find, or which I have found there before.

I am obliged to stay here myself to the middle of September, to have several seeds, which not can be ripe before; and when I have gathered them, I think to retourn from hence, and will have the honour to see you in the beginning or middle of October. *(He was, as usual, overly optimistic.)*

I have found great many trees and plants, which I not have seen before; but you have in Pensylvania, too, great many trees and herbs, that do not grow here: Poplar, Sweet and Sour Gum, Laurel, Chesnut, Mulberry trees, Black Walnut, Sassafras, Magnolia, and great many others you can't find here. The Oaks of all sorts have taken leave, only some small shrubs of Black Oak do grow here by this town.

I have made great many observations in all parts of the Natural History. If you do see Mr. EVANS, pray remember my most humble duty to him, and tell him that I hope to satisfy his curiosity in true maps of Canada: but the map of Canada he was so kind and write for me, had once (it was not far from it) thrown me in the other world. The reason was, that he has not put down a great river between Fort Ann and Crown Point, that runs in Wood Creek. My guides did not very well know the way, and we did go down this river, where such Indians did live that do kill all the English they see; but to our happiness we did by good time find that we were wrong, and returned.

Fifteen years ago, when the French King did send several of his learned men to Swedland to measure there a degree of latitude by the North Pol, our King in Swedland did let them have all things they wanted gratis, or for nothing. In recompense thereof, the French King have given orders to his gouverneurs here in Canada, that I too shall have everything as victuals, lodgings, men to carry me to which place I will, &c., for nothing. It is not permitted to me to pay any thing, but the French King he pays that all.

You can, sir, inform my man in several things where he can find some rare plants, pray do it. Show him all places, where you have seen some small Mulberry Trees, or Grapes, but especialement Mulberry Trees,—these I cannot have too many. I am persuaded it Will be a pleasure for you to assist me. When I do returne from hence, then I can inform and satisfy your curiosity in great many thing in all parts of Natural History.—My respect, sir, to madam, your wife. My man he can in great many things, too, satisfy your curiosity.

I am, sir, your most humble servant,
PETER KALM.

Québec, the 6th day of August, 1749.[34]

On the same day, Kalm sent a letter to Benjamin Franklin, an extract of which he printed in *The Pennsylvania Gazette* of October 12, 1749. Its glowing reports regarding the French, and especially the Jesuits, must have annoyed the English colonists who read it, especially James Logan, who was already suspicious of Kalm's motives in traveling to Canada. Kalm, alas, was often deficient in tact and diplomacy.

> I have found more learned Men in Canada, than I imagined had been in all America. The Jesuits in general excel in several Parts of Learning; and the King's Officers also are skillful in the Arts and Sciences. The new General Governor, Monsieur Jonquiere, who was taken Prisoner by the English in the last War, arrived here on Friday last from France. He was received with all imaginable Marks of Honour. All the Great Men met him at his Landing (when all the Cannon of the city were discharged) and attended him to the Cathedral Church, the Streets being lined on both Sides with soldiers. When he came to the Door of the Church, he was met by the Bishop and all the Priests in their finest Habits. The Bishop made him a long congratulatory Oration; and after he had kissed a silver Crucifix, he went into the church, the Bishop and Priests going and singing before him, carrying Candles and Crucifixes. There he assisted at the High Mass, which was perform'd by the Bishop himself. From the Church he went to the Castle, where all the Citizens and others came to pay their Reverence to him, with many Speeches and Orations. I had the honour to be invited to assist at all this Ceremony, and to dine in the Castle. In the Afternoon there was a great Procession through all the Streets, in honour of the Virgin Mary. Monsieur Gallissoniere, who was Vice Governor General, returns to France in about two Weeks. 'Tis said here that he will be made Secretaire d'Etat de France. He is the most learned Man in all Sciences, but especially in Natural History, that I have yet seen. It is hard to conceive where he could have acquir'd so much Knowledge. The new General Governor is a tall Man, between 60 and 70 Years of Age, of a benevolent Disposition, very agreeable in Conversation, &c.[35]

KALM SPENT SEVERAL DAYS BOTANIZING IN THE AREA AROUND LORETTE, a village three miles west of Québec, inhabited mostly by Huron Indians, who had been converted by the Jesuits and who now lived in many ways like the French settlers. The French government paid many Indians who helped Kalm to collect samples of plants.[36]

On August 15, Kalm returned to Québec, where he was able to join the many townspeople lining the streets to observe the elaborate procession that marched from church to church to celebrate the feast day of the Ascension of the Virgin

Mary. They were led by two boys ringing bells, "followed by a man carrying a banner with a painting of Christ on the Cross on one side and one of Mary, Joseph and the Christ Child between them on the other. Then came another man bearing a painted wooden image of the Savior on the Cross." They were followed by rows of priests, some carrying shrines, lanterns, or censers, boys in vivid costumes, and finally, the bishop and government officials.[37]

On the same day was the celebration of the arrival of the new governor-general. This was accompanied with a great deal of pomp and ceremony, which included all of the clergy and soldiers. Again, Kalm was invited to take part in the festivities, which he reported "lasted very long, and was as elegant as the occasion required."[38]

Kalm reported that the French in Canada liked to have their beer and wine served chilled or with pieces of ice, and he described several methods that they used. Sometimes bottles were wrapped in cloths soaked in cold water. Wealthy people kept ice houses made of stone into which snow was filled in winter and covered with water to make ice.[39]

From August 29 to September 7, at the suggestion of the governor-general and the vice-governor general, Kalm journeyed up the St. Lawrence with a party of French gentlemen, including the royal physician, Dr. Jean François Gauthier, who was knowledgeable in botany and who had drafted la Glassonnière's edict regarding the collection of specimens.[40] Dr. Gauthier shared with Kalm his notes on the weather of the area made between 1744 and 1746; however, Kalm found Gauthier's thermometer to be inaccurate.[41] They visited silver and lead mines near the Bay of St. Paul, stopping along the way to view the countryside. He also visited a place where red pine was used to make tar, just as in Finland.

Kalm reported the use of three kinds of boats in Canada: those made of the whole bark of a tree, carefully removed, and reinforced with ribs of wood; canoes; and bateaux, large, flat-bottomed, and used for carrying cargoes. The bottoms were made of oak, with sides of white fir.[42] Kalm had also found similar batteaux in Albany. They were long, had seats, and were rowed.

Kalm also described an Eskimo kayak that he observed in Québec. It was six feet long, made of skins with the hair removed. Several boards were placed inside to form the boat, which was covered with skin on top, with only a hole large enough for one person to sit in. The paddle had blades on both ends.[43]

Near Québec, several ships were being built, but an order had arrived from France prohibiting further building because it was found that those made of American oak did not last as long as those of European stock. Kalm reported that the farther north that oaks grew in America, the longer the wood lasted and withstood rot.[44]

Kalm found a great difference between the manners and customs of the French in Canada and those of the English colonists. In Canada, most of the settlers had originally come as soldiers; the English colonists came eager to earn a living as farmers, artisans, mechanics and craftsmen. The French had adopted many of the customs and dress of the Indians, with whom they lived in close proximity.[45]

In Québec, he found that the civility of the inhabitants was "more refined than that of the Dutch and English in the settlements belonging to Great Britain. On the street they raised their hat only to acquaintances and to those of the upper classes. [46] The gentlemen and ladies, as well as the poorest peasants and their wives, are called Monsieur and Madame." The Québecois, of both sexes, kissed each other when they met with acquaintances.[47] They, being more influenced by recent arrivals from France, were thought by Kalm to be more polite than those in Montréal.

Kalm always had an eye for the ladies. The French women in Canada were thought by the men to take "too much care of their dress" and to squander their fortune upon fashionable clothing. They took much time to maintain their fancy coiffures, which they curled in papers every night and powdered daily. He marveled that the upper-class women were able to walk in the high-heeled shoes that many of them wore. The peasant women, on the other hand, wore wooden shoes. All the women wore caps, short jackets, and their skirts "scarcely reached down to the middle of their legs."[48]

The ladies, too, seemed to find this tall foreigner attractive. The stolid and serious Kalm was embarrassed by the giggling provoked by his mangling of the French language. He thought the ladies of Québec somewhat too free and of a more becoming modesty at Montréal. He reported that "One of the first questions they put to a stranger is whether he is married; the next, how he likes the ladies in the country, and whether he thinks them handsomer than those of his own country; and the third, whether he will take one home with him."[49]

Kalm compared the French women favorably with those in England and in the English colonies, whom he had considered lazy. "The women in Canada on the contrary do not spare themselves, especially among the common people, where they are always in the fields, meadows, stables, etc. and do not dislike any work whatsoever."[50] He also noted that most of them had been taught to read and write and that many had excellent penmanship. He only found fault with their cleanliness, which he compared unfavorably with the religious scrubbing of floors of the English and especially the Dutch. Their lack of household cleanliness may have been one of the causes of the wide prevalence of bedbugs that Kalm found in Canada.[51]

Kalm reported that dogs were often used in Canada to pull carts that carried water or wood and in the winter to draw sleds, a custom that they had learned from the Eskimos. As in Pennsylvania, he found that the cattle and sheep brought from Europe did not grow as large or produce as fine coats in America. He attributed this to the scarcity of fodder in the winter.[52]

Although he was much impressed by the manners and behavior of the upper classes, Kalm acknowledged that the common people in the Canadian countryside were poor, subsisting on only the basic necessities: bread, water and brandy. He noted, however, that every farmer planted a little kitchen garden with vegetables and currant shrubs as well as a field of tobacco, which was smoked by everyone. "Notwithstanding their poverty, they are always cheerful and in high spirits."[53]

ON SEPTEMBER 11, Kalm left Québec in one of the king's boats manned with seven sailors bound for Montréal, which they reached on the twenty-sixth, stopping along the way to observe the countryside and to collect seeds. The hot summer weather was finally over, the asters and goldenrods were in bloom, and wild grapes were abundant. Autumn was imminent, and he hurried to collect as many seeds as he could.[54]

Kalm's original plan had been to return to Philadelphia via Fort Frontenac, which was at the end of the St. Lawrence River, just east of Niagara Falls, commanding the route into the Great Lakes. The governor of Montréal had expressed no objections to his plan. However, much to his disappointment, Kalm received a letter from the new governor-general of Canada denying his request to use that route, but indicating that every measure would be taken to provide him with all the comforts he desired on his return through Fort St. Frédéric.[55] Presumably, the new governor-general had not seen the letter from the French crown requesting Kalm's special treatment as a royal guest. It had been sent to his predecessor, la Glassonnière, who had now returned to France.

Despite the fact that the open hostilities between the French and the English had come to an end, there was still suspicion on both sides. In the letter accompanying the list of expenditures made by the French government to support Kalm's expedition, the author, a M. Bigot, declares that Dr. Gauthier, who accompanied Kalm all the time, "assures us that his observations had no other object than to learn about the minerals, vegetables and animals and to make a description of them."[56]

The new governor-general, still unsure of his position, clearly feared that information about French fortifications and troops might be conveyed to the English officials upon Kalm's return to New York. There was also concern regarding English capture of the lucrative fur trade with the Indians in that area. Kalm struggled with his poor command of written French to write a long letter to the governor of Montréal, hoping to convince him to countermand the governor-general's letter and permit him to go via Fort Frontenac, since, with the imminent onset of winter weather, there wasn't time for Kalm to return to Québec to plead his case and still have time to make the journey. He explained the fact that he had been specifically ordered by the Swedish queen and the Royal Swedish Academy of Sciences to travel to the coldest parts of Canada and to find and gather there seeds of plants that might grow in Sweden. He also said that he had been unable to procure a passport from the King of England because there had been some suspicions of his motives, implying that his loyalty was more to the French than to the English.[57]

Finally, Kalm was forced to give up his efforts and, after a mass said for his safe journey, he bade farewell to the de Couagne family who had been such gracious hosts. Kalm left Montréal October 10 on horseback on a raw and rainy day. He was accompanied by four carts, drawn by two horses each, provided at the King's expense. The provisions for the journey included tongues, chops, lamb, chickens, lard, beef, bread, butter and cheese, fifteen pots of wine and an additional barrel, a case of wine from the Canaries, salt, spices, apples, and candles. A total of 1404 livres had been spent by the French government to support Kalm's Canadian visit.[58]

On October 14, they set out in two canoes, one used for carrying their cargo. On the seventeenth they were able to make their way safely ashore against heavy squalls in a storm which continued through the next day. In the afternoon the storm abated, and rowing past them they saw the boats of English soldiers escorting French prisoners of war back to Montréal. Kalm was annoyed to discover that they had left Montréal three days after he had. His party was finally able to leave in the evening and rowed far into the night until they were within six miles of Fort St. Frédéric. They arrived there on the nineteenth under a cold and overcast sky that threatened snow. Here, Kalm and the four men that were to accompany him were well fed on ducks and venison and supplied with fresh bread for their journey. The next day the men rowed along the bay while he walked south past the last Canadian farm, stopping to gather seeds of sugar maples, American hornbeam, linden and ash.

Their return route took them through Lake George, then called Lac du Saint-Sacrement.[59] Bordered by high steep mountains that seemed to hang right over their heads, the shores were often so steep and rocky that it would have been impossible to land the canoe. They had to carry their canoe and all of their goods for a distance of a mile and a half past a large waterfall. The party was followed by an Iroquois man and his wife; the man was able to carry their canoe on his head the whole distance without any apparent effort. Along the way they found a lichen that his guides told him was occasionally eaten in dire necessity to sustain life. All along their route they were plagued by high winds that often prevented them from continuing for fear of capsizing the heavily loaded canoe, which carried enough food to sustain the men on their return trip. [60]

The area between the last farm south of Fort St. Frédéric and the first English farm near Fort Nicholson on the Hudson River was a no-man's land, without settlements. Even the Indians came only occasionally to hunt. Kalm and his guides encountered one native hunting party from whom they purchased fresh venison. During their journey through this wilderness, the guides told stories around the campfire at night of the atrocities committed during the recent war, including the scalping of captives while they were still alive. Kalm must have been frightened by these tales, for he wrote, "The long autumn nights are rather terrifying in these vast wildernesses. May God be with us!"[61]

Again, as on the journey northward, the path from the end of the lake through the fifteen-mile portage to the Hudson River was difficult to find. Fortunately, they found an Indian hunting party near the path. However, some of them were drunk from rum given them by the Englishmen who had passed through earlier, so Kalm and his party declined their offer to join them for a meal. The guides left their canoe on the lake shore for their return journey. They carried Kalm's belongings on their backs along the hilly trail, often stepping over fallen pine trees that obstructed the route. The party stopped at night to camp under the brow of a large cliff when they reached the Hudson River.[62]

Unfortunately, they had no boat to take them the remaining eight miles to Fort Nicholson, so they had to wait until daylight to be able to see the trail to go fetch a boat. They arrived at Fort Nicholson on October 26. The guides, who were to be paid by the French government, had been contracted to convey Kalm as far as Saratoga, but they had been delayed because of the winds on the lake. Therefore, Kalm dismissed them and let them return so that they could get home before the river began to freeze. They carried back many letters of thanks that Kalm wrote to those in Canada who had treated him so hospitably.[63] Kalm was left to return alone to Philadelphia.

CHAPTER NINE
Return to Philadelphia
October 26, 1749—May 1750

K ALM'S RETURN TO THE ENGLISH COLONIES was a distinct let down. The four guides paid for by the French were gone, and he was now all alone to cope with the rigors and expense of his journey. The Indian guides whom he solicited at Fort Nicholson demanded so much pay that he was unable to afford to hire them to accompany him to Saratoga. Finally, the man in charge of the trading post took pity on him and agreed to take him in his own boat to where another boat was to be found to continue the journey. When they arrived, they discovered that the boat had been taken, so Kalm was forced to leave all of his belongings in the woods overnight while he walked four miles along a wretched road to Saratoga, where he spent a sleepless night worrying that his precious cargo might be stolen or ruined. The next day was spent retrieving his goods and drying them out.[1]

No longer was Kalm the recipient of a generous all-expenses-paid trip; he was back to coping with budgeting the limited funds that he had been allotted. On top of that, he had fallen from visiting dignitary status to that of a foreigner who spoke English with an accent and who demanded services in a hurry but was not in a position to pay large sums in exchange. He was also convinced that "the inhabitant of Canada, even the ordinary man, surpasses in politeness by far those people who live in these English provinces, especially the Dutch. When I reached Saratoga and came in contact with the first English inhabitants who were of Dutch descent, I noticed a vast difference in the courtesy shown me in comparison with that shown me by the French; it was just as if I had come from the court to a crude peasant."[2] How much of this perception was truth and how much a result of his abrupt change in status? It may have been a bit of both.

Kalm came from a structured, highly organized society in which everyone knew his place, and beliefs and values were shared and clearly understood. The Swedish Lutheran Church was sovereign, keeping track of every inhabitant of every hamlet in the land. The priest made sure that everyone could read and understand the Word of God as interpreted in the catechism. The hierarchies of authority in the nation were clearly understood by every inhabitant. Directly beneath God was the king, and below him were the clear channels of secular and religious authority.[3]

Kalm had been eminently successful in such a society by working hard and following the rules. As a foreigner automatically conferred with high status, he was very comfortable in French Canada, a similarly hierarchical society, with governance centrally controlled from Paris. He valued the importance of religious observance and the role of science that he had observed in Canada. He found the freedom and democracy of the other American colonies messy and inefficient.

Kalm was disdainful of the Dutch in Albany and New York, who, after a century of living in a relatively egalitarian colony, tolerating immigrants of many nations and many beliefs, had little respect for titles and positions—except those gained from financial success. For almost a century, most of the residents of New Amsterdam had been accorded status as burghers, with a stake in their egalitarian community. The result was a type—worldly, brash, confident, hustling— that repelled Kalm.[4] He wrote approvingly that the French always referred to others as "Monsieur," the English as "gentleman," whereas the Dutch were unconcerned about formality of address.

Kalm also decried "the avarice, selfishness and immeasurable love of money of the inhabitants of Albany. . . . I was here obliged to pay for everything twice, thrice and four times as much as in any part of North America which I passed through."[5]

Kalm hired a cart and driver to go from Saratoga to Albany. The road was poor because many of the bridges had fallen into disrepair during the war, and in several places they had to ford rivers. Winter weather had set in, and wet snow fell fairly hard all day on the two as they drove along the muddy rutted roads. He arrived in Albany on October 29 and busied himself in gathering seeds of walnuts, chestnuts, squash and other plants from the nearby countryside. Then he had to wait impatiently until November 2, when a boat was ready to depart downstream. This was one of the last of the season to leave Albany, as the Hudson would soon be frozen.[6]

Kalm arrived in New York on November 8, close enough to his destination so that he began to receive letters and news. There he learned with great sadness of the death of his Swedish friend in Philadelphia, Peter Cock, who had been of such assistance to him during the previous autumn. It was Cock who had dealt with his bill of exchange and arranged for his funds.[7]

Kalm also received a letter from Abraham Spalding in London, who advised him not to leave for England in the fall because it would be unlikely that he could then continue directly to Sweden. He advised postponing his return until the spring. Kalm also received letters from Peter Collinson and one from Jungström, relating the events of his journey from Canada. He was also able to read his own letter to Franklin, written in Québec on August 6, 1749, regarding his visit to

Canada. Franklin, in his role as postmaster in Philadelphia, saw to the printing of this letter in several newspapers, including *The Pennsylvania Gazette, The New York Gazette* and *The Maryland Gazette.*[8]

Several times during his travels, Kalm faced a real dilemma caused by the difficulty of communication between Sweden and America. Mail took months to arrive at its destination—if at all—and the wait for an answer could take as long as a year. Kalm had anticipated leaving America in the autumn after his return from Canada or the following spring of 1750, although earlier he had petitioned the Royal Swedish Academy of Sciences to finance an additional year of exploration because of the delay in his arrival in America. They had not responded, and he felt that he had accomplished most of what he had been charged with doing. He had collected a great many seeds of native plants, including those of several species that he believed would thrive in Sweden: Three different species of walnut, an early-ripening maize, the sugar maple, pumpkin, cotton, beans, and watermelon.

However, while he was in Montréal the commandant of Fort Frontenac told him that wild rice grew near his fort. Kalm had only been able to obtain a gallon of those seeds; not sufficient to guarantee the possibility of growing enough in Finland to start an industry. He also learned that near Niagara the white mulberry and wild peach trees grew, as well as other useful plants. As a result, Kalm made a decision that, to accomplish all that he had been charged with doing, he must stay another year in America and obtain permission to travel to Niagara.[9] Therefore, he wrote to Count Tessin, President of the Royal Academy of Sciences, of his experiences in Canada, of his denial of access to Niagara and of his need for additional funds. He wrote similar letters to Linnaeus and Bielke, outlining his reasons for prolonging his journey, and to Spalding to request a draft of sixty pounds sterling.[10]

Another problem that Kalm faced was the lack of knowledge of the geography of North America among his patrons in the Royal Swedish Academy of Science. He dutifully wished to follow the instructions that they had set out for him, but the reality on the ground proved to be far different from what they had envisioned. For example, Linnaeus had written to Kalm that the academy wanted him to travel to Hudson Bay. Kalm responded that he too, when still in Sweden, had thoughts about such travel. However, the reality was that such a journey was undoable, dangerous, and not worth the effort, since few plants grew there. "The land is five times worse than the Lapland region that Master has written about. The wild people north of Québec never sow anything because of the cold climate but live off of meat . . . everything is *sterilissima terra* . . . nothing of value grows in the northern part of Canada; my time is too precious to waste it there."[11]

Despite the high cost of food and lodging in New York and his eagerness to return to friends in Philadelphia, Kalm had to remain there for several days to accomplish business. He had many letters to write, and they were to be sent by a ship that was soon to leave for London. He was also able to meet with Cadwallader Colden to report to him on his journey.[12]

Kalm left New York on November 14, arriving in New Brunswick the next morning. With luck, just as he jumped off the boat and was about to procure lodgings for a week until the next mail wagon was to leave, he encountered a man from Trenton who had just brought some travelers from there and was looking for passengers for his return trip. Thus, he was able to leave there at noon and was able to arrive safely in Trenton just before midnight, despite some fear of robbery along the dark road.[13]

Kalm arrived in Philadelphia on November 20, where he met two new pastors who had just arrived from Sweden and were staying at the home of Gustavus Hesselius. They were the Reverend Israel Acrelius, appointed dean of the Swedish congregations and pastor of the Christina parish, and the Reverend Erik Mathias Unander, who was to take over in Penn's Neck and Raccoon.[14] What a pleasure it must have been for Kalm to at last be able to speak in his own language instead of struggling with a foreign tongue.

On November 22, Kalm left for Raccoon. There he found that Jungström had been busy gathering seeds, as had others there who had promised to help him. He also found that there had been a great deal of sickness in New Sweden during the summer, which had been unusually hot. He reported that Mrs. Sandin had been ill, probably with malaria, but was now recovered.[15]

He returned to Philadelphia on November 25, and the next day he met with John Bartram, learning that he and his family had also been ill during the summer. Kalm also stayed overnight at Bartram's farm on the twenty-ninth and thirtieth; they probably continued their conversation long into the night.[16] Kalm eagerly reported on his findings about various plants and the environment in which he found them growing. He particularly noted how far north he found various plants and trees that he had seen growing in Pennsylvania and how tall they grew. Bartram reiterated his theory that all plants have a special latitude and climate in which they thrive best and that the further north or south that they grow, the smaller and more delicate they become. Kalm told him of seeing sassafras growing as far north as Fort Anne, but they were very small and did not bear seeds. As late as 1778, however, Kalm still insisted that "plants from lands lying further south, when planted in a land lying further north, gradually adapt and adjust their time of ripening to the locality which is their new home."[17]

Kalm also met with Franklin, who showed him several varieties of minerals that he had collected, including asbestos and a stalactite discovered in a cave in Virginia. He reported that Franklin used candles made of spermaceti for reading. They were considered superior to those made of tallow, wax or of bayberries (*Myrica*) because they did not drip or become soft when carried.[18]

It may be that Kalm complained of the cold that he had experienced the previous winter in Raccoon to Franklin, who loaned him one of his stoves. Kalm found it most satisfactory.[19] He wrote, "It kept the house quite warm, but then one had to use short wood in it. It proved often unnecessary to have a fire in the kitchen, and one could prepare chocolate and other food on the little stove."[20]

Kalm returned to Raccoon on December 4 and came back again to Philadelphia on the sixth, attending a Quaker meeting the next day. On December 10, he met with Lewis Evans to give him additions for his maps, and they compared notes on the summer weather and their recordings of temperature, particularly on the hottest days, in late June, when Kalm had been at Fort Anne.[21]

Kalm spent most of the rest of the winter in Raccoon, with occasional visits to Philadelphia. When he had left there the previous spring, Margaretha Sandin had still been a grieving widow, for whom he felt tender concern. It was now over a year since her husband's death, and time had probably lessened her grief. It was time for her to get on with her life and find a means of support for herself and her young daughter, Johanna Margaretha.

Franklin's model of his "Pennsylvania Fire-Place," now called the Franklin. (North Wind Picture Archives)

Her husband's parishioners had petitioned the Archbishop and Consistory of the Swedish church to provide her with the pastor's salary during the period between Sandin's death and the arrival of a new pastor. They wrote, "And as his bereaved, virtuous and godfearing wife is rather dear to us and close to our hearts, we make so bold as to, in all humility and respect, express a tender and dear petition, that she with the poor, fatherless child may enjoy *Intervallum*, until another teacher is appointed or chosen for us; particularly as she is a poor and abandoned stranger in this country."[22]

The new pastor had now arrived from Sweden, and presumably he and his family would have expected to occupy the manse, leaving her and her daughter without a home or a means of support. Kalm, as a friend and fellow student of her late husband, was an appropriate and timely match.

We can assume that Kalm, in his eagerness to succeed as a naturalist in Sweden, had spent little time courting women. As an impecunious student, he lacked the resources to think of marriage. All of his thoughts for several years had been to plan for the great journey of exploration that he was to make, and, of course, that would have been impossible had he married, since Linnaeus had stipulated that all of the "apostles" had to be unmarried. Since he left Raccoon, however, Kalm had enjoyed the flirtations and attention of the many beautiful French women in Québec who were so intrigued by the tall reserved foreigner. Several of them had even asked whether he would marry them. The attention must have turned his head and emboldened him into thinking of marriage.

We know the result; less than three months after his return, Kalm was married to Anna Margaretha Siöman Sandin in February, 1750, in the Gloria Dei (Old Swede's) Church in Philadelphia.[23] In an early chapter of his book, Kalm described the process of obtaining a marriage license in Pennsylvania from the governor, at a charge of five and twenty shillings. The couple then gives the license to the clergyman who keeps it permanently. In the "license, he declares that he has examined the affair and found no obstacles to hinder the marriage, and therefore allows it. The license is signed by the governor; but, before he delivers it, the bridegroom must come to him in company with two creditable and well known men, who answer for him that there really is no lawful obstacle to his marriage. These men must sign a certificate, in which they make themselves answerable for, and engage to bear all the damages of, any complaints made by the relations of the persons who intend to be married."[24]

Perhaps Hesselius was one of the men who signed the license for Kalm and his bride. The church records for that year are, unfortunately lost. One wonders whether their marriage was celebrated with a wedding party, perhaps with one or more musicians playing a fiddle so that the dancers could join in a traditional polska.

Soon after his arrival in Philadelphia in 1748, Kalm had been taken by his fellow countryman, Peter Cock, to visit James Logan at his estate, Stenton, but as it was late in the evening, they decided not to call.[25] It was not until more than a year later, after his return from Canada, on February 28, 1750, that Kalm went with Franklin and finally met the wealthy and influential agent of the Penn family.[26] Logan was in poor health; four months later he would suffer a stroke that prevented him from speaking; he died in 1751.[27] Logan wrote of this visit to Peter Collinson:

Facing page: Gloria Dei (Old Swede's) Church in Philadelphia.
(American Swedish Historical Museum, Philadelphia, Pennsylvania)

I have spent most of this day for the first time with thy friend Kalm accompanied with B. Franklin, and I know not what to make of him, nor of his Journey to Canada, where, after the whole last winter Spent at a Swedish Woman's House near Newcastle, he Spent near five Months, and dined many times at the Governor's at Québec, without Seeing during the 8 Months or more that he had been here, any one person that I could hear of, but B. Franklin and Jno. Bartram, and he talks of returning to Canada again, but on what business I cannot learn.

Logan describes the settlement of New Sweden and the conquest by the Dutch and later the English. He goes on to say:

The Swedes are not much encreased and in my time here (now above 50 years) are much Anglified as our Term is, nor if we had a War now with France should we have any reason to apprehend the French in conjunction with the Swedes were they to joyn them.[28]

Logan's skepticism regarding Kalm and his snide reference to Kalm's stay with Margaretha in Raccoon must be interpreted in the light of Logan's previous governmental role and his patriotic concern about a possible attack by the French on Pennsylvania or the other English colonies. He was also involved in huge land speculations in the western part of the colony which were threatened by French incursions into the Ohio Valley. These attacks had been instigated in 1749 by the Canadian Governor-General, the Comte de La Galissonnière, whom Kalm so admired when they met in Québec.[29] Logan suspected that Kalm might be spying for the French, since his patron, Count Tessin, President of the Royal Swedish Academy of Sciences, was a leader of the pro-French party in Sweden. Logan apparently suspected that Kalm spent so much time in New Sweden in order to convince the inhabitants to side with the French in case of an attack.[30]

Kalm may logically have felt that Logan could not have been of much assistance to him, given his declining condition, and thus had not been in any haste to meet him the previous autumn. He had (as Franklin pointed out to Logan in a letter written in November 1748[31]) attempted to make a call at the Stenton estate a month after his arrival in Philadelphia, and a visit with Franklin earlier in February had been postponed because Franklin was lame.[32] In addition, Logan and Bartram had apparently had some disagreement prior to 1743, when Bartram complained in a letter to Collinson that Logan had influenced the decision by William Penn not to support annual expeditions by Bartram.[33] By the time of Kalm's visit, they had little contact with each other. Bartram may well have convinced Kalm that it would not be worthwhile to spend time with Logan.[34]

Nevertheless, it was impolitic of Kalm to have neglected making a courtesy call to Logan earlier in his stay. This omission was typical of Kalm's single mindedness to accomplish his botanical tasks that made him careless of performing the polite gestures that might have made him more successful in navigating the political waters in America and later back in Sweden.

We have much less information about Kalm's activities from the time of his return to Philadelphia than before because he was never able to publish a third volume of his travels. He spent the remainder of the winter and much of the spring in Raccoon enjoying the delights of a newly wed. He was also able to write up his notes and to sort out and pack for shipment to Sweden the seeds, specimens of insects and small animals preserved in alcohol (a praying mantis, a mole, turtles, snakes), and such curiosities as a humming bird's nest[35] that he had gathered.

Kalm, always keenly interested in observing different religious practices, traveled in May through eastern Pennsylvania to visit the pietistic German Mennonite community at Ephrata in Lancaster County, based on a celibate and ascetic mode of life. The community had just built, without the use of nails or any other metals, a great, steep-roofed, three-story church shingled to the ground. Kalm also traveled to Cape May and along part of the Jersey shore to look for plants from that sandy environment, as well as to Wilmington.[36] This may be when Kalm discovered the American lotus, *Nelumbo lutea* in a creek in South Jersey. John Bartram collected it for his garden and later sent specimens to his patrons in England.[37]

Kalm wrote again to the Royal Swedish Academy of Sciences outlining his proposal for a return to Canada. He was probably anxious that they might turn down his request, for as recently as February 15, 1750, he had written to Linnaeus to justify the extension of his stay and the cost to the Royal Swedish Academy of Sciences. "I don't doubt that everyone thinks that this journey is expensive. I do as well, and nobody thinks more about that than I do."[38]

Linnaeus had written to him with concern that most of the seeds that he had collected were from plants that were native to areas too far south to be able to thrive in Scandinavia. Kalm wrote to assure him that all of his seeds were from plants that grew in cold climates.

Fortunately, his letters had their desired effect, and on February 10, 1750, the academy granted him an extension.[39] He could now plan for his trip to Niagara.

CHAPTER TEN
Niagara Falls
June 24, 1750—February 1751

THE SWEDISH MINISTER IN PARIS was able to obtain permission for Kalm to travel to the Great Lakes. After a profitable winter spent sorting and packing his seeds and dried specimens and doing more local exploration, he set out again on horseback on June 24, bound for Niagara Falls. Jungström was left behind to collect more seeds.

Kalm rode his horse north along the east side of the Hudson River but made a brief detour to visit Cadwallader Colden at his estate, Coldengham, on the west side of the river west of Newburgh.[1] He was at Albany on July 22 and then spent July 24 to August 4 with Colonel William Johnson, whom he had met the year before on his way to Montréal.

This time Kalm was a guest at Johnson's estate, Mount Johnson (later fortified and called Fort Johnson), forty miles west of Albany, where he lived with his common-law Mohawk wife. The large and elegant two-story house had been completed only a few months before Kalm's arrival. It was graced with paneling, mantles and banisters carved from cherry and black walnut in semi-classical designs, and the library contained books on natural philosophy and English history.[2] Mount Johnson was a stopping point for anyone traveling west along the Mohawk Trail toward the trading post of Oswego.[3]

Kalm wrote of Johnson:

This gentleman lives among the savages and has in many ways gained their respect and love. Many villages receive most of their support from him and the savages regard him as their father. Knowing they will be well received, they often travel long distances just to see him. They know he will supply their needs for it is his desire to do well by all. No less laudable is his high regard for the sciences; he has an ardent passion for them and derives great satisfaction in their advancement. As this gentleman has lived among the savages for many years, no one is more familiar with their mode of life than he.[4]

Johnson's biographer, James Thomas Flexner, wrote the following description of him, perhaps based more on myth than reality:

Fort Johnson.
(New York State Library)

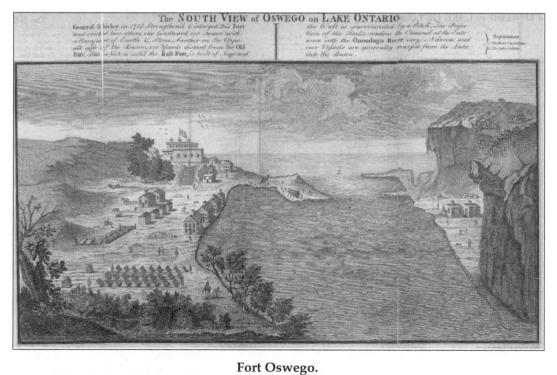

Fort Oswego.
(Edmund Bailey O'Callaghan, *O'Callaghan's Documentary History of the State of New York*)

In character, Colonel William was gargantuan: physically overwhelming, of tremendous appetites. His prowess in drinking is testified to by his death from cirrhosis of the liver; rumor found reason to assert that he had fathered seven hundred children, on women Indian and white. He was addicted to the outdoors, hunting, fighting, and fishing, but also to the arts of peace.[5]

According to Flexner, Johnson was efficient at organizing the agricultural communities of settlers in the Mohawk Valley. He was a tyrant in his territory, "violent upon occasion" but also benevolent. "Untutored, he was highly intelligent, able to defeat not only regulars in battle but politicians in the schemes of power." He was able to be at home in two cultures. "Sir William was a well-adjusted European man; Warraghiyagey (his Mohawk name) thought and acted as an Indian. These two personalities lived together without strain in one keen and passionate heart."[6]

Johnson entertained the Swedish traveler with such hospitality and was so helpful in assisting him that Kalm wrote the following words of thanks and admiration to his host. "If God spare my life, I shall an other time have a better opportunity to let the world know your great qualities, and when I have only said the half of them and of your kindness, every body shall find, that they greatly do surpass all others and put the mankind in admiration."[7]

Kalm had difficulty understanding someone as unusual as Johnson and marveled that a man of his culture could live happily in such a remote location. He wrote to Johnson from New York on his return trip that "a new sorrow did darken my heart, when I remembered that you, Dear Sir, yet did live as a David in the tents of Kedar, & as a child of Israel in the middle of the Sons of Enakim, where the most, if not all, which on all sides live round about you, look upon you with a more sowr eye & darker face, than a bull can do; I wonder, Sir that you don't grow ten times sick in a day in a such place."[8]

From Mount Johnson, Kalm's route took him through the territory controlled by the six nations of the Iroquois. Johnson provided him with an excellent interpreter, William Printup, whose family had lived for generations with the Indians. A horse was purchased for Printup as well as gifts to give to Indians met along the way. These included a store of tobacco and of cinnabar, which they used to paint their faces and sometimes their hair. The journey was "very difficult and quite adventurous."[9] Kalm slept some nights in the woods, once in the home of a "stingy German" and some nights in Indian dwellings, where he was plagued by lice and bedbugs. They arrived at the English-owned Fort Oswego on August 13. It was a busy trading area; by 1739, one hundred and fifty traders were reported to be lodged there, purchasing furs from the Indians and selling them English goods.[10]

Kalm stayed at Fort Oswego for five days as the guest of Captain John Lindesay and his wife, to whom he had been recommended by Johnson. They later provided him with seeds of wild oats, *fol avoine*.[11] From Oswego Kalm traveled in a batteau across Lake Ontario with a guard of Indians that had been provided for him by order of Johnson.[12] The voyage took six days of rowing along the shore, arriving at Fort Niagara on August 23.[13] Kalm later wrote to Franklin that the French at Fort Niagara at first mistook him for an English officer on a spying mission, but as soon as he showed them his passports they "received me with the greatest civility."[14]

The first eyewitness written description of the falls of the Niagara River had been written by Father Louis Hennepin, a Recollet priest, who accompanied René-

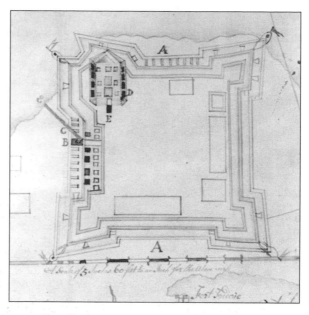

The 1727 "French castle" at Fort Niagara.
(The Old Fort Niagara Association, Inc., Niagara Falls, New York)

Robert Cavalier, Sieur de La Salle, on his journey in search of the Mississippi River. His *Description de la Louisiane,* published in 1683, became an instant best-seller. As was the fashion among travel writers of the day, he greatly exaggerated what he saw. He insisted that the ground under the fall "was big enough for four coaches to drive abreast without being wet." Hennepin claimed that the waterfall was 500 feet high or higher, almost three times its actual height.[15]

Kalm sent a scientific description of Niagara in a letter to the Swedish librarian and journalist Carl Christoffer Gjörwell, which was translated and added as an appendix to the Benson translation of Kalm's *Travels*.[16] He also wrote a letter to Benjamin Franklin from Albany on September 2 describing his trip to Niagara Falls. He suggested in his letter that "If you, Sir, find this worth to give a copy of it in your News Paper, pray turn it in better English: I am but a poor English man, and now I have no Dictionary to run to for help."[17] Franklin did, indeed, edit the letter and published it in his *Pennsylvania Gazette* on September 20, 1750. It was also reprinted in the *Gentlemen's Magazine* and the *Virginia Gazette* and the following year in London as an appendix to Bartram's description of his 1743 trip to Onondaga.[18]

On the morning of August 24, fortunately a bright clear day, Kalm set out from the Fort. He was accompanied by two French officers as well as by Daniel Jonquiere, who had lived next to the land trail around the falls for the previous

Gent. Mag. Feb. 1751

a. The Place where a piece of Rock was broken from, which while standing turn'd the Water obliquely across ye Fall as in Popple's Map.

A View of the Fall of N.

ten years and was in charge of overseeing the goods shipped between Lakes Erie and Ontario. When they arrived at the trail, Kalm saw more than two hundred Indians carrying heavy packs of furs over a distance of about nine miles. He marveled that this sight was said to be an everyday occurrence. In the letter, Kalm provided a precise description of the falls.[19]

Kalm denied the accuracy of Father Hennepin's estimate of the height of the falls as more than 500 feet and suggested that the estimate he had obtained when he was in Montréal from Etienne Rocbert de La Morandière, the king's engineer in Canada, of 137 feet was correct. He also corrected Hennepin's estimate of the

Page 18 Vol XXI.

b *Two Men passing over ye east stream with Slaves.*
c. *The Indians reascending their Ladder.*

"A View of the Fall of Niagara," engraving on paper from *Gentlemen's Magazine*, originally published in London in 1751 along with Kalm's letter to Franklin. (Castellani Art Museum of Niagara University Collection. Generous donation from Dr. Charles Rand Penney, partially funded by the Castellani Purchase Fund, with additional funding from Mr. and Mrs. Thomas A. Lytle, 2006)

distance at which the roar of the falls could be heard. The most was about 15 leagues; under favorable wind conditions the noise could be heard at the fort.[20]

Kalm did allow himself to express some superlatives. "When all this water comes to the very fall, then it throws it self there down perpendiculair; the hairs will rise and stand upright upon your head, when you sees this; I can not with words express how amazing this is; you can not see it, without to be quite afraid, seeing a such great quantity of water falling down perpendiculair to a surprising height."[21]

Kalm mentioned that the bodies of animals and waterfowl caught by surprise and carried over the fall were found on the shore below. He also told the story of two drunken Indians who had accidentally been marooned for nine days on the island above the falls and how they were rescued. A passing party of Indians who spotted them conferred with the French officers, who suggested that the current was less strong and the river more shallow at the east end of the island. They provided the rescuers with iron poles, which they drove into the river bottom to hold onto to avoid being swept along by the current. In this way they were able to walk across and provide the starving pair with food and to guide them back to shore. Later hunting parties would occasionally use this method to cross onto the island to harvest deer and elk that were seen to be marooned there.[22]

Kalm went on to give further descriptions of the area. He ended his letter with a declaration that his description was completely truthful, with no exaggeration. "I can not make the nature otherwise than I find it; I like more, that man shall say some hundred years here-after, that they find every thing then, as I have said, than that I should be look'd upon as one false wonder-maker."[23]

During the return trip from Oswego, Kalm was able to collect seeds from plants that he had not encountered before and also paid several people who promised to collect more seeds and send them to him later. He also paid an Indian who traveled with him and demonstrated some of the traditional uses of the plants that they encountered. On his return from Niagara and Oswego, he again stopped to visit with Johnson. There he told him about various discoveries he had made during his trip.[24] He spent only one night at Coldengham on his way south along the Hudson, earger to return home to Margaretha.[25] Kalm arrived back in Philadelphia on October 6 after a successful journey of a little over thirteen weeks despite difficulties with runaway horses and the high cost of food and lodging among the Dutch. In his accounts, he explained the exorbitant charges, "This is unheard of but the Dutch are stingy. They are worse than Jews!"[26]

Kalm still had to sort and pack the seeds and dried specimens that had been collected. This was a complicated process to ensure that they would arrive safely. Collinson and Bartram had developed appropriate methods for preserving different kinds of seeds to make sure that they did not rot. Early in their correspondence, Collinson had sent instructions and a supply of the appropriate paper for preserving dried specimens.[27] However, until Nathaniel Bashot Ward invented the Wardian case—a sealed glass box that stabilized humidity and temperature— live plants seldom survived and many seeds rotted.

It was now too late in the season to consider embarking on a voyage to England through the stormy winter Atlantic, only to wait in England until spring to go through the Baltic to Sweden. It seemed more profitable to remain in Philadelphia, lodging again with Mistress Durburow,[28] and continue to collect seeds. Kalm visited Bartram several times during the autumn and winter. He also spent much time during the winter months working on copying and supplementing the diary notes that he had made during his travels.

CHAPTER ELEVEN
Native Americans

LIKE MOST EUROPEANS OF HIS ERA, Kalm was curious about the natives of North America. One of the prevailing views in Europe was that the Indian was barely a man, who neither "tamed the seas or guided the rivers or worked the land."[1] In the best-selling *Histoire Naturelle* (*Natural History of Man*), published in 1749, George-Louis Leclerc, Comte de Buffon, wrote of the inhabitants of the New World:

> The Savage has weak and small organs of generation; he has neither hair nor beard and no ardor for his female. The most intimate society of all, that of the same family, only contains weak links for them; the connection of one family to another does not exist; thus, no fellowship, no republic, no social unit. The physical side of love defines their morals; their hearts are icy, their society cold and their rule hard."[2]

Buffon, of course, had not been to America. He chose to ignore the many accurate descriptions of Indians that had been sent back by Jesuit missionaries to New France.

Kalm was again fortunate in his choice of Philadelphia as a destination (rather than New England) to gain information about Native Americans. The reports in his journal present a fairly open-minded view of Indians. The English colonists whom he met in Pennsylvania and New York were relatively better disposed toward Native Americans than would have been those in the New England colonies who had suffered through the ravages of King Phillip's War.

Quaker-Indian relationships were unique among the English colonies. William Penn maintained a deliberate strategy of fairness in his dealings with the Indians. He wished to maintain peaceful relations and was careful to deal with them on terms that they found acceptable. Land was occupied by the colonists in Pennsylvania usually only after clearly understood treaties were drawn up with the local tribes.[3]

Until recently, the accepted interpretation of historians was that Penn's treaty resulted in almost seventy-five years of peace and stability between Indians and colonists in Pennsylvania, bringing about a great increase in the wealth and population of the colony. However, the next generation of the Penn family became greedy and was not so kindly disposed to the Indians.

Kalm's Swedish friend, the painter Gustavus Hesselius, had painted the portraits of two Lenape chiefs, Lapowinska and Tishcohan, signers of the Walking Purchase Treaty of 1735-1737, in which William Penn's sons, John and Thomas, acquired a vast track of land in Pennsylvania. These paintings were commissioned by John Penn, who paid Hesselius sixteen pounds for the portraits; it is thought that he presented these portraits to the two chiefs in order to gain favor with them and secure the release of lands promised to his father in the Treaty of 1686.[4]

More recent interpretations of Pennsylvania history suggest that there was occasional violence between the Indians and the colonists and that tension between the cultures was the norm, rather than harmony.[5] Tension arose over misunderstandings about the meaning of land purchases and deeds, which the colonists understood in terms of English common law to be perpetual and exclusive. Indians, on the other hand, thought that agreements were temporary and that land could be shared.

Author/historian Michael Mackintosh suggests that violence between the Lenapes and the settlers in New Sweden was avoided because of the relative weakness of both sides and the fact that both groups were fairly widely dispersed.[6] The Swedes were more concerned with the menace from other European colonies than from the few remaining Lenapes, many of whom had died from the diseases brought with the first wave of European explorers. In addition, the ethnic Finns who constituted a large portion of the New Sweden settlers had much in common with the Lenapes in that they had subsisted at home on slash-and-burn agriculture supplemented by hunting and fishing, were dependent upon woodcraft, built log cabins, similar to Indian long houses, and enjoyed saunas, similar to Indian sweat lodges.[7]

The Lenapes, whom the Swedes encountered in the Delaware Valley, endowed all of the parts of nature with powers, personalities and souls. They believed that they shared reciprocal obligations with the forces of life on the earth.[8] This view of nature created another source of tension between the settlers of Pennsylvania and the local Indian tribes. The Europeans believed in the Great Chain of Being, that God had created the world for man to have dominion over all. Consequently, resources were there to be exploited.

Kalm discussed the Indians' religion with one of his Swedish informants, who "thought it very trifling." He recounted a story that the man told about walking with an Indian and encountering a red-spotted snake on the road. When the Swede went to get a stick with which to kill the snake, "the Indian begged him not to touch it, because it was sacred to him. Perhaps the Swede would not have killed it, but on hearing that it was the Indian's deity, he took a stick and killed it, in the presence of the Indian, saying: 'Because thou believest in it, I think myself obliged to kill it.'"[9]

Kalm recounted an Indian creation legend. "A large turtle floated on the water. Around it gathered more and more slime and other material that fastened itself to it, so that it finally became all America. The first savage was sent down from heaven, and rested on the turtle. When he encountered a log he kicked it, and behold, people were formed from it."[10]

Kalm's French hosts in Canada were also even-handed in their evaluation of the native population. French treatment of Native Americans in Canada was much more humane than that of many of the English colonies. The famous verdict of nineteenth-century historian Francis Parkman was that "Spanish civilization crushed the Indian; English civilization scorned and neglected him; French civilization embraced and cherished him."[11]

French fur traders learned the Indians' languages to be able to trade with them. The Jesuit missionaries learned their languages to convert them to Catholicism and lived for long periods of time in Indian villages. Both learned ways of survival in the wilderness from the natives.[12] The French were successful in dealing with the Indians because they did so on Indian terms rather than trying to impose upon them the norms of French society. They were willing to fulfill the expectations of their Indian allies by marrying into Indian families and serving as mediators of disputes among Indian groups.[13] Although brandy was prized by the Indians above all European goods, its sale was prohibited under severe penalties from the French government.[14]

Most of the Puritans of New England scorned the Indians. The Puritans believed that they were creating a "City on a Hill," according to God's plan.[15] They assumed that the presence of the heathen Indians was merely an obstacle to the progress of civilization.[16] They built their homes and grew their crops just as their ancestors in England had done, learning few skills from the Native Americans. Few Englishmen married Indian wives, whereas intermarriage, as Kalm reported, was common among the French Canadians.

The French were not perceived by the Indians as so much of a threat as the English colonists because the primary French interest was in trade, especially the fur trade. The English colonists, in contrast, were mainly farmers, who cleared land for cultivation and brought with them large animals that were unfamiliar and threatening to the Indians. In addition, the French population in the middle of the eighteenth century was only about hundred thousand, as compared with almost a million in the English colonies.[17]

Kalm provided an extensive description of the trade between the French and their Native-American trading partners. Many French traders from Montréal traveled long distances into the interior and encountered great danger to trade for furs with Indians, living with them to make sure that they would not sell to the English. Money was not exchanged; wampum was the only medium of exchange used other than barter.

French traders brought muskets, powder, shot and balls to trade with the Indians. By the mid-eighteenth century firearms had supplanted bows and arrows. Other items for trade included kettles of copper or brass, hatchets, knives, scissors, needles, flint, earrings of brass or tin, looking glasses and burning glasses, glass beads, and brass and steel wire. Cinnabar was used by the Indians for red body paint and verdigris for green. They also purchased tobacco if they could not grow it themselves. In addition, the Indians wanted pieces of white cloth striped with blue or red to wrap around them, blue or red cloth to be made into skirts for the women, and cloth to wrap around their legs. None of the clothing was ever washed and was worn until it wore out. In exchange, the French traders received many different kinds of skins.[18]

Kalm was able to obtain extensive information from Bartram, Evans and Colden, who had spent time with Native Americans, as well as two men who were fluent in their languages: Colonel William Johnson and Conrad Weiser.

Johnson was later appointed the northern Indian superintendent for the British because of his knowledge and extensive experience. Johnson felt that Englishmen, who were mostly ignorant of the customs of the Indians, would grow to admire and respect them if they knew them better. He described them as holding high principles, seldom succumbing to the temptation to steal. Johnson wrote, "Their ideas of right and wrong and their practices in consequence of them, would, if more known, do them much honour."[19]

Cadwallader Colden—who had advised Kalm about a route to Canada—had written the only substantial account in English of the Indians in the region, *History of the Five Indian Nations*, originally published in New York in 1727. Peter Collinson had arranged the publication of the second, enlarged edition of Colden's *History* in London (1747) with his *Papers Related to the Indian Trade* as an appendix. He had presumably shown the book to Kalm during one of their visits.[20] In his book, Colden tried to convince European readers that the Indians were not simply barbarians and savages. "Instead, he offered the opinion that—although they could be fierce and formidable enemies—they possessed a nobility and honesty that often surpassed that of the European settler. The latter had, he believed, often victimized and debauched the Indians and was primarily responsible for acquainting them with all the treachery and deception that the Indians often resorted to as a means of self-defense."[21]

Franklin was so impressed by Colden's book that he agreed to help him sell the books that had not been sold by his English publisher. Kalm was probably reflecting the views of Colden, who considered the Indians as "examplars of the 'Original Form of all Government'" and noted that "each nation was an 'absolute republic,' and that authority and power were derived, in effect, from the consent of the governed."[22] Colden was also impressed by the Iroquois' sense of equality; he wrote that they had "such absolute notions of liberty that they allow of no kind of superiority of one over another, and banish all servitude from their territories."[23]

Bartram, too, gave favorable views of the Native Americans whom he had met during his trip with Lewis Evans and Conrad Weiser to a meeting with the Iroquois in July 1743. Weiser, Bartram and Evans traveled on foot and by canoe through Pennsylvania north to Oswego, New York, to the Central Council Fire of the Six Nations in the large village of Onondaga. Bartram would certainly have discussed this trip with Kalm and perhaps given him a copy of his journal, which was published in England in 1751.[24]

Weiser had been ordered to make a treaty of peace between the Iroquois and the colonial government of Virginia. Weiser, whose father had originally emigrated from Germany to Schenectady, New York, had lived for eight months at age seventeen in a Maqua (Iroquois) village and learned their language. His expertise in Indian language and customs was acknowledged in 1731 by James Logan, who appointed him to serve as an Indian interpreter and agent for Pennsylvania.[25]

Although in his journal Kalm doesn't mention meeting him, it is likely that he and Weiser would have met several times. Weiser was also a good friend of Franklin and of Johnson. Perhaps one occasion was during Kalm's 1750 visit to the Ephrata cloister, near Weiser's homestead. Christian Daniel Claus mentions in his journal that Kalm and Weiser had agreed to meet in Onondaga or at Colonel Johnson's home during Kalm's trip to Niagara. Whether they did or not is unclear. He probably just missed meeting Weiser, who passed on his way to Onondaga the next day. Kalm had already left for Albany.[26]

When the English traded with the Indians for furs, they gave them a better price than did the French, and, in addition, they offered them rum or brandy, which the French did not, according to Kalm.[27] Often the English took advantage of Indians who had become drunk from rum. Kalm noted that many Indians "frequently attain a great age," that is, unless they succumb to the use of brandy introduced by Europeans.[28] In addition to introducing Native Americans to the use of alcohol, Kalm reports that "The Europeans have taught the Indians in their neighborhoods the use of firearms, and so they have laid aside their bows and arrows, which were formerly their only arms, and use muskets. If the Europeans should now refuse to supply the natives with muskets, they would starve to death, as almost all of their food consists of the flesh of the animals which they hunt."[29]

Kalm reported: "Everyone was of the opinion that the American savages were a very good-natured people, if they were not attacked. Nobody was so strict in keeping his word as a savage. If any one of their allies came to visit them they showed him more kindness and greater endeavors to serve him than he could have expected from his own countrymen."[30]

Kalm recounts a story that he probably heard from Colden. The governor of New York often met with sachems of the Iroquois when the colonists intended to make war on the French. At one meeting, the subject turned to the attempts of the English to convert the Indians to Christianity. One of the Indian chiefs complained that the French sent better men to instruct the Indians than did the English, and some of the white men had taught the Indians to drink to excess. "He then entreated the governor to take from them these preachers, and a number of other Europeans who resided amongst them, for, before they came among them the Indians had been an honest, sober, and innocent people, but now most of them had become rogues."[31]

During the winters of 1748-1749 and 1749-1750, Kalm collected a great deal of information from older inhabitants of New Sweden regarding their recollections of the Indians whom the early settlers had encountered. However, this was second-hand and often third-hand, derived from tales that these men had heard from their parents or grandparents. As Kalm writes, by the time of his visit, one had to travel about 120 miles from the coast before reaching the first Indian village. "And it is very possible for a person to have been at Philadelphia and other towns on the seashore for half a year without so much as seeing an Indian."[32]

In March of 1749, Kalm visited a 91-year-old Swede named Nils Gustafson in hopes of learning more about the early days of New Sweden. Gustafson reported that the settlers had bought their land from the many Native Americans who lived in the area and who then moved further inland or died of smallpox.[33] Some of the settlers had been killed and scalped by Indians. One had tried to kill Gustafson's mother, but she was able to resist them until help arrived. However, he said that, in general, most of the natives lived peaceably with the Swedes.[34]

At first the settlers bought corn from the Indians, but later the Indians became lazy, Gustafson said, and instead of laboring to grow their own, the Indians bought corn from the Swedes. Gustafson said that the Indians were fond of turnips, which had been introduced by the Swedes.[35] Surprisingly, Kalm writes, "Nobody around here had ever heard of *rutabagas* or Swedish turnips."[36] After the Swedes were able to increase the number of hogs which they raised, by letting them graze free in the woods, the local Indians began to catch and eat them. Sometimes they bought hogs and tamed them to follow them as they moved from place to place. The Indians also became fond of cow's milk.[37] Kalm learned from Colonel William Johnson that the Iroquois had learned to drink tea as the Europeans did.[38]

From conversations with some of the older Swedes, Kalm learned about the tools used by the Native Americans before the arrival of Europeans and access to iron implements. They used "sharp stones, shells, claws of birds and wild beasts, pieces of bones, and other things of that kind, whenever they intended to make hatchets, knives, and similar instruments."[39]

The early settlers came across many of the native implements when plowing in the fields or digging. Hatchets were made of stone in the form of six-inch wedges, sharp at one end, with a notch all around the thick end. The handle was made by splitting a stick and inserting the stone between the sides, then tying it in place. Sharp pieces of flint or quartz or a sharp shell were used for cutting or scraping. Arrowheads were made of flint or quartz or bones or claws of animals.

John Bartram showed Kalm a decorated clay pot that had been made by Native Americans. Those who lived near the seashore pounded the shells of snails and mussel and mixed them with the clay. Others, who lived further inland pounded "mountain crystals" and mixed them with clay. The pots were poorly fired, for they were quite soft. Since the arrival of Europeans, the Native Americans whom Kalm met used iron pots and had forgotten the art of pottery.[40]

Pots or kettles for cooking were either made of clay or of different kinds of pot stone, *Lapis ollaris.* They had holes on either side to insert a stick so that the pot could be held above the fire. Stone was also used to fashion pipes for smoking tobacco.[41] Fish hooks were made of bone or bird's claws. Fire was made by rubbing two sticks together.[42]

The Conestoga Indians living in the area of New Sweden used the perennial plant Indian hemp or dogbane, *Apocynum cannabinum*, to make ropes and fishing nets as well as bags, pouches, quilts and linings. Kalm reported that the ropes made from this plant were strong and long-lasting, even in water.[43] When Kalm traveled through the Iroquois territory on his way to Niagara, he saw Indian women preparing hemp by rolling the filaments on their bare thighs. The threads and strings were then dyed red, yellow or black and worked into fabrics.[44] Farther north, wood nettle, *Urtica canadensis*, or the bark of white linden, *Tilia heterophyla*, was also used to make ropes, strings and pouches. The bark of leatherwood, *Dirca palustris*, was also used to make rope and baskets.[45] Sleeping mats for sleeping were made of bulrushes, *Schoenopleactus* or *Scirpus*.

Native Americans used white ash, *Fraxinus americana*, to make baskets, boxes, bushels and brooms. It was easily split, was tough, and could be bent in any way that they wished.

Before the arrival of Europeans, when the Indians wished to fell a tree, they used fire rather than tools to accomplish their task. They controlled the extent of burning by using wet rags and water.[46]

Although Kalm admired the Indians, he also expressed his strong belief in utility and technology when comparing European tools with primitive ones. "They could not hollow out a tree with their hatchets, or do a hundredth part of the work which we can perform with ease by the help of our iron tools. Thus we see how disadvantageous the ignorance and inconsiderate contempt of useful arts is. Happy is the country which knows their full value!"[47]

Early on, the French recognized the superiority of the light birch bark Indian canoe for exploration of North American waterways.[48] Kalm admired the Indian birch bark canoes and provided extensive descriptions of how they were constructed. They were usually made with six strips placed close and seamed together by cross-stitched spruce roots or ropes. Melted resin then was used on the outside seams. The inner side of the bark becomes the outer side of the canoe. These canoes were difficult to navigate and subject to frequent tears from a rough stone. Repair materials of bark and resin were always brought along.[49] The oars were usually made of maple.

Naturally, Kalm was interested in the farming practices and the diet of Native Americans because his charge was to find American plants that could be of use in Sweden. He noted that Indians who lived in the northern part of Canada subsisted solely on meat and fish. However, those who lived farther south had a varied diet, consisting of native vegetables such as corn, beans, pumpkins, squashes and melons.[50] In addition, they ate various fruits and nuts that grew wild in the woods: walnuts; chestnuts; mulberries; soursop or custard apple, *Annona reticulata*; chinquapins; hazelnuts; peaches; plums; grapes; persimmons, *Diospyros virginiana*; serviceberry, *Amelanchier canadensis*, and various berries. The flesh of fish and game constituted a large part of their diet. Kalm was especially interested in their use of wild rice, *Zizania aquatica*, which he hoped to be able to grow in the lakes of Finland. [51]

Kalm noted that Old World grains (wheat, barley, rye and oats) were "entirely unknown" before the arrival of Europeans, "nor do the Indians at present ever attempt to cultivate them."[52]

Immediately after his return to Finland, Kalm published an article in the *Transactions of the Royal Society* about the Indian staple, corn.[53] He called it "the lazy man's crop" because it was one of the most productive plants in the whole world.[54] Kalm could find no mention of maize growing wild in North America, nor were the Indians to whom he spoke able to tell him where their forefathers first found maize, although there were many folk tales about its origin.

Kalm was aware that, although the same species grew all along the Atlantic seaboard, there were many cultivated forms of the plant, which were adapted to the various climates and soils of the eastern woodlands. Maize grew well in the sandy soils that Kalm found in the coastal plain of New Jersey, and he noted that maize seedlings easily tolerated America's unpredictably late spring frosts. In his article, he claimed that maize found in Virginia but planted in New England would at first ripen with great difficulty unless the summer was unusually long. But it could be "trained" eventually to mature earlier and earlier so that it would become tolerant of the shorter growing season.[55]

Kalm described the Indian practice of planting bean seeds one or two weeks after planting corn so that the maize could serve as a prop on which the beans could lean and twine. They also planted sunflowers along with the corn.[56]

Kalm gives a detailed description of how maize was preserved. The Indians who had lived in the area of New Sweden allowed "their maize ears to dry in a moderate smoke, and afterward hang them up under the ceiling in their huts. The ears remain good for many years, both for food and planting. . . . They dug a deep pit in the ground in a dry place, covered the bottom and walls, or sides, with dry bark, and put dry grass on the bark at the bottom. Then they placed the maize in the pit. They also put dry grass at the sides next to the bark and then covered the top with soil."[57]

The Indians roasted ears of young green corn and even ate green ears when they were raw, which Kalm said tasted "as good as sweet-sugared milk."[58] Their bread was made by grinding "the maize in a large dry wooden mortar to grits or coarse flour. . . . Then they make a dough that they fill either with American blueberries, blackberries or wild grapes, which they collect and dry in great quantities during the summer for this purpose. From this dough small cakes are baked. These are first cooked in water like dumplings and then roasted and baked on a hot stone, or only cooked in water without the later baking and roasting. They are sometimes wrapped in leaves and blades of herbs and buried in ashes. A fire is built over them and in this manner they are baked. This is a dish especially used for important celebrations and big feasts, when they have some stranger for whom they wish to show their highest respect. Such bread tastes good and is usually eaten while it is warm."[59]

Kalm also described a concentrated food invented by the Indians and called *quitzera* by the Iroquois; maize grits were mixed with maple sugar and fat. This was kept in a sack and used when traveling, mixed with water.[60]

Pumpkins were a common food among the Indians, who boiled them whole or roasted them in ashes. The pulp was used to make pancakes or Indian pudding. They also preserved them by cutting them in slices that were dried by the sun or by a fire. These kept well and were used on their journeys.[61]

The sap of sugar maples was cooked until the desired thickness was obtained and used as a drink, for various confections and in preserving fruits. Kalm suggested that the Swedish maple be similarly used to obtain syrup.[62] The Indians prepared a sweet drink by drying and crushing hickory nuts and black walnuts and pounding them into fine flour that they mixed with water.[63]

Kalm described several native plants that were used for food by the Native Americans. One of these was the groundnut, *Apios americana*, a member of the pea family that was used extensively as a food source. Another was arrowhead, *Sagittaria latifolia*, the root of which was roasted and used in a great variety of ways. Kalm reported that it tasted somewhat like potato but was rather dry. Another Indian plant that Kalm mentioned was tuckahoe, *Peltandra virginica*, which the Indians used instead of bread and in a variety of other ways. It is poisonous unless cooked. If consumed raw, it makes the mouth and digestive tract feel as though hundreds of tiny needles are being stuck into it. Kalm wondered how early men in various parts of the earth had learned to eat various species of arums only when cooked when their initial taste would have been so offensive.[64]

Still another food source that Kalm mentioned was the dried or cooked seeds of golden club, *Orontium aquaticum.* The Indians made extensive use of huckle-berries, *Vaccinum sp.,* which they ate raw or dried in the sun and later mixed with corn bread batter. If necessary, the Indians smoked Canadian lousewort, *Pedicularis canadensis,* instead of tobacco and ate the leaves as an early spring green.

Another Indian food that Kalm wrote about is the clam, which the Native Americans came to the seashore annually to dig and then dry for future use. Oysters and clams provided a large part of the Indian diet in the summer. Kalm reports sights of great piles of oyster shells in various places along the seashore. He also explains their use of the clam shells as money, wampum, and as ornamentation for both men and women. The purple part of the shells was most valued. He mentions that the Indians formerly made their own wampum, but at the time of his visit it was mostly made by Europeans, especially the Dutch in Albany, who had a profitable business of making wampum, which was still used as a medium of trade.[65]

During his voyage north along the Hudson River, Kalm often saw Indians in birch bark canoes catching the plentiful sturgeons. They used torches at night to attract the fish and then harpooned them. The women sliced and dried the fish in the sun for use as food in the winter. These Indians were living on an island in temporary wigwams built simply of four posts covered with a roof of bark but without walls; they slept on deerskins.[66]

The Indians' lives were determined by the seasons of the year and the food then available, Kalm reported. "At one time of the year they live on the small store of corn, beans, and melons, which they have planted; during another period, about this time (July 20), their food is fish, without bread or any other meat; and another season they eat nothing but game, such as stags, roes, beavers, etc., which they shoot in the woods and rivers. They, however, enjoy long life, perfect health, and are more able to undergo hardships than other people. They sing and dance, are joyful and always content, and would not for a great deal exchange their manner of life for that which is preferred in Europe."[67]

Autumn was the time for hunting for the Indians. Entire families, including wives, children and dogs went along. On his return from Montréal, Kalm passed an Indian hunting party camped for the night with their canoe upside down on the shore. In the woods they had made shelters from poles covered with bark; the sides were protected from wind with an old blanket. Between the two tents they had a fire on which they cooked the venison that they had just killed. The carcasses of the deer were hung up to dry, as were the skins.[68]

The Indian women whom Kalm saw were dressed in a short blue petticoat bordered with red that reached to their knees. Over it they wore a blouse. Their black hair was tied with ribbons, and they wore large earrings and necklaces of wampum which hung down on their breasts. As they worked, they squatted on their knees, with the feet bent out. They were making articles of clothing from skins to which they sewed porcupine quills sometimes dyed with black or red.[69]

The warriors whom Kalm had just missed encountering on his route to Fort St. Frédéric wore shirts painted in vermilion, which also adorned their faces. They wore earrings, which were so heavy that they had to hold them when they jumped up and down. Several of the men wore rattlesnake skins around their waist with the rattles still attached.[70] Indian men "could not be persuaded to use trousers, for they thought that these were a great hindrance in walking."[71] Kalm reported that the Indian "men, upon the whole, are more fond of dressing than the women." "They constantly carry their looking glasses with them on all their journeys, but the women do not."[72]

The Hurons who lived in Lorette, near Québec, painted their bodies with various figures, using the charcoal of speckled alder, *Alus incana, subsp. rugosa,* to tattoo themselves. After his visit, Kalm reported that they wore a white- or blue-striped shirt and a sort of serape over their shoulders. Around their neck they wore a string of wampum with a large "French silver coin" at the end. Kalm found their shoes, made of skins, very similar in construction to those worn by women in Finland. Instead of stockings they wrapped their legs in pieces of blue cloth. Their bodies were tattooed with various designs such as figures of snakes. The Indian men whom Kalm saw along Lake George plucked the hair from the front part of their heads so that they appeared to have high foreheads.

The Indians smoked tobacco in pipes made of young shoots of dogwood. "Both Indians and French took these shoots or branches, removed the outer bark so that they became smooth, then bored out the soft kernel and used the branches for their pipe stems." They wore a small pouch made of skins around their neck in which they carried tobacco, which was mixed with the bark of red osier dogwood.[73]

Kalm also reported that the Native Americans customarily buried food along with the body of a deceased person.[74]

At Fort St. Jean, Kalm was able to see some Indian dances. The men danced first and then the women, accompanied by a drum beat and singing. When a man danced, he wore only a cloth tied around his waist and drawn up between his legs covered by a short apron or skirt. He held an axe in his hand while stepping to the beat of the drum. In the war dance, the dancer imitated many of the moves that would be used during a search for an enemy and during battle, and the singing was punctuated with the horrible-sounding war cry. The women danced together in a row, moving in unison with simple steps. Sometimes they all danced in a ring, with the men foremost.[75]

Kalm described the Indians skill in stalking enemies or animal prey without being observed by their target. They wore green grass tied around their head as camouflage and imitated the sounds of their animal prey. He admired their ruggedness and ability to travel long distances with few clothes and no bedding.[76]

In Québec, Kalm was provided with a guide to teach him about how the Indians made use of wild plants. The guide had been born to English colonists and had been captured as a child and brought up in an Indian village, where he married an Indian woman. This had been a common practice during the wars, resulting in many children in Canada with mixed blood. The guide, like most of the other captives, was unwilling to return to live with his family, despite their entreaties. Kalm found that "The free life led by the Indians pleased them better than that of their European relations; they dressed like the Indians and regulated all their affairs in their way. There is on the contrary scarcely one instance of an Indian adopting the European customs. They always endeavored to return to their own people again, even after several years of captivity."[77]

KALM reported that the houses of the Indians whom he visited on his way to Niagara were hung with human skulls, the trophies of war that indicated how many enemies had been slain. However, he found the Indians nearly always friendly and hospitable, "for they exhibit greater hospitality than most of the Christians. A stranger has scarcely time to enter their dwelling before the Indian mistress offers food, while her husband tries in his way to entertain the visitor."[78]

Kalm was not always so positive in his assessment of Native Americans. During his stay in Québec, he conversed at length with several of the Jesuits who had journeyed extensively among the Indians. He asked them whether they had found any who had been Christians before the arrival of Europeans and none had. He speculated that a more civilized nation may have inhabited North America in previous times because "a few marks of antiquity" had been discovered by European explorers. However, he declared,

"The Indians have always been as ignorant of architecture and manual labor as of science and writing. In vain does one seek for well-built towns and houses, artificially built fortifications, high towers and pillars, and such like among them, which the Old World can show from the most ancient times. Their dwelling places are wretched huts of bark, exposed on all sides to wind and rain."[79]

CHAPTER TWELVE
The Search for Cures

"I HAVE CAREFULLY COLLECTED ALL I COULD ON THIS JOURNEY, concerning the medicinal use of the American plants and the cures some of which they reckon infallible in more than one place," Kalm reported.[1]

He was, of course, ignorant of the bacterial or viral cause of disease, and he reported many speculations as to the cause of various ailments. Because of their lack of understanding of the causes of disease, the colonists tried many different cures. Almost all of these we now know were of little or no value, and many, such as excessive blood-letting and use of purgatives, were actually harmful.

Kalm describes many "infallible cures" for various diseases. For example, two prescriptions for dysentery were a "fried red English cheese eaten on a sandwich" and a tea of cinnamon and brandy and burnt sugar.[2] One of the few cures that he mentions that is still known to be of value is *Cinchona* bark, from which quinine is derived. It was found by Jesuits in Peru, who introduced it to Spain for the treatment of malaria. Kalm was told that the roots of the tulip tree, *Liriodendron tulipfera,* were as efficacious as *Cinchona* in the treatment of malaria.[3]

Kalm frequently described what he called "fever and ague," which was most likely malaria. Kalm reported that intermittent fevers were rare in Québec but common near Fort St. Frédéric and Fort Detroit. He indicated that the illness was more prevalent in Philadelphia than in New York and that the inhabitants thought that the cause was "vapors arising from stagnant fresh water, from marshes, and from rivers."[4] He also suggests that "the carelessness with which people eat quantities of melons, watermelons, peaches and other juicy fruit in summer, was reckoned to contribute much towards the progress of this fever, and repeated examples confirmed the truth of this opinion."[5]

Although American colonists did associate swamps and hot summer weather with the cause of malaria, they did not understand that mosquitoes were the vector for the dissemination of the disease. Both in the English colonies and in French Canada, Kalm was told that native Europeans lived longer than did the second or third generation born in America. Although Indians often lived to be quite old, he noted that Europeans in America were unlikely to live to old age. Some attributed this difference in mortality to the variability of the American climate.[6] Perhaps it was because of the debilitating effect of malaria. The disease itself rarely causes death on its own. Instead, malaria weakens the individual's resistance to other diseases. Although the majority of the colonists probably did not die directly of malaria, their weakened condition from periodic malarial attacks would have made them especially vulnerable to other diseases and to infection after child-birth.

Kalm noted that many of the people in New Sweden seemed to have lost most of their teeth; he ascribed it to drinking tea, especially if they drank it when very hot.[7] In discussions with Cadwallader Colden, who was a physician, Kalm asked him about his observation regarding the noticeable loss of teeth among the general population in America. Colden ascribed the widespread loss of teeth to the prevalence of scurvy, which he believed to be contagious.[8] We now know scurvy is due to dietary deficiency, a lack of vitamin C.

Kalm also speculated on the reasons why Americans seemed to have much larger families than did Europeans. He gave several examples of men and women who had produced large numbers of descendants. Kalm pointed out that men in America were free to marry at a young age because so much fertile land was available at reasonable prices. It was possible for anyone to make a living and support a family. He also pointed out that taxes were low. In addition, he was impressed by the freedoms of Americans: "The liberties he enjoys are so great that he considers himself as a prince in his possessions."[9]

BENJAMIN FRANKLIN published many practical volumes in addition to his more famous *Poor Richard's Almanack.* His third medical publication was an American edition of the English *Dr. Short's Medicina Britannica or a Treatise on Such physical Plants as are generally to be found in the Fields or Gardens in Great Britain, containing a particular account of their nature, virtues and uses.* Franklin reprinted this volume in 1751, during Kalm's stay in America, with a preface and appendix by John Bartram. Franklin had asked Bartram to review Dr. Short's list of plants and indicate which ones grew in American fields or gardens.[10] Bartram also prepared brief annotations throughout *Short's Medicina Britannica,* indicating whether the European medicinal plants were available in North America or whether there was a native North American substitute.[11]

In addition, Bartram's seven-page booklet, "Description, virtues and uses of sundry plants of these northern parts of America, and particularly of the newly discovered Indian cure for the venereal disease" was published separately in 1751 but was usually bound with the former book.[12] Presumably, Kalm and Bartram would have discussed these plants and their uses at length.

The plants that Bartram named as growing in America, with their currently accepted botanical names, as well as other native medicinal plants that are known to have been grown in his garden are listed in Table 1.[13]

Kalm is mentioned as a source of information on the use of two of these

Correct scientific names and currently used common names of American plants that John Bartram listed in his appendix to Dr. Short's *Medicina Britannica*

Gillenia trifoliata – bowman's root
Uvularia grandiflora – largeflower bellwort
Chamaelirium luteum – fairywand
Aralia racemosa – American spikenard
Aralia nudicaulis – wild sarsaparilla
Polygala senega – Seneca snakeroot
Caulophyllum thalictroides – blue cohosh
Iris versicolor – harlequin blueflag
Verbena hastata – swamp verbena
Cimicifuga racemosa – black cohosh or bugbane
Asclepias tuberosa – butterfly milkweed
Collinsonia canadensis - richweed
Sanguinaria canadensis – bloodroot
Veronica virginica – thymeleaf
Lobelia inflata – Indian tobacco
Polemonium reptans – Greek valerian
Anemone americana – round-lobed hepatica
Podophyllum peltatum – mayapple
Passiflora incarnata – purple passionflower
Opuntia humifusa – devil's-tongue
Echinacea purpurea – eastern purple coneflower
Eryngium yuccifolium – button eryngo
Liatris spicata – dense blazing star
Chelone glabra – white turtlehead
Geranium maculatum – spotted geranium
Asarum canadense – Canadian wildginger
Solidago canadensis – Canada goldenrod
Uvularia perfoliata – perfoliate bellwort
Aletris farinosa – white colicroot
Triosteum perfoliatum – feverwort
Liriodendron tulipifera – tuliptree
Apocynum cannabinum – Indianhemp
Lycopodium complanatum – ground cedar
Antennaria margaritacea, now known as *Anaphalis margaritacea* – pearly everlasting
Veronica spicata – spiked speedwell
Eupatorium perfoliatum – common boneset
Lobelia siphilitica – great blue lobelia

plants: *Apocynum* [14] and *Lobelia siphilitica*, as well as four other species of *Lobelia*. Bartram writes of *Apocynum*, "Peter Kalm saith it is excellent for the hysteric Passion."[15]

Kalm considered himself fortunate to have learned about the Indians' use of lobelia as a cure for syphilis and other venereal diseases from Colonel Johnson during his visits to Mount Johnson on his way to and from Niagara. The Indians believed that if they revealed their secret to Europeans, the cure would no longer be effective. According to Kalm, "Many of the French have attempted to bribe the savages with money or by other means to reveal the cure, but their efforts are useless."[16] Through stratagems suggested by Kalm, Johnson was able, at great "trouble, expense, and persuasive arguments," to obtain from three different Indian women the method they used to cook the roots of *lobelia* to prepare a curative beverage for their patients. The recipes were quite similar.

Kalm was so impressed with the reports of the healing powers of *lobelia* that he sent from Philadelphia a detailed account of its description and use to the Royal Swedish Academy of Sciences. It was published in their proceedings in 1750 and entitled, "Lobelia as a Sure Cure for Venereal Disease." This article was the first of the seventeen articles that Kalm published on American subjects in the proceedings of the Academy, *Kongl. Svenska Vetenskaps Academiens Handlingar*.[17]

In his article, Kalm reported that Native Americans had suffered from syphilis even before the arrival of Europeans, according to an elderly Indian informant. They considered "this disease one of the easiest to cure."[18] In retrospect, this supposed easy success may have been due to various factors. The early symptoms of syphilis are quite varied and can often be confused with those of other diseases. The chancre of primary syphilis usually disappears without treatment. The Native Americans may not have understood the fact that syphilis has a latent period that may last for many years before the onset of the tertiary phase of the disease.

Kalm also described horse balm, *Collinsonia canadensis*, which was named for Peter Collinson. Conrad Weiser had told Bartram that Native Americans used it as a liniment for pain or as a cure for rattlesnake bite. Bartram told Kalm that this plant was "an excellent remedy against all sorts of pain in the limbs, and for a cold, when the affected parts were rubbed with it."[19]

Kalm had been specifically charged with finding several medicinal plants in America: wild sarsaparilla, *Aralia nudicaulis*; sassafras, *Sassafras albidum*; Seneca snakeroot, *Polygala senega*; and American ginseng, *Panax quinquefolium*. Sassafras root was used as a tea for various ailments and as a treatment for sore eyes.

Snakeroot had been considered a cure for snakebite. However, in a letter to Linnaeus, Kalm wrote that "*Polygala* protects you from their bites no better than anything else." He described an incident in which an Indian was said to have been bitten by a rattlesnake and, despite the use of *Polygala*, was dead within two hours.[20] Kalm described snakeroot in an article published in 1752. It was used by the Indians as a tonic, as a treatment for pleurisy and as a thickening for broth.[21]

Kalm reported that the French used ginseng root as a cure for asthma, as a stomachic, and to promote fertility in women. In Canada, ginseng was collected by the Indians and sold to merchants who shipped it to China. There it was used as an aphrodisiac and sold for high prices. It was not found north of Montréal.[22]

The Indians also collected maidenhair fern, *Adiantum capillus-veneris*, which was sent to France, where it was highly valued. It was used to make a tea for coughs in Albany as well as by the Indians.[23] Black cohosh or bugbane, *Cimicifuga racemosa*, which Kalm mentioned as being effective against pleurisy and inflammation, is now under investigation as a selective estrogen receptor for use in the treatment of menopausal symptoms.

Kalm reported that the leaves of arborvitae, *Thuja occidentalis*, were used to make a poultice for rheumatic pains.[24]

The following plants[25] from Kalm's Herbarium were mentioned by him as having medicinal properties:

- Sicklepod rock cress, *Boechera Canadensis*, was called scurvy grass by the English colonists and was used as a remedy for that illness.
- Sarsaparilla, *Aralia nudicaulis*. "The root is effective against illnesses of the chest," wrote Kalm.
- Butterfly milkweed, *Asclepia tuberose*, was also called pleurisy root.[26] It was also used by the Indians.
- Swamp dogwood, *Cornus racemosa*. "The decoction of the bark is good against gout, urethritis, aching legs."
- Red osier dogwood, *Cornus serica*. "The decoction of the bark is good against gout, as well as cystorrhea."
- Witch hazel, *Hamamelis virginiana*. "The steam from the decoction of the bark is exceptionally effective against eye problems."
- Hairy hawkweed or queendevil, *Hieracium gronovii*; the root was considered as a good remedy for toothache and snake bite.
- Littleleaf buttercup, *Ranunculus abortivus*; was used by Indian women to induce abortions. The root was also used as a treatment for syphilis.
- The crushed leaves of the tuliptree, *Liriodendron tulipifera*, were used as a balm on the forehead to treat headache and for malaria.
- Mayapple, *Podophyllum peltatum*. Although highly toxic except for the fruit, it was used by the Indians as a strong laxative, and to treat worms. The root is currently used in cancer medications and may have commercial potential as a cultivated plant.
- The bark of speckled alder, *Betula incana, subsp. Rugosa*, was used to make red, brown and black dye, and a decoction of the bark was "excellent for leg wounds."
- Bloodroot, *Sanguinaria Canadensis*, was effective against contusions and against menstrual suppression. It was also used as a red dye plant.

CHAPTER THIRTEEN
Kalm as a Scientist

KALM was one of the first people trained as a scientific observer to use Linnaeus's classification system to report on the flora and fauna of North America. When evaluating Kalm as a scientist, the modern reader must keep in mind the fact that botany as a science had not yet been defined.[1]

Kalm considered himself a natural philosopher whose aim was to observe, collect and describe information about all of the aspects of the natural world and to assist in the task of organizing it systematically. It was only through such tedious and detailed collection and organization of data about natural phenomena from all over the world that theories would eventually emerge through a systematic comparison of specimens and by the development of schemes of classification.[2]

Kalm took careful measurements of the temperature every morning during his journey, and when he was in Canada, made sure that the temperature in Philadelphia would still be recorded by Bartram. Kalm noted that winters in Philadelphia were as severe as those in Sweden, but that they did not last as long, nor did the snow remain as long. The summers were much hotter and more humid, and the growing season lasted longer.[3] He found American weather to be inconsistent and too often changing. He deplored the frequent damage caused by hurricanes.[4] When a late frost hit Raccoon on May 1, Kalm was careful to note which plants were damaged by the cold.[5] He pointed out that native trees were seldom damaged by frost, whereas many of those whose flowers were killed were European introductions.[6] He noted that in Albany there were frequent late frosts, but that autumn lasted a long time. He had been told that the Hudson froze there in winter to a thickness of three or four feet.

Kalm seldom quantified his data, except for measuring temperature and barometric pressure, estimating the distance between towns, and reporting the latitude and longitude of locations and the dimensions of waterfalls. He simply tried to describe, as best he could, the natural world as he found it. Neither Kalm nor his mentor Linnaeus understood quantitative sciences such as astronomy or mathematics and did not carry out controlled experiments based on mathematical analyses.[7]

Kalm did not conduct scientific experiments, except, for example, to rub the sap of dogbane (*Apocynum androsaemifolium*) on his skin to see if it would create blisters, as it did to a soldier in Canada. He also observed the effects of poison ivy, *Toxicodendron radicans*. During their first year in America, Jungström was immune to its effect, but suffered greatly the next year. Kalm notes, "Hence it appears that though a person be secure against the power of this poison for a while, yet in course of time he may be affected by it just as much as people of a weaker constitution."[8]

Although Kalm was trained to observe nature carefully and scientifically, there are many instances in his accounts in which the modern reader would consider him gullible, as did botanists Juel and Harshbarger, writing at the beginning of the twentieth century.[9] Kalm reported verbatim what his various informants told him without verifying the accuracy of their statements. For example, Kalm reported that his Swedish friend Peter Cock had seen a snake swallowing a little bird, thus apparently confirming the then widespread belief that snakes were able to charm birds and small animals into succumbing to them.[10] He insisted that, although he had never seen it, most people in America believed that snakes had this power and many had told him of their own experiences of seeing this happen.

The very fact that Kalm had been sent to Canada was, of course, based on Linnaeus's belief in the supposition that lands in the same latitudes would have basically the same climate and growing conditions. Linnaeus did not realize that ocean currents affect climate and that soil types were not the same worldwide. Linnaeus believed that what was crucial to a plant's survival was an inherent range of temperature tolerance; he emphasized the importance of the role of the lowest winter temperature that a plant would tolerate.

Linnaeus also believed that plants could be "tamed" to grow in the climate of Scandinavia, and he convinced the Swedish establishment that this could be done. A given plant species that was exposed to colder temperature ranges could be changed to become hardier, he thought.[11] Kalm, reflecting his master's idea, wrote to Linnaeus from England suggesting that English saplings should first be planted in southern Sweden and then gradually moved farther north.[12]

Kalm, not understanding the physiology of trees, also believed that a way to protect them from winter damage was to pluck the leaves off the trees beginning in the middle of September to "decrease the sap in the trees so that the cold has less opportunity to exert all its strength and violence on them."[13]

It would not be for more than a half century until Alexander von Humboldt would develop the concept of isothermal lines, based on the records of temperature in different parts of the world kept by observers such as Kalm. It would also be many years until, because of the observations of Franklin and others, the effect of the Gulf Stream on the climate of Europe was fully understood.

It was not until more than a century had passed that the cumulative worldwide knowledge—accumulated from hundreds of collectors like Kalm—would provide sufficient data for the sub-science of plant geography to be developed by Alexander von Humbolt, Alphonse de Candolle, Asa Gray, Joseph Hooker, and especially by Charles Darwin.[14]

Kalm was sent to university to become a Lutheran minister. Despite his switch to natural philosophy, his conceptual framework was based upon an unwavering belief in Christian scripture. He believed in an immutable natural order, a system of regular, constant and universal relations among created beings, ultimately founded in the will of God. His basic assumptions were the notions of continuity, purpose and plan, as well as the fixity of species.[15] It was believed that the results of scientific investigations could provide proof of the existence of God and His wisdom and skill in creating the universe.

As Linnaeus immodestly expressed it, *"Deus creavit. Linnaeus disposuit."*[16]

One wonders how much Kalm's conversations with John Bartram, Benjamin Franklin and other Deists challenged Kalm's orthodox Christian faith. Bartram was selective in his reading of the Bible, rejecting miracles that defied the laws of nature and seeking confirmation of truths that he knew empirically to be true. Bartram had no use for the clergy. He was disowned by the Darby Meeting for heresy in his disbelief in the divinity of Christ.[17]

Linnaeus, too, had sometimes run afoul of theologians and, to avoid censure, had to compromise the reports of his observations. His friend Fabricius wrote: "He dared not publish many important observations relating to the general arrangement of nature because he was afraid of the excessive violence of the Swedish divines. . .who, too faithful to their own arguments, do not consider that nature, as well as revelation, proclaims. . .the hand of that great master who formed both."[18]

Kalm also tried to avoid confrontation with theologians. In a letter to Pehr Wargentin, the secretary of the Royal Academy, on June 3, 1748, he wrote, "The Lord's intention in giving us the Bible was to help us to blessedness and not to tell us whether the oceans are decreasing or not. The Scriptures must be quoted sparingly where natural science is concerned, in order not to give atheists and the godless grounds for despising and poking fun at a priceless book."[19]

Kalm struggled to fit his observations into the framework of his belief in the literal interpretation of the Bible, especially the account of Noah and the flood. An early entry into his journal indicates this concern, "Many of the savages who are yet heathens are said to have some obscure notion of the Deluge. But I am convinced from my own experience that not all are acquainted with it."[20]

Kalm was puzzled by the presence of shells far from the shore. Near Fort St. Frédéric, he found petrified shells of what he called *"Ostreae pectines"* embedded in a black rock, along with snail shells and corals.[21] Kalm "asked Mr. Benjamin Franklin and other gentlemen who were well acquainted with this country, whether they had come upon any evidence that places which were now a part of the continent had formerly been covered with water." He was told that there were such places and speculated, "Are not these reasons sufficient to make one suppose that those places in Philadelphia which are at present fourteen feet and more under ground were formerly the bottom of the sea, and that by several violent changes, sand, earth, and other things were carried upon them? Or, that the Delaware formerly was broader than it is at present? Or that it has changed its course?"[22]

Several of the Swedes in the Raccoon area also believed that their region had once been covered by the sea. Kalm concluded that "a great portion of the province of New Jersey, in ages unknown to posterity, was part of the bottom of the sea."[23]

Bartram pointed out to him that shells he had found on northern mountain tops were of species that were now only found alive on the shore much farther south.[24] He and Bartram spent much time discussing the meaning of the shells found so far from the sea. Kalm reported that "Mr. Bartram has not only frequently found oyster shells in the ground, but has likewise met with such shells and snails as undoubtedly belong to the sea, at a distance of a hundred or more English miles from the shore. He has even found them on the ridges of mountains which separate the English plantations from the habitations of the savages."[25] "A vast quantity of petrified shells are found in limestone, flint, and sandstone on the same mountains."[26]

Kalm's keen observation of geological formations was already evident early in the journey from England to Philadelphia. On the third day of the voyage, when the *Mary Gally* passed Dover, Kalm noted his agreement with the opinion that William Camden expressed in his *Brittania* of 1586 that the chalk hills on either side of the English Channel must at one point have been joined together.[27] He was also correct in his speculation that the fossils that he identified in the flint at Little Gaddesden were of marine origin and that chalk underlies London and its surrounding area.[28]

However, the development of the science of geology and its theories describing how geologic formations occur was still in the future. During his voyage up the Hudson River, Kalm had many questions about the origin of such streams, but not many answers. He was puzzled that the north-and-south-flowing river bisected mountain ridges that ran east and west. He wondered why the river flowed so directly for such a long distance along the same meridian and was so deep, with no sign of rapids or shallow rocky beds.

Kalm also speculated on why the summits of the Berkshire Hills were barren, assuming, mistakenly, that they were too hot, dry and windy for plants to grow there.[29] These "excessively high and steep mountains" were probably the highest mountains that Kalm had ever seen; his previous European travels were in relatively flat Sweden, Finland, and western Russia. The highest hills he had seen in England were the Chilterns. Thus, he had no measure of comparison regarding the height of mountains or how high the tree line actually was.

Kalm was undoubtedly familiar with the view of America that was then current in Europe: That America was indeed a New World and that, although God had been content with one great inundation of the Old World and had permitted Noah to start that world anew, in America there had been several later floods, and the people, plants and animals that remained were the remnants of these later devastations.[30]

There are many places in Kalm's account of his travels in which he makes observations that attempt to either confirm or reject the theories then current among European scientific circles. One of these, proposed notably by the Comte de Buffon, is that American plants and animals were inferior in size and fertility to those in Europe. Buffon had provided a scientific and philosophical explanation of the supposed backwardness of the New World because of the successive floods. "So swampy was the soil, so rank the vegetation, so thick the forests, so miasmic the air, that the sun could not penetrate to the ground below, and the waters could neither evaporate nor drain away."[31]

Kalm seemed to support this view in an unsubstantiated comment early in his account, when he talks about the trade between England and Philadelphia. He is puzzled that woolen cloth is not manufactured in the colony and speculates that it may be because "the breed of sheep which is brought over degenerates in process of time and affords but a coarse wool."[32] It may be that he attributed this degeneration to the careless practices of American farmers who did not enrich the soil of their pastures. Few other comments in Kalm's journal would corroborate Buffon's theories, but he did not openly refute them. That task would await Jefferson's *Notes on Virginia*.

Kalm reported that the seeds for the spring wheat that grew well in Canada were originally imported from Sweden or Norway because the seeds from France failed to grow. There had also been a successful experiment of substituting Swedish winter wheat and winter rye for the French varieties, which did not survive the cold winters.[33]

Kalm provided a list of the trees that he found in the Philadelphia area and the environment in which they grew, listing them in relative order of occurrence. This list is useful to modern naturalists who wish to determine the changes that have occurred over time in particular populations of trees.[34]

Kalm tried to determine whether the size of plants is affected by their latitude. Because Kalm was able to travel a considerable distance north from Wilmington, Delaware, to Montréal and Québec, he was able to observe the differences in the growth and variety of trees and other plants as he journeyed from a southern to northern climate. Early in his visit, he inquired of Bartram as to whether he believed Mark Catesby to have been correct in his observation that American trees decreased in size as they grew farther north. Bartram responded that "There are some trees which grow better in southern countries, and become smaller as you advance to the north. If their seeds are planted farther north, they will not grow as tall and eventually not at all. In addition, there are some trees that prefer a more northerly climate and will not grow as well in the south."[35] Bartram had also told him that alders, *Alnus spp.*, were smaller further south of Philadelphia—where they were shorter than in Europe—but they were taller and thicker in the north.[36]

Kalm was able to confirm Bartram's conclusions during his travels. For example, the sassafras, which grew tall in Pennsylvania, "hardly reached the height of two or four feet" if planted near Oswego. The same was true of tulip poplars.[37] Kalm reported that sugar maples, which grew to great heights in Canada, would only grow on north-facing slopes in Pennsylvania and would not attain as great a height.[38] He found that alders in Canada grew almost as tall as those in Sweden.[39] He listed a dozen trees that he had seen in Pennsylvania that he did not find north of Albany; in addition to the more northerly location, he wrongly attributed their absence to the fact that the river flowed from north to south and thus did not carry seeds in the opposite direction.[40] On his journey south to Philadelphia from Canada, he made note of each time he saw a plant or tree that he had not previously encountered north of that point.

Kalm summarized his findings concerning Canadian plants, "the further you go northward, the more you find the plants are the same as the Swedish ones: thus, on the north side of Québec, a fourth part of the plants, if not more, are the same as the wild plants in Sweden."[41]

Kalm mentions a number of conversations with Benjamin Franklin about various scientific topics, but a surprising gap in Kalm's journal is the lack of any mention of electricity. Kalm's visit to Philadelphia took place during the years of Franklin's famous experimentations with electricity. His *Experiments and Observations on Electricity, Made at Philadelphia* was published in London in 1751.[42]

Kalm frequently mentions minerals that were found in the areas that he visited, such as copper, iron, asbestos and soapstone. In several places he visited mining operations. He was clearly interested in the economic value that mineral deposits could bring to a nation.

In this era before the invention of chemical dyes, cultivation of dye plants was an important source of revenue for areas such as the low country of South Carolina, where indigo began to be widely cultivated at this time to obtain its dark blue dye. Kalm was probably aware of the British bounty that was placed by the English Parliament for Carolina indigo as a result of their fear of competition from the French following the 1748 Peace of Aix-la-Chapelle.[43] Kalm reported that a number of American plants were used as red dyes, including the bark of chestnut oak, *Quercus prinus or montana*,[44] and speckled alder, *Alnus incana subsp. rugosa*, as well as bloodroot, *Sanguinaria canadensis*, and bedstraw, which the French called "tissoyanne rouge," *Galium tinctorium*. The red berries of sumach, *Rhus glabra*, were used as a red dye, as were those of the American pokeweed, *Phytolacca americana*. Goldthread, *Coptis trifolia*, which provided an excellent red pigment, grew near Niagara Falls. The bark of sassafras, *Sassafras albidum*, was used in "dyeing worsted a fine lasting orange color, which does not fade in the sun. They use urine instead of alum in dyeing, and boil the dye in a brass boiler, because in an iron vessel it does not yield so fine a color."[45]

The bark of the red maple, *Acer rubrum*, was boiled to give a dark blue color to worsted and linen.[46]Alder bark was used for red and brown dye, and woolen and linen cloth was dyed yellow with hickory or black oak bark. Field sorrel ,*Rumex acetosella*, was used for a black dye.[47]

A modern reader is struck by the number of times that Kalm mentions the presence of insects and the harm that they caused, perhaps because we are so used to being protected from their irritations by screening. Kalm implied that insects were more troublesome in America than in Sweden; he often complained of the swarms of mosquitos. He found their bites more irksome than those he had experienced in Sweden.[48]

Kalm reported on an infestation of insects that had devastated the crops of peas in Pennsylvania and New Jersey and was spreading north to New York. He carefully sent a sample of the insect to Count Tessin, the President of the Royal Swedish Academy, and to Linnaeus. Linnaeus was already familiar with the insect, which he called *Bruchus pisi*, the pea beetle.[49]

Other insect that Kalm found troublesome included the caterpillars of gypsy moths and clothes moths, cockroaches, wood lice, and noisy crickets. When he slept in the huts of Indians, he was plagued with fleas, brought in by the many dogs, which they kept.[50] In Canada, he was bitten by bed bugs.

In 1756, after his return to Finland, Kalm wrote an article about periodical cicadas or seventeen-year locusts, *Cicada septendecim*, based on observation made of their emergence in New Sweden in 1749. Bartram and Collinson had carried on a correspondence about these insects since 1737.[51] Certainly Kalm must have queried his friend about them. In addition, two of the pastors in New Sweden, the Reverend Andreas Sandel, of the Gloria Dei Church in Philadelphia and the Reverend Andreas Hesselius of Holy Trinity Church in what is now Wilmington had both kept notes in their diaries of the May 1715 invasion of the locusts, with which Kalm must have been acquainted.

According to many people whom Kalm queried, honey bees had been brought to America by the English. Several of the English and Swedish farmers kept beehives.[52]

Kalm was interested in several American animals that did not exist in Europe.

He wrote extensively about the skunk, *Mephitis mephitis;* however, he assumed that its noxious odor was from its urine rather than its specialized musk. Kalm also suggested that, although gray foxes were native to America, red foxes had been introduced from Europe. He mentioned that there were two species of wolf: yellowish or pale gray and dark brown or black. He also described squirrels, flying squirrels, muskrats, beavers, mink, raccoons and chipmunks, as well as many species of birds. Kalm also published an article on rattlesnakes.

Kalm sent several shipments of seeds to the Royal Swedish Academy of Sciences; one in October of 1748 contained seeds of wild grapes as well as chestnuts and hazelnuts packed in boxes of sand. The following autumn, he sent two separate lots of the seeds of some 408 species, many collected in Canada. The accompanying lists noted where the plant had been found and its use. It arrived at the Royal Academy on June 23, 1750, and the seeds were distributed to several naturalists or gardeners, including Linnaeus and Bielke.[53]

Kalm preserved three sets of his collection of dried North American herbarium specimens. One, containing about 380 specimens, was destroyed in the great Åbo fire of 1827 that burned down a large part of the city. The specimens that he gave to Linnaeus are now at the Linnean Society of London. Several years after his return, Kalm presented the third herbarium of 380 North American plants to Queen Lovisa Ulrika, who had supported his travels.[54] On the back of the gold-rimmed sheets Kalm wrote the names given to the plants by either Linnaeus or himself and their use. This herbarium is now in the Museum of Natural History at Uppsala. Additional specimens are elsewhere—in the Thunberg Herbarium at Uppsala University, at the Bank Herbarium at The Natural History Museum, London, and at the University of Helsinki.

Kalm remained a faithful and subservient disciple of Linnaeus to the end of his life. Although he did discover many hitherto unnamed species during his American travels, he left the verification and naming of them to Linnaeus. He gave one dried specimen of every plant that he brought home to Linnaeus.

Linnaeus's most important work, *Species plantarum*, published in 1753, is regarded as the starting-point for the Latin binomial, or two-word, names of plants. In earlier publications, Linnaeus had identified about 250 species from North America. However, in *Species plantarum*, some seven hundred North American species are listed, of which seventy-five were new to science. Kalm was mentioned as the discoverer of ninety of them, of which sixty were new to science. In later works, Linnaeus listed two more plants that had been found by Kalm.[55]

Kalm's unfinished and unpublished "Flora of Canada," mentioned by Linnaeus in his *Species Plantarum*, probably perished in the Åbo fire.[56] Kalm was more interested in the practical application of what he had learned about the cultivation and use of plants, rather than in writing a detailed scholarly catalog of plants. He wrote in a letter to C.C. Gjörwell in 1764, "Natural history alone without consideration of its use in human life is pure balderdash and not a jot better than allot of metaphysical ravings."[57]

Linnaeus named several plants for Kalm, the most important being *Kalmia*. Mountain laurel, *Kalmia latifolia,* is a widespread native plant of which there are now about eighty recognized cultivars. It is the official state flower of Pennsylvania and Connecticut. Kalm was not the first European naturalist to describe the plant. Mark Catesby illustrated it in his book, *The Natural History of Carolina,* which Kalm purchased during his stay in England.

Four other species of plants were named for Kalm: *Hypericum, Lobelia, Bromus,* and *Pachylepis kalmii.* Kalm's St. Johnswort, *Hypericum kalmianum,* is a three-foot shrub native to Great Lakes region, and *Bromus kalmii* is a native American brome grass that grows in damp or wet places. An insect, *Hygus* or *Cimex kalmii,* is also named for him. Linnaeus wrote of Kalm's definition of three genera (*Lechea, Gaultheria* and *Polymnia*) and a diagnosis of one species (*Tilia americana*). A dissertation published under Linnaeus's direction in 1751, entitled *Nova plantarum genera,* included information in its first chapter about plants that Kalm found in America, *Genera americae septentrionalis.*

CHAPTER FOURTEEN

Kalm as an Environmentalist
The Contrast between Native Americans and European Colonists

PART OF HIS CHARGE as professor of economics and docent in natural history when Kalm returned to Åbo Akademi was to introduce improved farming methods to Finland. Much of the commentary in the account of his stay in England dealt with agricultural practices there. English farmers employed some of the most advanced methods in Europe at that time, according to Kalm. He clearly admired the results and hoped to emulate English practices in Sweden and Finland wherever possible. From his experience of trying to improve the poor soil at Lövsta with the addition of manure and other organic material and with the results he had seen on English farms, Kalm became convinced of the need for farmers to constantly add to the fertility of their farmland.

In America, however, he found little to emulate, except, perhaps, the practice in the cities of Philadelphia and New York of holding regular farmers' markets where fresh produce could be purchased directly from the producer. He found that the only thing he could learn was from the "gross mistakes and carelessness of the future" displayed by the colonists, whether English, Swedes, Germans, Dutch or French. He deplored the wasteful practices of the Pennsylvania farmers. "Their eyes are fixed upon the present gain, and they are blind to the future."[1] He compared the colonists' treatment of the land unfavorably with that of the Indians, who cleared only a small part of the land for agriculture and left the remainder in its natural state.[2] Kalm contended that the depth and richness of the soil that the early settlers found misled them into being "careless husbandmen."[3]

In his native Finland, it had been the practice for farmers in outlying areas in the east to use the cut-and-burn method of clearing the land, then to move on after the soil was exhausted. Eventually, it was recognized that this method was wasteful, and strict laws with harsh penalties were passed against this practice.[4] Kalm even believed that such burning adversely affected the climate.[5] To his dismay, he found that farmers in America were doing the same thing.

> Formerly when a person had bought a piece of land, which perhaps had never been plowed since Creation, he cut down a part of the wood, tore up the roots, tilled the ground, sowed seed on it, and the first time he got an excellent crop. But

the same land after being cultivated for several years in succession, without being manured, finally loses its fertility of course. Its possessor then leaves it fallow and proceeds to another part of his land, which he treats in the same manner. Thus he goes on till he has changed a great part of his possessions into grain fields, and by that means deprived the ground of its fertility. He then returns to the first field, which now has pretty well recovered.

"It being customary here to let the cattle go about the fields and in the woods both day and night, the people cannot collect much dung for manure. But by leaving the land fallow for several years a great quantity of weeds spring up in it, and get such strength that it requires a considerable time to extirpate them. This is the reason why the grain is always so mixed with the seed of weeds. The great richness of the soil which the first European colonists found here, and which had never been plowed before, has given rise to this neglect of agriculture, which is still observed by many of the inhabitants.[6]

Kalm deplored the colonists' practice of burning their fields in March to clear them of dead leaves to allow the shoots of grass to spring up. He found that the fires consumed indiscriminately some valuable tree shoots and destroyed the seeds of annual grasses that had once provided a lush crop of hay.[7] Kalm had identified a number of native plants that could be used to create "the richest and most fertile meadow," if only they received "a little more attention and assistance from their unexperienced owner."[8]

Kalm suggested that, by using these native plants, American farmers could provide better food for their cattle, which he found grew "poorer daily in quality and size because of hunger." [9] He also deplored their lack of knowledge about horticulture.

On my travels in this country I observed several plants, which the horses and cows preferred to all others. They were wild in this country and likewise grew well on the driest and poorest ground, where no other plants would succeed. But the inhabitants did not know how to turn this to their advantage, owing to the little account made of Natural History, that science being here (as in other parts of the world) looked upon as a mere trifle, and the pastime of fools.[10]

As correct as he was in his assessment, Kalm failed to acknowledge the differences in the supply of manpower in the countries that he visited. In his native Sweden and Finland, great effort was needed to wrest a living from a difficult environment, and labor was in short supply. In England, where he deplored what looked to him like the laziness of farmers spending many hours a week relaxing in pubs, there was a surplus of labor. David Freeman Hawke contrasts the situation in England with that of the American colonists. "It was a land of underemployed people who averaged about four hours a day at their work. America might be a land rich and fat, but it asked more work than that from someone who expected to survive."[11] Pennsylvania was chronically short of workers, thus the reliance of so many farmers on indentured servants.[12]

From interviews that Kalm conducted with elderly colonists, Swedes and Englishmen, he learned that wild birds and fish had decreased in numbers significantly since these people were children. "In their youth the bays, rivers and brooks were quite covered with all sorts of water fowl, such as wild geese, ducks, and the like. But at present there was sometimes not a single bird upon them. About sixty or seventy years ago, a single person could kill eighty ducks in a morning; but at present you frequently waited in vain for a single one."[13]

Kalm still was able to see immense numbers of wild pigeons in the uninhabited area north of Albany, New York.[14] One of the articles that he published in the proceedings of the Royal Swedish Academy of Sciences described the wild passenger pigeon, now, unfortunately, extinct. This species was once incredibly abundant and was used by the American colonists and the Indians as a common and delicious food source. As late as the early part of the nineteenth century, John James Audubon reported seeing schooners in New York harbor piled high with mounds of passenger pigeons that had been caught upriver and brought for sale in the city's markets for a penny a piece.[15]

Kalm related that in the middle of March, 1740, the numbers of the pigeons while in flight were said to have "extended 3 or 4 English miles in length, and more than 1 such mile in breadth, and they flew so closely together that the sky and the sun were obscured by them." There were so many birds that they broke the limbs of trees on which they roosted, and the ground below was covered with their dung. They fed on acorns, chestnuts, beechnuts, mulberries, elm seeds, grain (except for corn) and other fruit and seeds. During his travels up the Hudson to Canada, Kalm saw these pigeons "in countless numbers. Their young had at this time left their nests, and their great numbers darkened the sky when they occasionally rose en masse from the trees into the air." Their cooing disturbed his sleep, as did the sound of branches crashing to the ground because of the weight of countless pigeons. Kalm ascertained their summer range to be in Canada but not more than 20 French miles north of Québec, the northernmost range of the oak and beech trees, whose nuts they ate. In the winter, they migrated farther south in the interior of the continent except when a lack of sufficient food drove them toward the coast.[16]

Kalm learned from the Iroquois who lived at Onondaga that the pigeons had a special fondness for alkaline deposits of salt. The Indians netted them while they were eating this salt.[17] However, he reported that "While these birds are hatching their young, or while the latter are not yet able to fly, the savages are in the habit of never shooting or killing them, nor of allowing others to do so, pretending that it would be a great pity on their young, which would in that case have to starve to death."[18]

Kalm again contrasted the colonists' wastefulness with the condition before the arrival of Europeans. He wrote, "The few Indians that lived here seldom dis-

turbed the birds" because they did not have guns to shoot them. "And consider-
ing that they cultivated their small maize fields, caught fish, hunted stags,
beavers, bears, wild cattle, and other animals whose flesh was delicious to them,
it will soon appear how little they disturbed the birds." In contrast, the colonists
cut down the forests and "have by hunting and shooting in part extirpated the
birds, in part frightening them away. In spring the people still steal eggs, mothers
and young indifferently, because no regulations are made to the contrary. And if
any had been made, the spirit of freedom which prevails in the country would not
suffer them to be obeyed."[19]

Kalm also noted that trees that were used for especially desirable lumber were
already disappearing. Houses in Philadelphia were covered with very light and
durable shingles made from Atlantic white cedar, *Chamaecyparis thyoides.*
"Swamps and morasses formerly were full of them but at present these trees are
for the greatest part cut down and no attempt has as yet been made to plant new
ones."[20] In Carolina, he was told, the forests of longleaf pine had been largely
destroyed in order to make tar.[21]

Much of the trade of Philadelphia was with the West Indies. Kalm reported
that "The true mahogany which grows in Jamaica is at present almost all cut
down." In exchange for West Indian products, such as sugar, molasses, rum, indigo and mahogany, Philadelphians sent black walnut and oak planks from New
Jersey, "the forests of which province are consequently more ruined than any
other."[22]

Kalm was also aware of the importance of balance in nature as well as the law
of unintended consequences. He repeated a story told to him by Benjamin
Franklin. New Englanders passed laws encouraging the extermination of black-
birds which they believed destroyed their corn. "The consequence was, the Black-
birds were diminished but a kind of Worms which devoured their Grass, and
which the Black-birds had been used to feed on encreased prodigiously; Then
finding their Loss in Grass much greater than their saving in corn they wished
again for their Black-birds."[23]

CHAPTER FIFTEEN
Return to Sweden
February 24—August 28, 1751

KALM left America with great reluctance. He bade goodbye to several of his American friends at a dinner party in Darby, outside of Philadelphia.[1] He wrote to Linnaeus, "I have now come to the end of my travels in this country which I find more difficult to leave than I can express. If I could follow my own desires I should like to be here for many more years in order to go all over and explore all places carefully, but my purse says otherwise."[2]

The return journey of the party now included Margaretha Kalm, her daughter Johanna, and Jungström, as well as a pair of opossums, a tortoise, a guinea pig,[3] and a large amount of baggage. The trip began on February 24, 1751, when they set out from Philadelphia. They had to travel by land to New Castle, Delaware, because the Delaware River was still frozen. They had with them not only all of the seeds and dried herbarium specimens that had been collected recently but a supply of food and other necessities for the journey, including two pounds of raisins to be eaten to avoid constipation during the voyage.[4] Just before the ship embarked, fresh provisions were purchased, including pigs, poultry, geese, eggs, milk, lemons and butter.[5]

Kalm also took some 150 live specimens of different rare and valuable perennial plants and young trees that he was able to water and care for during the voyage. There were also trunks containing rocks and miscellaneous curiosities.[6] Finally, there were several books (in addition to those he had brought with him), including one of Franklin's almanacs, a Swedish catechism for the Delaware Indians, and the octavo sheets of his journal that was later transcribed into ten volumes, extending to May 15, 1751.[7]

He was assisted by a friend in haggling with Captain Shirley for a reduced fare of only eighty pounds. The voyage across the stormy Atlantic was difficult, and twice the waves were so high that his cabin was half-filled with sea water. The possums were forced to swim around in it. As a result, perhaps, of too much salt from the water or a bite from the ill-natured female, the male died. However, the couple had mated several times, and Kalm wrote to Linnaeus that he was hopeful that she might survive to bear her young.[8] She (or perhaps an offspring) did survive and became a nuisance later, chewing up chairs, tables, chests and books. He offered the animal to Linnaeus, saying that it had become as tame as a cat or dog and was excellent at catching rats.[9]

Near the mouth of the Thames the ship struck a sandbar and began to leak. In great fear, Kalm packed in a small satchel his most precious belongings, a few seeds, and his diary and record of expenditures, and prepared to disembark. Fortunately, the ship was able to continue to Margate, and on March 26, Kalm, Margaretha and the child landed and proceeded to London by coach, leaving Jungström behind to come later with the cargo. The ship docked a week later, and the precious cargo was safely unloaded in good condition and stored in a warehouse that Kalm rented for that purpose.[10]

They stayed in London until the end of May. During this time, Kalm visited the friends that he had made during his previous stay in England: Collinson, Mortimer and Warner. They had already read the account of Niagara Falls in the letter published by Franklin, which had become a literary success in London.[11] They were certainly eager to hear of the results of his journey. Warner reported that the seeds that he had received from Kalm had germinated, and Kalm was able to see for himself that they were growing well in Warner's garden.[12] On the same ship had come a letter from Franklin to Collinson in which he wrote, "Our Friend Mr. Kalm, goes home in this Ship, with a great Cargo of Curious Things. I love the Man, and admire his indefatigable Industry."[13]

Collinson wrote to Bartram on April 24, 1751, with the following request:

> Pray remember the *Faba AEgyptiaca*, that our friend KALM found in West Jersey: specimens of leaf, flower and fruit.
>
> He and his wife arrived safe here. We have had many conferences. He desires his service; commends thee in most things, but much blames thee for not enriching thy journal (of the expedition to Lake Ontario) with as many curious articles which he has collected from thy mouth, and which, had he come time enough, he would have added.[14]

Kalm and Jungström also spent time sorting the seeds into two lots, one that would go with Kalm to Gothenburg and then by land to Stockholm. The other would go directly to Stockholm with Jungström.

Kalm arrived in Stockholm on June 3, where he and his family stayed for most of the summer, finding lodgings in the house of a Madame Åkerman. He busied himself making paper bags from morning till evening and filling them with seeds. These were distributed free at the Royal Swedish Academy of Sciences to anyone who wished to try growing them. Shortly after his return, Kalm wrote a small octavo pamphlet of forty-eight pages to describe the planting and care of the various seeds. Published in Stockholm in 1751, it listed those plants that Kalm thought might survive the Scandinavian climate and were likely to provide economic benefit. For each plant he described the general area in which he found it, its use, and the type of soil and other conditions required for each. He recommended Philip Miller's *Gardener's Dictionary* as an excellent source of general advice on the theory and practice of gardening.[15]

Kalm also had to present his long expense account to the Royal Academy. It consisted of fifty-three pages in small quarto in the form of a brief travel diary, beginning on October 13, 1747, when he had set out for Gothenburg. It is divided into sections according to the currency which he used: Swedish, Norwegian, English sterling, and Pennsylvania money. It also includes Jungström's account of his return from Canada and his summer in Pennsylvania in 1750. Kalm was worried that the academy would not approve the large bill that he presented to them. On October 19, 1751, he wrote to Pehr Wargentin, the secretary of the academy, "You seem to believe that I have spent damn huge sums, but I can assure you that I could not live cheaper than I have. Nobody in England and America believed that I and a servant could manage on so little money."[16]

Among the many items that Kalm brought back with him from America were two copies of Lewis Evans's 1749 map of Pennsylvania, New Jersey, New York and Canada. One of them was a personal copy, and the other, with a Latin inscription from Evans, was given to the library of the Royal Swedish Academy of Sciences. At Kalm's request, Evans also drew up a map of those parts of North America through which Kalm had traveled. Kalm noted in a letter to the secretary of the Royal Academy that Evans had indicated the location of Raccoon as *T. Suecicum*, meaning "Swedish temple."[17]

Linnaeus was eager to see his student and to discover what he had learned in America. In May, before Kalm's arrival, he had written to his friend Dr. Abraham Bäck describing his eagerness to see Kalm. "Take fire-brands and throw them after Professor Kalm that he may come without delay to Uppsala, for I long for him like a bride for one o'clock at night."[18]

Kalm wrote twice to Linnaeus from Stockholm before he had a chance to visit with him. Both letters indicated his nervousness regarding whether or not the Master would acknowledge him as having been the discoverer of new and as yet unnamed plants. He feared being labeled as a plagiarist if he himself claimed such an honor, emphasizing his deference to Linnaeus. But he believed that one important measure of the success of his journey would be the number of new plants whose discovery was attributed to him.

Upon his return to Stockholm Kalm wrote to Linnaeus, pleading for his recognition and approval.

> May God grant that Master find as many herbs in my collection worthy of being described publicly (as do I) since I, from the bottom of my heart, would long for the honor of having them described in print for the learned world by you, gentle Master. The number of herbs Master deems of value to describe will present clear evidence of how Master has liked or disliked my travels; the more useful herbs

described, the more Master will give testimony to the diligence with which I have undertaken my travels. And remember a hundred times that I have a new appointment where I will have so much to do at first that I will have no time to think about my *Flora Amerikae Septentr*. Remember that my body is worn out and that I am a mere mortal; remember that you owe the public to reveal what you know; remember to give me *nomina specifica* for all my herbs and publish them in your name; finally, it is Master's duty and on his conscience to make known every herb he receives that merits it. I would be the most common person in the world if I didn't count it as the greatest honor to have Master do that."[19]

In July, crippled from gout but unwilling to wait until his former student was able to visit him, Linnaeus came by boat to Stockholm to see him.[20] Kalm was later able to spend a week in Uppsala with Linnaeus and left him a large collection of his harvest of seeds as well as a full set of dried pressed specimens.[21] He and Margaretha left for Turku and his new duties on August 28.[22]

CHAPTER SIXTEEN
Life as Professor at Åbo
August 29, 1751—November 16, 1779

P ETER KALM was a different man from the naïve young disciple who had started out from Stockholm almost four years before. He had been treated with respect by people of importance in three countries and had survived innumerable hardships. He was now a married man with a wife and child to support and a respected position to fill.

But the mission was still not complete. He had to assure that the seeds that he brought back with him were planted and tended and that at least some of them would grow to become the basis of new ways for improving the economy of his homeland. Despite Kalm's eagerness to plant the seeds and live plants that he had brought back with him, he was forced to wait until the next spring. No garden was available.

Kalm and Margaretha arrived in Åbo at the end of August and found rented lodgings, where they stayed until the spring of 1752. He then borrowed money to obtain his own larger house at 26 Linnankatu[1] (Slottsgatan) to accommodate his growing family. A son, Pehr Gabriel, was born that year.[2] The home was across the Aura River from the cathedral and just a few blocks' walk from the Akademi buildings, with a garden large enough for his own private collection.[3] The land, once cultivated, had reverted to meadow, so he spent a lot of time fencing, cultivating and manuring the garden.[4]

A plot of land belonging to Åbo Akademi had been used as a garden many years before, but it had been neglected; some houses had been built there, and the remainder had reverted to its natural state. Before Kalm's return, a large part of what was called the "Bishop's Plot" had been reserved for use as a university garden but was not to be available until construction of the new bishop's palace was completed in 1757.

Kalm's frustration was evident in an indignant letter that he wrote two months after his arrival in Åbo in October, 1751, to the secretary of the Akademi, "The poor seeds cannot hang onto clouds."[5]

In the spring of 1752, Kalm was finally given use of a small house and property belonging to the Crown in Seipsalo off the island of Hirvensalo. About twen-

Top: The house at Seipsalo, Kalm's "America in miniature." Above: A plaque on the corner of the house at Seipsalo, indicating that Kalm lived there. Right: The cathedral in Åbo (Turku). Below: Åbo Akademi buildings. (Photos by the author)

Left: An American oak tree planted by Kalm on the banks of the Aura River. Above: The barn at Seipsalo. Above: The view from the house at Seipsalo. (Photos by the author)

ty miles from the center of the city, Kalm was given use of the property as a plantation for his American plants on the condition that he pay rent to the Crown. The
Rikstag granted an annual sum to the University for planting, so that Kalm's
expenses were covered. It stipulated that "observations and experiments in crop-
raising, the care of pasturage, forestry and other branches of agriculture should
be a model and a source of instruction to young scholars."[6] Only useful plants
were to be grown there.

The climate at Seipsalo was a bit warmer than in Åbo and thus more favorable for success. The property was on a little granite skerry now part of the larger island, but then separated from it for about a half-mile by a shallow tongue of
the sea. When he went to stay at Seipsalo for a few days, he had to bring with him
someone to row him across in a small boat. He also had to bring a cook to prepare
meals and hired a farmhand to help him with the work.[7] He trained several
helpers only to find that, once trained, they left to work elsewhere for wages higher than he was able to pay.[8]

The cottage, where he lived with his family during the summers, was on the
top of a knoll, with outbuildings behind. The gardens were spread out below
down a gentle slope facing south toward the bay beyond.

Kalm was able to report to the Rikstag in the summer of 1755:

> The most suitable place for a plantation was found and seeds of the most useful
> American plants were sown in the spring of 1752. My joy was the greater and my
> industry increased accordingly when a large number of shoots came up in the
> same summer and the rest the following summer. The same hand that had gath-
> ered the seeds in America was able to sow them in Finnish soil and care for them.
> I have since frequently watered these shoots myself and have spent whole days
> weeding the ground around them, fearing that others would not have done it as
> carefully as was necessary. I have had many an anxious moment while caring for
> these plants. This place has become for me America in miniature where I receive
> new life every summer as I look on all this greenery, which seems to wish to show
> its gratitude and bring joy to him who has cared for the plants so tenderly and so
> untiringly.[9]

Finally, when the Bishop's palace in Åbo was completed in 1757, Kalm was
able to oversee the building of Finland's first true botanical garden on the banks
of the Aura River near the ancient Åbo Cathedral.[10] All that remains of that garden today is a large American oak tree behind the present Sibelius Museum; Kalm
is memorialized with a plaque.

Kalm still continued his experimental gardens at Seipsalo during the summers. In addition to growing his American plants and other exotics, Kalm raised
a crop of gooseberries. He picked them himself and made them into jam, which
he then brought back to show to his students, much to the amusement of some of
his colleagues.[11]

Kalm's first task, after distributing his seeds and arranging for a proper garden, was to ready his journal for publication. He was permitted to devote his time to that task for a year, until the end of 1752, when he was obliged to take on his academic obligations. First, he had to decide what form his account would take. He discussed with many people whether to present his information in diary form with daily observations of what he had seen and done or whether he should choose the more difficult method of organizing his information by subject. Linnaeus was in favor of the diary form, which Kalm chose because it meant less work for him.[12]

Kalm also saved some botanical information for what he hoped to publish as a *Flora americana* or perhaps as *Flora canadensis*, but that work never materialized. Although Kalm was conscientious about keeping his journal and reporting all that he had seen, he seemed to have little interest in the cataloging, organizing and theorizing that Linnaeus did so well. These tasks were put off for some later time that never seemed to arrive.

The first volume of his travels was sent to Stockholm at the beginning of 1752; presumably, it would have been largely completed in America before his return and simply required some editing. First, it had to be read by members of the Royal Swedish Academy of Sciences.[13] Despite Kalm's impatience to see his work in print, *En Resa til Norra America* was not published by Lars Salvius in Stockholm until 1753. The second volume came out in 1756, and the third one in 1761, ten years after Kalm had returned to Finland.

Kalm put aside editing the remaining material for many years but did take it up again in 1774, and by early in 1776, it was ready for publication.[14] Unfortunately, Salvius had died, and another publisher could not be found because, by that time, interest in Kalm's journey had faded and the initial volumes had not been a great commercial success.[15] Kalm's flat and turgid writing style and masses of detail were not exciting to the ordinary Swedish reader. He did not have the gift of storytelling that naturalist William Bartram exhibited in his account of his travels in Florida and the Carolinas.

There seemed to be more interest in Kalm's work abroad, where travel literature was immensely popular. Two translations into German were published within a year, and an abridged description of Pennsylvania, based upon a German translation, was published in French in 1768 by de Surgy as *Histoire naturelle et politique de la Pensylvanie*.[16] A Dutch version appeared in 1772.

The first English translation of *Travels in North America by Peter Kalm* was made by Johann Reinhold Forster and his sixteen-year-old son Johann Georg Adam and was published by Samuel Eyre in Warrington in 1770 and in London in 1771; it was republished in 1772 and again in 1812, in a collection of traveler's tales. The elder Forster, a Fellow of the Royal Society, had been one of the natural philosophers who joined Captain Cook's *Endeavor* on its Pacific voyage. Upon his

C. Philips, Jacobsz. inv. del. et fec. 1772.
Te UTRECHT by J. v. Schoonhoven & Comp. en G. v. de Brink. Jz.

return, he was appointed to fill the vacancy left by the departure of Joseph Priestley from the Dissenting Academy of Warrington.[17]

The part of the journal dealing with Kalm's stay in England, omitted from Forster's translation, was published by Joseph Lucas, a geologist, in 1892. Canadian versions were published in French by M.L.-W. Marchand,[18] in 1880 by T. Berthiaume, and by Jacques Rousseau and Guy Béthune in 1977.[19]

Kalm also managed to publish, between 1749 and 1778, seventeen scientific articles in the proceedings of the Royal Swedish Academy of Sciences on such American topics as a drink prepared from spruce needles, ticks, a description of a North American grasshopper and the rattlesnake and cures for its bite. Among the articles dealing with American plants were one on the mulberry; another on Indian corn: how it is planted and cared for in North American and about the manifold value of this grain; on the properties and value of the North American black walnut; and on the properties and value of the American tree which is called hickory.[20] Later, after he had lost interest in his American subjects, he turned to a description of the plants of Finland; *Flora Fennica* was published in 1765.[21] It included a list of 925 plants known to exist in Finland.[22]

Kalm's first university lecture took place on November 27, 1752 and was on the observations he had made during his travels and how they might apply to the benefit of the Finnish economy. His words were so eagerly awaited by the students that they serenaded him with a band on the evening of his initial lecture. During his first term, his classes had more students enrolled than those of any of his colleagues. He remained a popular teacher, as his subject of economics, or more broadly, applied natural science, was of great general interest.

A total of 147 students prepared theses under Kalm's direction.[23] Some of them dealt with regional and parish descriptions, but many of the students chose to amplify topics related to Kalm's travels. Six of the students clearly derived most of their information from him. For example, Daniel Backman presented a thesis on July 13, 1754, on "The Benefits which Our Dear Fatherland Might Have Derived from the Colonies in America Formerly Called New Sweden."[24]

One of his students searched for a substitute for coffee that could be made from native plants; this had been a pet topic of Linnaeus, who decried the Swedish custom of sociability over a cup of coffee.[25] Kalm's student suggested a mixture of wheat, rye, beans, peas and hazelnuts. Other students pursued Kalm's interest in hedgerows and his many descriptions of the various living fences that he had seen on his travels. It was during Kalm's professorship that the Great Partition, the conversion of scattered strips in open fields into unitary holdings, took place in Finland.[26] Kalm himself published a paper on the use of cockspur hawthorn as a hedge around fields, meadows and vegetable gardens.

Facing page: Frontispiece of Dutch translation of En resa til Norra America.

Kalm considered replication of Native American birch bark canoes for their possible use in the many lakes and rivers of his homeland. Birch bark was traditionally used in Finland for many other purposes, such as making baskets and even shoes. When he returned to Finland, one of his students, Anders Chydenius, wrote a master's thesis on the subject of the American Indian canoe, published in 1753. In 1752, during a visit to Åbo, Swedish King Adolf Fredrik, consort of Queen Lovisa Ulrika, rode in an Indian-style birch bark canoe built by Kalm's students. However, it was soon discovered that the bark of Finnish birches was not strong enough to use in making canoes.[27]

Kalm was also interested in the promotion of silviculture to diversify Finland's forests and to promote the principles of conservation. In England he had seen the poor consequences of insufficient timber for construction and firewood. He urged a rational forest policy. Shortly after his death, a plaque was affixed on the home in which he had lived with the words "Att spara skogen landets rikedom" (to conserve the woodland the nation's wealth). He also encouraged his students to pursue the improvement of Finland's grasslands and to promote the wider cultivation of fruit trees and bushes.

Kalm had many friends in Åbo, especially his former teacher, Johan Browallius, who had been appointed bishop of the diocese and ex officio vice-chancellor of the university. He died in 1755 and was succeeded by Carl Fredrik Mennander, a former physics professor and later a bishop, who remained a friend and supporter of Kalm until the end of his life. Eighty-five letters of Kalm to Mennander have been published, evidence of their friendship. Kalm established a garden next to the city home of Mennander, as well as at his country estate, Ala-Lemun.[28]

Another of Kalm's friends in Åbo was Johan Leche, a fellow student of Linnaeus, who had been appointed professor of medicine in 1748. He and Kalm both sent information on Finnish plants to Linnaeus, which he included in his *Flora Suecia*. Count Carl Gustaf Tessin, who had championed Kalm's travel to America when he was president of the Royal Swedish Academy of Sciences, had become chancellor of Åbo Akademi and also continued to support him.

But not everyone at the Akademi was Kalm's friend and supporter. He also had a rival in the person of Pehr Adrian Gadd, who became professor of chemistry, physics and economics in 1758.[29] During Kalm's absence in America and while he was writing up the results of his journey, the younger Gadd had been appointed docent in natural history and economics.[29] Presumably, he was given Kalm's classes to teach until Kalm completed the editing of his diaries. This added burden became the basis of Gadd's jealousy, which stayed with him the remainder of his life. Unfortunately, both men pursued many of the same interests, and their outlook was similar. A rivalry ensued, for example, in the growth of mulberry trees for potential silk production; of course, both were unsuccessful.[30] Kalm had introduced the American mulberry, and Gadd grew another variety. Gadd is known today as the father of chemistry in Finland.[31]

Martti Kerkkonen, a Finnish scholar who wrote extensively about Kalm and edited his journals, wrote an article in Swedish in 1953 in which he speculated that a certain painting by Johan Tobias Sergelin of "a professor from the University of Turku" was of Kalm. The painting was donated to the Satakunta Museum in 1899. However, in a more recent article, Jari Niemelä has suggested that the portrait bears a close resemblance to a later drawing of Gadd done by Sergelin and now at the Swedish National Museum. Although the portrait has been reproduced many times and represented as Kalm, the evidence seems to indicate that it is most likely of Gadd.[32]

Kalm suffered the letdown common among people who have had exciting experiences and traveled to far-off places and then must adjust to life back home. Foremost, Åbo was a very provincial place in the 1750s, far from centers of scholarship. Kalm and a few colleagues had tried to start a Finnish Scientific Society in 1753, but there were not enough contributors or funds to sustain interest.[33]

Not only did Kalm have to struggle with the lack of resources, but enduring the long cold winters was, he wrote, like "living in a dark sack." He complained that the climate in Åbo was colder than in Uppsala or Stockholm. "the summers have been short and at the same time very cold; the winters, on the other hand, like an eternity with severe and long-lasting chill."[34]

After his first year or two in Finland, Kalm began to realize that many of his responsibilities included work that was routine and dreary. In addition, he found many obstacles in his way: the lack of resources, the climate, and the fact that so few of his plants survived. He was no longer able to make new and exciting discoveries. Early in 1753 he wrote to Linnaeus, "Pray help me, dear Doctor: what the deuce is the good of my being stuck here in Finland; in the whole of last summer I found scarcely a single plant that I hadn't seen earlier in Sweden."[35]

Kalm did receive an invitation written in Latin to move to St. Petersburg to take the chair of botany at Petropolitana, but he declined.[36]

When Kalm left America, it was with great regret. He began to dream of returning. He thought that he had found only a tenth of the plants that could be found in Pennsylvania, Maryland, Virginia and Carolina, and his observations of birds, fish, insects and minerals were incomplete. He wrote, "I find life easiest when I can find new plants every day and new things in the field of natural history. In a word, I want nothing more than to go back to America and my dear wife is even more emphatically determined that we should go back."[37]

Of course, it was out of the question that the Swedish government would finance another trip when he still had not completed his assigned task in Finland, and he had to fulfill his academic obligations. However, the government did maintain Lutheran pastors in New Sweden. Pastor Israel Acrelius, whom Kalm had met upon his arrival in Philadelphia, was now eager to return home. Perhaps Kalm could replace him. Although other pastors thought of the assignment to New Sweden as a hardship post, Kalm would relish spending seven more years

St. Mary's Church. (Photo courtesy of Marian Kirkko)
Below: Entrance , churchyard and cemetery. (Photos by the author)

there and using his spare time to gather plants.[38] To this end, Kalm prepared himself for ordination; he had already fulfilled many of the requirements as an undergraduate and had preached to the congregation in Raccoon during his winters there.

He was ordained in 1757, but his dream of returning to America would not be realized. His new status, however, did result in an increase of his income. According to university rules, three professors might obtain benefices at the three churches in the diocese of Åbo if they were members of the clergy. He was appointed to "the living" of the fourteenth-century stone church of St. Mary. This meant that he was the senior clergyman and would obtain the salary provided by the state for that office. The family moved to the vicarage, which was a comfortable half-hour's walk from the university and cathedral precinct. The religious duties were not heavy and could be delegated to assistants. He was also able to manage the church farm and to keep a small garden near the house.[39]

Kalm was ill for several months in the autumn and died on November 16, 1779, disappointed that his goals had not been attained. The university garden was filled with weeds, and none of the American plants there had brought economic value to the country. He had not been able to complete publication of his last volume, and many in his circle of friends were gone. His body is assumed to be buried under the floor of the St. Mary's Church, and a small plaque has been placed on the wall above commemorating his life.[40]

Before his death in 1779, Kalm entrusted his papers to Salomon Kreander, his assistant and successor at both Åbo Akademi and at the St. Mary parish,[41] with the proviso that Kreander edit and publish the remaining parts of the diaries. Some money was raised by public subscription for that purpose, but no publication materialized. The Kalm papers were turned over to the Åbo Akademi library in 1826 by Kreander's son-in-law. The following year they were consumed by the great fire that burned down a large part of the city, by then known also by its Finnish name of Turku.

The most recent English translation of *Peter Kalm's Travels in America*, published in 1937, was that by Adolph Benson, Professor of German and Scandinavian at Yale University. It included new material from Kalm's diary notes from October 16, 1747 to January 11, 1750, that had been found in 1899 by Georg Schauman at the library of the University of Helsinki. Six of the ten folios of the diaries had, fortuitously, been borrowed from the Åbo Akademi library by Professor J. F. Wallenius before its contents were consumed in the fire of 1827. These newly found materials had already been included in another Swedish edition published by Elfving in 1929. The first volume of the original travel journals, now in the University of Helsinki Library, was edited by Martti Kerkkonen in 1966, by Kerkkonen and J. E. Roos in 1970, the third by Roos and Harry Krogerus in 1985, and the fourth and last one by Roos and Krogerus in 1988.[42]

On his return from Niagara, Kalm had been able to provide Lewis Evans with information that enabled him to prepare a new map, the *Brevis Delineatio*, which showed the Mohawk Valley, the western portion of the St. Lawrence Valley, and especially the western portion of the south shore of Lake Ontario, "the Lake to the North West."[43] Kalm had planned to include Evans's map in the projected fourth volume of his travels. When that publication no longer seemed possible, the map was finally engraved, under the direction of Kreander, in 1784, five years after Kalm's death. Most of the copies perished in the great fire of 1827, but one was discovered in a second-hand bookshop in Helsinki in the 1930s and was presented to the United States Library of Congress by the Finnish government.[44]

CHAPTER SEVENTEEN
The Outcome of Kalm's Journey

URING THE FIRST YEAR OR TWO after his arrival in Åbo, Kalm was optimistic about the success of his plantings. He believed what he had been taught by the master, Linnaeus, that plants could get used to the colder climate and could be "tamed" or "adapted."[1] In the instruction pamphlet that he had written for those experimenting with his American seeds, he had written, "If the same seed is carefully hoarded and planted, the plant will by degrees adapt itself to the climate. Maize in Carolina where the summers are long takes 6 whole months to ripen, just as if it instinctively knew that there was no need to grow rapidly; but the same maize in Canada takes only 3 months and sometimes less, hurrying just as if it knew the summer was short and it had no time to lose. The same is true of many other plants."[2]

In a report to the Rikstag in July 1755, Kalm noted that some American plants had been killed by the cold winter, but he was still hopeful for the survival of others. However, by the time that the University Botanical Garden was founded in 1757, only a minority of the plants there were from America.[3] By 1760, only fifteen of the seventy American species that he had planted remained.[4] Kalm and his colleagues, Gadd and Leche, had all tried to grow maize, but after ten or fifteen years of attempts, ears of corn successfully ripened only a few times.[5] By 1768, Kalm mentions only twenty American plants that he had been able to cultivate successfully: bird, cluster or Virginia chokecherry, *Prunus virginiana*; pignut hickory, *Carya glabra*; black walnut, *Juglans nigra*; Canada goldenrod, *Solidago canadensis*; milkweed, *Asclepias syriaca*; shadbush, Canadian serviceberry or juneberry, *Amelanchier canadensis*;[6] black raspberry, *Rubus occidentalis*; and Virginia creeper, *Parthenocissus quinquefolia*, now ubiquitous in Scandinavia; as well as cockspur hawthorn, *Crataegus crus-gali*; apples; plums; cherries; maize; pumpkins; watermelons and various other melons.[7] However, none of these were of much commercial value in Finland.

Kalm had been charged by the Royal Swedish Academy of Sciences to obtain from America "two species of mulberry trees that grow on hills among birches, firs, and spruces, which we here in the North in the future could have for silk cultivation just as well as in Europe's southern countries."[8] Bartram informed Kalm that red and white[9] mulberry trees grew wild in the forests of North America.

Kalm asked him why the inhabitants had not set up silk manufacture. He was told that the labor required to feed silk worms was too expensive for such a labor-intensive industry to be economical. However, Kalm wrote, "from the trials of a governor in Connecticut, whose estate lay far north of New York City, it is evident that silk worms thrive very well here and that this kind of mulberry tree is very good for them. The governor brought up a great quantity of silk worms in his courtyard; and they succeeded so well and spun so much silk that they gave him a quantity sufficient for clothing himself and all his family."[10] The governor of Montréal also showed him four or five mulberry trees (*Morus rubra*) that had been planted there twenty years before. However, they did not grow wild farther north than the area of Albany.[11]

Despite several attempts, American mulberry trees did not survive in Finland, although they did in southern Sweden.[12] The mulberries that Kalm had planted in Åbo were killed in the winter of 1770-1771.[13] Although a Central European species of mulberry was successfully cultivated by Gadd and Leche, Kalm was not to see the establishment of a Finnish silk industry.

Kalm noted that grapevines grew wild in the area near Philadelphia. When he inquired of Bartram as to why vineyards were not planted for wine he received the same explanation: the lack of sufficient labor. In addition, Kalm found that the North American grapes mostly produced a rather sour wine that was not as agreeable in taste as wine made from European grapes.[14]

In Philadelphia, Kalm enjoyed eating sweet potatoes, which he said "almost melt in the mouth. They grow very fast and very well here; but the greatest difficulty consists in keeping them over winter, for they stand neither cold, great heat, nor wet." Unfortunately, those which he brought back with him to Finland rotted from dampness in the ship.[20]

Kalm succeeded in bringing back the seeds of wild rice, which Linnaeus and the Royal Academy had requested, but nothing came of the idea that a commercial crop could successfully be raised on Finland's lakes.

Linnaeus had also asked for American oaks, sassafras, walnuts, chestnuts, hay grasses and magnolia.[15] Kalm found that sassafras was used in Pennsylvania for dyeing fabrics an orange color.[16] However, it did not grow north of the Hudson River, and he thought it "useless to attempt to plant sassafras in a very cold climate."[17]

Kalm reported that "no native grass or plants are found in North America suitable for meadow cultivation. All such plants must be introduced from Europe."[18] Of course, Kalm had not had the opportunity of seeing an American prairie.

In addition to his disappointment over his lack of success in growing American plants, Kalm suffered even more disappointment regarding the cultivation of his favorite genus of grasses after the untimely death of his patron, Sten Carl

Bielke in 1753. Only five years later, Linnaeus wrote to say that he had occasion to visit Bielke's estate at Lövsta and found that all of Kalm's careful plantings of various grasses and other foreign plants were neglected and had now "gone wild."[19]

The outcome of Kalm's efforts was that Linnaeus's theory that plants could be "trained" to acclimatize themselves to a more northerly climate was disproved, as was the notion that plants from similar latitudes could easily be transplanted from one continent to another. However, Kalm, who was uninterested in theorizing, never pointed out that the premise on which his journey was made was false. He dared not refute the master, nor was it in his character to do so. It would have been too painful to acknowledge that his primary task ended up in failure.

However, Kalm's efforts did spark a widespread interest in Finland in the cultivation of foreign plants. Kalm was also able to influence some of his students to follow in his footsteps of exploration. One of these was Erik Laxmann, a Finn born in Karelia, the eastern part of the country, which was annexed by Russia five years after his birth. Laxmann attended Åbo Akademi for only a short time in 1757, but he developed a friendly relationship with Kalm while he was there. Kalm may have instilled in him an interest in obtaining Siberian plants that might be acclimated to grow in Finland, which may have influenced his future explorations.[21]

Back in America, there was much disappointment at the fact that Kalm seemed to have forgotten the people there who had given him so much help. Bartram wrote to Collinson on March 20, 1753, "P.S. We are all surprised that we have not one letter from Peter Kalm whome we are ready to tax with ingratitude."[22] However, in a letter written to Collinson on June 26, 1753, Franklin mentions the receipt of a letter from Kalm.[23]

In another letter, to Philip Miller written on April 20, 1755, Bartram wrote:

> I have an account that he hath published, lately, two books containing all our North American plants which KALM observed, when he was with us. I showed him many, that he said were new Genera, and that Linnaeus must make many alterations, when he was by him more truly informed of their true characters, as I should soon see when they were printed. I long to see these books,—to see if they have done me justice, as KALM promised me. Dr. Gronovius promised to send them to me, as soon as they came to his hand."[24]

Of course, Bartram would not have been able to understand the Swedish, and the English version was not published until just a few years before his death in 1777. However, there was no excuse for Kalm's lack of courtesy in not writing to thank his hosts. But the hostilities between the French and the English had resumed soon after his return to Finland, and he may have written more than once, only to have the letters lost at sea.

Kalm was also accused of not acknowledging much of what he had learned from Bartram. In a letter to Bartram, dated Stockholm, July 2, 1769, Carl Magnus Wrangel wrote, "I have not been like Professor KALM, in taking the honour to myself of what belongs to others. I have given my dear friend, Mr. JOHN BAR-TRAM, Jr., his due."[25] The Reverend Wrangel was sent to America in 1759 to serve as dean for the Swedish Lutheran communities in the Philadelphia area and became a close friend of Bartram. Upon his return to Sweden he became chaplain of the Royal Court and was probably responsible for instigating Bartram's correspondence with Queen Lovisa Ulrika. He gave testimony supporting Bartram's election to the Royal Swedish Academy of Sciences.[26] Wrangel's criticism does not seem justified, because Kalm repeatedly mentioned Bartram as the source of much of the information in his journals. He also faulted Bartram, as did others, for not himself documenting his vast store of knowledge of American plants and animals.

Franklin was especially critical of Kalm's reports when he read a copy of the Forster English translation. The Colden family, too, expressed annoyance at some of the statements Kalm had attributed to them. In a letter to David Colden, on March 5, 1773, Franklin wrote,

> Kalm's Account of what he learned in America is full of idle Stories, which he pick'd up among ignorant People, and either forgetting of whom he had them, or willing to give them some Authenticity, he has ascrib'd them to Persons of Reputation who never heard of them till they were found in his Book. And where he really had Accounts from such Persons, he had varied the Circumstances unaccountably, so that I have been asham'd to meet with some mention'd as from me. It is dangerous conversing with these Strangers that keep Journals.[27]

It is hard to assess the validity of their criticism. On the one hand, it is clear that Kalm was often gullible and took people's stories at face value. On the other hand, we have noted his lack of political finesse, and some of the criticism may have resulted from Kalm's negative reports of what he found in the culture of the British colonists and his clear admiration for the French whom he met in Canada. One must remember that Franklin's letter was written in 1773, just before the outbreak of the American Revolution, when his patriotic fervor was rising to a fever pitch.

Not all of the American comments on Kalm were entirely negative. Alexander Garden wrote from Charles Town, South Carolina on May 5, 1755, "greatly pleased, at the same time chagrined, at the account . . . of Dr. Kalm, the Swede, who is just now publishing his collection, made in our colonies, in the Swedish language, by the particular desire of his king. This will not only give them the glory and honour of such public undertakings, but the sole advantage of what observations he may have made. This looks as though we are obliged to strangers to point out our own richness, and shows us the advantages of what we ourselves possess."[28]

Despite the failure to accomplish the task that Linnaeus had assigned him of bringing back American plants that would improve the Swedish economy, Kalm's travels were of value. Fortunately, Kalm was a very thorough and methodical person, and his diary and the resulting volumes that he culled from it have been a treasure trove of information for scholars of colonial America. Kalm made entries for most days, and each includes precise details of the weather. Keeping such an extensive diary was often tedious and tiring, but he felt strongly that it was his duty to do so because of the faith that his sponsors had shown in him. He wrote in the preface to his journal that daily "examination of all that one sees and its immediate recording on paper is as exhausting as any other kind of labor."[29]

Unfortunately, Kalm's journal is written as a consecutive narrative, so that many topics are dealt with helter-skelter and not grouped together. There is considerable repetition regarding topics that particularly interested him, mainly practical details regarding how tasks were done. His writing style lacks elegance and humor; he sticks to the facts as he sees them, with little interpretation. As a result, his *Travels* have never enjoyed the broad readership they might have had if his writing style had been more engaging or if the material had been better organized.

Among his many accomplishments, Kalm can be credited for the first accurate written description of Niagara Falls and an important comprehensive study of North American natural history. He was not to be the savior of the motherland, but a Boswell recording the details of life in the lands that he visited, warts and all, for the benefit of posterity. It was his faithful recording in simple unvarnished language of everything that caught his interest during his journey that has made his work of value. Kalm's importance to posterity is from the extensive and clear descriptions that he made of daily life in England, Pennsylvania, New Jersey, New York, Montréal and Québec in the mid-eighteenth century, including dress, diet, manners, agriculture, religious observances, construction of public buildings and private homes, fences, transportation and trade.

It is interesting to note that a century after his journey, Kalm's journal caught the attention of a fellow natural historian and conservationist. Henry David Thoreau made extensive use of the three-volume Forster translation of Kalm's *Travels*, which he had borrowed from the Harvard library on August 11, 1851. He copied a number of passages into his Canada notebook and volumes four and five of his Indian notebooks. Thoreau also quoted or alluded to Kalm's work in *Cape Cod* and *A Yankee in Canada*, as well as in his journal entries of 5 and 6 September 1851. In March 1856, Thoreau read the 1751 London publication of Bartram's *"Observations on the Inhabitants, Climate, Soil, Rivers, Productions, Animals, and Other Matters Worthy of Notice, Made by Mr. John Bartram, in His Travels from Pensilvania to Onondago, Oswego and the Lake Ontario, in Canada.* To which is annexed a Curious Account of the Cataracts of Niagara, by Mr. Peter Kalm, A Swedish Gentleman Who Travelled There."[30]

KALM was but a minor figure in the panoply of men of the European Enlightenment who traveled the world collecting descriptions and specimens of the world's riches and filling in the details of scientific knowledge of the natural world. He added many North American plants to the list of known species. He may have lacked the creative imagination and literary style of a William Bartram, but he was steadfast and courageous in accomplishing his mission despite all of the many obstacles that he faced. Like Thoreau, we are indebted to him for his clear description of the natural world that he found, so much of which is now sadly lost to us. He can justly be counted as one of the first to raise the alarm over the human destruction of the American environment.

Notes

PKT: Benson, Adolph B. *Peter Kalm's Travels in North America: The English Version of 1770.* 2 vols. New York: Wilson-Erickson Inc., 1937.
KVTe: Kalm, Pehr. *Kalm's Visit to England on His Way to America in 1748.* Translated by Joseph Lucas. London, 1892.

CHAPTER ONE
Linnaeus's Vision

1. PKT, 7.
2. Carl Linné was elevated to the nobility in 1761, becoming von Linné.
3. Niemelä, Jari, *Vain hyödynkö tähden?* (Helsinki: Suomen Historiallinen Seura, 1998) 347, 352-3.
4. Koerner, Lisbet. *Linnaeus: Nature and Nation* (Cambridge: Harvard University Press, 1999), 6.
5. Roberts, Michael, *The Age of Liberty: Sweden 1719-1772* (Cambridge: Cambridge University Press, 1986), 16.
6. Koerner, 4-5.
7. Koerner, 102.
8. Roberts, 16.
9. *Ibid.*
10. Crosby, Alfred W., *Germs, Seeds and Animals: Studies in Ecological History* (Armonk, NY: M.E. Sharpe, Inc., 1994), 168 (quoting Thomas, Dorothy Swaine, *Social and Economic Aspects of Swedish Population Movements, 1750-1933* [New York: The Macmillan Co., 1941], 150-1).
11. Crosby, 150-151.
12. Crosby, 161.
13. Crosby, 153.
14. Landes, David S. *The Wealth and Poverty of Nations: Why Some Are So Rich and Some So Poor* (New York: W. W. Norton & Company, 1998), 169.
15. Wuorinen, John H. *A History of Finland* (New York: Columbia University Press, 1965), 77.
16. Crosby, Alfred W., Jr. *The Columbian Exchange: Biological and Cultural Consequences of 1492* (Westport, Connecticut: Greenwood Press, 1972), 171.
17. Hindle, Brooke, *The Pursuit of Science in Revolutionary America, 1735-1789* (Chapel Hill: University of North Carolina Press, 1956), 12.
18. *Ibid.*
19. Bailey, L.H., *How Plants Get Their Names.* 1933. (New York: Dover Publications, 1963), 19-22; 52.
20. Kastner, Joseph, *A Species of Eternity* (New York: Alfred A Knopf, 1977), 34.
21. Bailey, 18-21.
22. Bailey, 24-5.
23. Blunt, Wilfrid, *The Compleat Naturalist: A Life of Linnaeus* (New York: The Viking Press, 1971)

24. Blunt, Wilfrid, 14ff
25. Hindle, 12-35; Stafleu, Frans A., *Linnaeus and the Linnaeans: The spreading of their ideas in systematic botany, 1735-1789* (Utrecht, Netherlands: International Association for Plant Taxonomy, 1971), 9.
26. Dewitt, F. Dawtrey, *The Romance of the Apothecaries' Garden at Chelsea* (third edition) (London: Cambridge University Press, 1928) 69.
27. Dewitt, 71-73.
28. Hindle, 16.
29. Blunt, 131.
30. Koerner, 105.
31. Roberts, 215.
32. Blunt, 168-9.
33. Lindroth, Sten, "The Two Faces of Linnaeus," in Tore Frängsmyr, ed., *Linnaeus: The Man and His Work* (Berkeley: University of California Press, 1983), 55.
34. Koerner, 114; Blunt, 183.
35. Koerner, 113-4; Blunt, 183.

CHAPTER TWO
Peter Kalm

1. Koerner, 115.
2. Ibid.
3. Kerkkonen, Martti. *Peter Kalm's North American Journey: Its Ideological Background and Results* (Helsinki: Finnish Historical Society, 1959), 68-69.
4. Blunt, 187.
5. Colden, Cadwallader, *The Letters and Papers of Cadwallader Colden.* Vol. IV (New York: AMS Press, 1973), 257-8.
6. Wuorinen, John H. *A History of Finland* (New York: Columbia University Press, 1965), 76.
7. Kerkkonen, 47.
8. Wood, Gordon S. *The Americanization of Benjamin Franklin* (New York: The Penguin Press, 2004), 25.
9. Wuorinen, *A History of Finland,* 95; after the great fire in Turku in 1827, the University was moved to Helsinki, which had become the capital of the Grand Duchy after Finland came under Russian rule. The present Åbo Akademi and Turku University were founded in the early part of the twentieth century.
10. Kerkkonen, 49-50.
11. Kerkkonen, 51.
12. Wuorinen, 94.
13. Kerkkonen, 50; Kalm's letters to Linnaeus, in the file that the Archiacter labeled "Pehr Kalm," are in the collection of the Linnean Society in London, as are Kalm's letters to Bielke written after 1742.
14. Kerkkonen, 53.
15. Ibid.
16. Kerkkonen, 53-54.
17. Ibid.
18. Kastner, 34.

19. Leikola, Anto. "Linnaeus, Kalm and the Finns," A paper delivered at the conference "Thinking through the Environment." Turku University and Abo Akademi, September 16, 2005, 3.
20. Eriksson, Malin, "Sten Carl Bielkes och Pehr Kalms försöksodlingasr vid Lövsta," unpublished paper, Swedish University of Agricultural Sciences, 2005.
21. Private communication, Malin Eriksson, November 7, 2005.
22. Kerkkonen, 42.
23. Kerkkonen, 39.
24. Kerkkonen, 56-63.
25. Kerkkonen, 64-6.
26. PKT, vi-viii.
27. Kerkkonen, 66-67.
28. Kerkkonen., 66.
29. Kerkkonen. 67.
30. Kalm to Linnaeus, *The Linnaean Correspondence*, http://linnaeus.c18.net/Letters/letter_list.php, #1593, 9 February 1748.
31. Kerkkonen, 69.
32. Acrelius, Israel, *A History of New Sweden* (Ann Arbor: University Microfilms, Inc., 1966) 339.
33. PKT, vi-viii.
34. PKT, 550.
35. Kerkkonen, 76.
36. Hildebrand, Bengt. *Pehr Kalms Amerikanska Reseräkning* (Helsinki: Svenska litteratursällskapet i Finland, 1956), 38.
37. Mead, William R. *Pehr Kalm: A Finnish Visitor to the Chilterns in 1748* (Trowbridge, Wiltshire: The Cromwell Press, 2003), 16; Hildebrand, 37.
38. Larsen, Esther Louise. "Lobelia as a Sure Cure for Venereal Disease," *American Journal of Syphilis, Gonorrhea and Venereal Disease*. XXIV (1940): 17-18.
39. Larsen, 22.
40. Kerkkonen, 73.

CHAPTER THREE
England

1. KVtE, ix.
2. Kerkkonen, 74.
3. Kerkkonen, 76.
4. KVtE, ix.
5. Hildebrand, 14-19.
6. Mead, 10.
7. Mead, 11.
8. KVtE, ix.
9. Fänge, Ragnar, "Introduction: Early Hagfish Research." In Jens Peter Lomholt, Roy E. Weber and Mans Malte, eds. *The Biology of Hagfishes* (London: Chapman and Hall, 1998), xiii-xiv.
10. KVtE, 6.
11. KVtE, 122.

12. Schwartz, Richard B. *Daily Life in Johnson's London* (Madison: The University of Wisconsin Press, 1983), 8-9.

13. KVtE, 37.

14. KVtE, 3.

15. Kalm to Linnaeus, *The Linnaean Correspondence*, http://linnaeus.c18.net/Letters/letter_list.php, #1593, 9 February 1748.

16. Mead, 10.

17. Kalm to Linnaeus, *The Linnaean Correspondence*, http://linnaeus.c18.net/Letters/letter_list.php, #1594, 24 March 1748.

18. Hildebrand, 23-24.

19. Sometimes called "King George's War" or a prelude to it (since in the New World those two wars were not distinctly separate), the strangely named "War of Jenkins' Ear" had an improbable and superficial origin and an unusually tragic ending. In 1731, a Spanish coast guard sloop off Havana boarded the English privateer, the *Rebecca*, captained by Robert Jenkins, as it made its way from Jamaica to London. The Spanish found no evidence of privateering, but repeatedly tortured Jenkins, and a Lieutenant Dorce finally sliced off his ear with his cutlass and told him to take it to King George as a token of what they had in mind for the king. Seven years later Jenkins was invited by a certain party of warmongers to display his pickled ear to Parliament, thereby inflaming British and American colonial opinion against Spain. The government of Hugh Walpole duly, but reluctantly, declared war. The press and later historians could not resist naming the war for its theatrical beginning. www.regiments.org/wars/18thcent/39jenk.htm.

20. Kerkkonen, 79.

21. Frick, George Frederick and Stearns, Raymond Phineas, *Mark Catesby the Colonial Audubon* (Urbana: University of Illinois Press, 1961), 87.

22. Kalm to Linnaeus, *The Linnaean Correspondence*, http://linnaeus.c18.net/Letters/letter_list.php, #1594, 9 February 1748.

23. KVtE, 88-89.

24. KVtE, 138.

25. Kerkkonen, 79.

26. Hildebrand, 27.

27. Hildebrand, 26.

28. KVtE, 188-9.

29. Ibid.

30. Hildebrand, 40.

31. Stearns, Raymond Phineas, *Science in the British Colonies of America* (Urbana: University of Illinois Press, 1970), 527.

32. Stearns, 516.

33. Stearns, 104.

34. Stearns, 516.

35. Stearns, 134.

36. Hindle, 7-8.

37. Stearns, 516.

38. Frick, 86.

39. Stearns, 528.
40. Dewitt, 63; information sheet, "A Brief History," provided to visitors to the Chelsea Physic Garden.
41. Hildebrand, 25.
42. KVtE, 109-19.
43. Dewitt, 64.
44. Stearns, 259.
45. KVtE, 108.
46. Hildebrand, 31.
47. KVtE, 90.
48. KVtE, 91-2.
49. Dewitt, 50-51.
50. KVtE, 98.
51. KVtE, 100; upon his death, Sloane's collection became the nucleus of the British Museum.
52. KVtE, 19.
53. KVtE, 114-15.
54. KVtE, 26.
55. KVtE, 26.
56. KVtE, 46-7.
57. KVtE, 50-51.
58. Berkeley, Edmund and Berkeley, Dorothy Smith, *Dr. John Mitchell: The Man Who Made the Map of North America* (Chapel Hill: The University of North Carolina Press, 1974), xviii.
59. Stearns, 542.
60. Berkeley and Berkeley, *Dr. John Mitchell*, 40-45.
61. Berkeley and Berkeley, *Dr. John Mitchell*, 66-69.
62. Berkeley and Berkeley, *Dr. John Mitchell*, 85.
63. Berkeley and Berkeley, *Dr. John Mitchell*, 124.
64. Stearns, 539.
65. Stearns. 541-543.
66. KVtE, 114.
67. KVtE, 116.
68. KVtE, 120.
69. KVtE, 53.
70. Berkeley, 127.
71. KVtE, 17, 188.
72. Stearns, 286-288.
73. Stearns, 317.
74. Stearns, 318.
75. Stearns, 318-322.
76. KVtE, 118-9.
77. Chaplin, Joyce E., "Mark Catesby, a Skeptical Newtonian in America." in *Empire's Nature: Mark Catesby's New World Vision.* ed. Amy R. W. Meyers and Margaret Beck Pritchard. (Chapel Hill: University of North Carolina Press, 1998), 11.

78. Chaplin, 47.
79. Chaplin, 51.
80. KVtE, 57.
81. Berkeley and Berkeley, *Dr. John Mitchell*, 109.
82. KVtE, 58.
83. KVtE, 112-13.
84. Berkeley and Berkeley, *Dr. John Mitchell*, 121; Schwartz, 114.
85. Stearns, 602.
86. KVtE, 66-7.
87. KVtE, 68.
88. KVtE, 87.
89. Hildebrand, 33.
90. Chancellor, E. Beresford, *The XVIIIth Century in London: An Account of its Social Life and Arts.* 1920 (London: B. T. Batsford Ltd., 1933), 90-107.
91. KVtE, 334.
92. Kalm to Linnaeus, *The Linnaean Correspondence*, http://linnaeus.c18.net/Letters/letter_list.php, #1595, 6 March 1748.
93. KVtE, 71.
94. KVtE, 7-8.
95. KVtE, 235.
96. KVtE, 36.
97. KVtE, 28-9.
98. KVtE, 54.
99. Schwartz, 100.
100. KVtE, 54.
101. Wuorinen, 182-3.
102. Mead, 95.
103. KVtE, 328.
104. KVtE, 95.
105. KVtE, 337.
106. Mead, 122-3.
107. Hildebrand, 30-40.
108. Hildebrand, 30-40.

CHAPTER FOUR
Why Philadelphia?

1. Slaughter, Thomas P., *The Natures of John and William Bartram* (New York: Alfred A. Knopf, 1996), 22-23; Bartram, William, "Some Account of the Late Mr. John Bartram, of Pennsylvania." In *Travels and Other Writing* (Library of America, 1996), 577; Goetzmann, William H., "John Bartram's Journey to Onondaga in Context," in *America's Curious Botanist: A Tercentennial Reappraisal of John Bartram 1699-1777.* ed. Nancy C. Hoffman and John C. Van Horne (Philadelphia: The American Philosophical Society, 2004), 97.
2. Berkeley, Edmund and Dorothy Smith Berkeley, eds., *The Correspondence of John Bartram: 1734-1777* (Gainesville: University Press of Florida, 1992), 627.
3. Crévecoeur, J. Hector St. John de, *Letters from an American Farmer.* [London: J. M. Dent & Sons, 1782], (New York: E. P. Dutton, 1912), 191.

4. Berkeley, Edmund and Dorothy Smith Berkeley, *The Life and Travels of John Bartram: From Lake Ontario to the River St. John* (Tallahassee: University Presses of Florida, 1982), 67.
5. Stearns, 307.
6. Hindle, 21.
7. Stearns, 89.
8. When Logan died, he left his magnificent collection of 3,000 volumes to form the Loganian Library in Philadelphia, for which he built a home and left an endowment.
9. Hindle, 200-202.
10. Hindle, 20; Armstrong, Alan W., "John Bartram and Peter Collinson," in *America's Curious Botanist: A Tercentennial Reappraisal of John Bartram 1699-1777.* ed. Nancy C. Hoffman and John C. Van Horne (Philadelphia: The American Philosophical Society, 2004), 28.
11. Armstrong, 32.
12. Bell, Whitfield J., Jr., "John Bartram: A Biographical Sketch," in *America's Curious Botanist: A Tercentennial Reappraisal of John Bartram 1699-1777.* ed. Nancy C. Hoffman and John C. Van Horne (Philadelphia: The American Philosophical Society, 2004), 3.
13. Bartram, William, 579.
14. Slaughter, 54-56.
15. Hindle, 26.
16. Kalm to Linnaeus, *The Linnaean Correspondence,* http://linnaeus.c18.net/Letters/letter_list.php, #1597, 28 May 1749.
17. PKT, 61.
18. Hindle, 26.
19. PKT, 61.
20. PKT, 62.
21. When Kalm traveled to New York, he learned of that city's problems in obtaining good drinking water.
22. PKT, 32.
23. PKT, 27-28.
24. PKT, 30.
25. PKT, 33.
26. Bridenbaugh., Carl and Jessica, *Rebels and Gentlemen: Philadelphia in the Age of Franklin.* 1942 (New York: Oxford University Press, 1962), 72-83.
27. PKT, 19.
28. Bridenbaughs, 6.
29. PKT, 20.
30. PKT, 33.
31. PKT, 24.
32. PKT, 20-24.
33. PKT, 19.
34. PKT, 675.
35. PKT, 225.
36. PKT, 677.
37. PKT, 33.

38. PKT, 32.

39. PKT, 17.

40. Commager, Henry Steele, *The Empire of Reason: How Europe Imagined and America Realized the Enlightenment* (New York: Anchor Press/Doubleday, 1977), 16-17.

41. Morgan, Edmund S., *Benjamin Franklin* (New Haven: Yale University Press, 2002), 72.

42. Brands, H.W., *The First American: The Life and Times of Benjamin Franklin* (New York: Doubleday, 2000), 326; Dray, Philip. *Stealing God's Thunder: Benjamin Franklin's Lightning Rod and the Invention of America.* New York: Random House, 2005.

43. Isaacson, Walter. *Benjamin Franklin: An American Life* (New York: Simon & Schuster, 2003), 104.

44. PKT, 25.

CHAPTER FIVE
Arrival in Philadelphia

1. PKT, 14.

2. PKT, 7.

3. PKT, 57, 95.

4. Bridenbaugh, Carl. *Cities in Revolt: Urban Life in America, 1743-177.* (New York: Alfred A. Knopf, 1955), 39.

5. PKT, 16.

6. Franklin, Benjamin. *The Papers of Benjamin Franklin.* ed. Leonard W. Labaree, Whitfield J. Bell, Jr., Helen C. Boatfield, and Helene H. Fineman. vol. 3 (New Haven: Yale University Press, 1961), 300.

7. PKT, 17.

8. Franklin, 323.

9. PKT, 1; Hildebrand, 43.

10. Polis, Crystal A. and Robert E. Savage, "Calming John Bartram's Passion," in *America's Curious Botanist: A Tercentennial Reappraisal of John Bartram 1699-1777.* ed. Nancy C. Hoffman and John C. Van Horne (Philadelphia: The American Philosophical Society, 2004), 57.

11. PKT, 39.

12. PKT, 40.

13. Fry, Joel T., "John Bartram and His Garden," in *America's Curious Botanist: A Tercentennial Reappraisal of John Bartram 1699-1777.* ed. Nancy C. Hoffman and John C. Van Horne (Philadelphia: The American Philosophical Society, 2004), 157.

14. Fry, 158.

15. PKT, 63.

16. Berkeley and Berkeley, *Correspondence of John Bartram*, 293.

17. Hindle, 32.

18. Kalm to Cadwallader Colden, September 29, 1748. *The Colden Papers—1748-1754,* 77.

19. Faragher, John Mack, *A Great and Noble Scheme: The Tragic Story of the Expulsion of the French Acadians from Their American Homeland* (New York: WW Norton, 2005), 245-77.

20. Kalm to Linnaeus, *The Linnaean Correspondence*, http://linnaeus.c18.net/Letters/letter_list.php, #1596, 14 October 1748.

21. Kerkkonen, 93.
22. Anderson, Fred and Andrew Cayton, *The Dominion of War: Empire and Liberty in North America 1500-2000* (New York: Viking, 2005), 44.
23. PKT, 96-7.
24. PKT, 100.
25. Hildebrand, 49.
26. Hildebrand, 57.
27. PKT, 206.
28. PKT, 208.
29. PKT, 209.
30. PKT, 209.
31. PKT, 204-5.
32. PKT, 204-6.
33. Hildebrand, 40.
34. PKT, 37.
35. Hildebrand, 42.
36. Hildebrand, 44.
37. PKT, 115; Kalm had written to Colden on September 29, 1748, presumably to make arrangements.
38. PKT, 125.
39. Franklin, n.319.
40. Hoermann, Alfred R., *Cadwallader Colden: A Figure of the American Enlightenment* (Westport, Connecticut: Greenwood Press, 2002), 2-7.
41. Stearns, 494-6.
42. Stearns, 559-565.
43. Hoermann, 29.
44. Brands, 168.
45. Kelley, Joseph J., Jr., *Life and Times in Colonial Philadelphia* (Harrisburg, Pennsylvania: Stackpole Books, 1973), 37.
46. Kelley, 322.
47. PKT, 129.
48. PKT, 103.
49. PKT, 134.
50. Morgan, Edmund S., "Secrets of Benjamin Franklin," In *The Genuine Article: A Historian Looks at Early America* (New York: WW Norton & Co., 2004), 176-7.
51. PKT, 143.
52. PKT, 90-91.
53. PKT, 172-3.
54. Franklin, 321.
55. Franklin, 323-4.
56. Franklin, 329.
57. PKT, 154-161.

CHAPTER SIX
New Sweden

1. Wuorinen, John H., *The Finns on the Delaware 1638-1655: An Essay in American Colonial History* (New York: Columbia University Press, 1938), 24.

2. Norman, Hans, "A Swedish Colony in North America," in *New Sweden in the New World 1638-1655.* ed. Rune Ruhnbro (Stockholm: Wiken, 1988), 7-8; Johnson, Amandus, *The Swedes on the Delaware 1638-1664* (Philadelphia: The Lenapé Press, 1914), 70-93.

3. Shorto, Russell, *The Island at the Center of the World: The Epic Story of Dutch Manhattan and the Forgotten Colony that Shaped America* (New York: Doubleday, 2004), 88-9.

4. Wuorinen., *The Finns on the Delaware*, 3, 47.

5. Wuorinen., *The Finns on the Delaware*, 48-9.

6. Spady, James O'Neil, "Colonialism and the Discursive Antecedents of Penn's Treaty with the Indians," in Pencak, William A. and Daniel K. Richter, *Friends and Enemies in Penn's Woods: Indians, Colonists and the Racial Construction of Pennsylvania.* (University Park, Pennsylvania: The Pennsylvania State University Press, 2004), 21.

7. Shorto, 182; Johnson, 114.

8. PKT, 714; Shorto, 280.

9. Johnson, 82.

10. Johnson, 124-5.

11. Wuorinen, *The Finns on the Delaware*, 54.

12. Wuorinen, *The Finns on the Delaware*, 13.

13. Wuorinen., *The Finns on the Delaware*, 15.

14. Wuorinen, *The Finns on the Delaware*, 16-17.

15. Wuorinen, *The Finns on the Delaware*, 19-20.

16. Wuorinen, *The Finns on the Delaware*, 21-22; Beijbom, Ulf, "Sweden's First Voyagers to America," in *New Sweden in the New World 1638-1655.* ed. Rune Ruhnbro (Stockholm: Wiken, 1988), 75-76.

17. PKT, 717, 731-2.

18. Weslager, Clinton Alfred, *The Log Cabin in America: From Pioneer Days to the Present* (New Brunswick, New Jersey: Rutgers University Press, 1969), 152.

19. Weslager, 150.

20. Kelley, 24.

21. www.colonialswedes.org/History/History.html, 2, The Swedish Colonial Society, 29 November 2006.

22. PKT, 712.

23. Johnson, 209; PKT, 714.

24. Johnson, 142-6.

25. Johnson, 240.

26. Johnson, 244; Rydén, Josef, "Johan Printz of New Sweden," in *New Sweden in the New World 1638-1655.* ed. Rune Ruhnbro (Stockholm: Wiken, 1988), 58-70.

27. Johnson, 275-6.

28. Shorto, 277-9.

29. Beijbom, 84.

30. Kelley, 24.

31. www.colonialswedes.org/History/History.html, 3.

32. Shorto, 280.

33. Waldron, Richard. "New Sweden: An Interpretation," in Joyce Goodfriend, ed., *Revisiting New Netherland: Perspectives on Early Dutch America*; Leiden: Brill, 2005, 71.

34. PKT, 82.

35. PKT, 83-84.

36. www.colonialswedes.org/History/Chronology.html, 6.

37. Franklin, n282; 324.

38. Kerkkonen, 96.

39. Acrelius, Israel, *A History of New Sweden* (Ann Arbor: University Microfilms, Inc., 1966), 338.

40. PKT, 176-177.

41. PKT, 177.

42. PKT, 178.

43. Translation by Dr. Peter S. Craig, October 18, 2006, from a document in a bound book at the Landsarkivet at Uppsala, Sweden, under the title of "Uppsala domkapitel F VII:2, folios 63-64.

44. Hildebrand, 44.

45. Acrelius, 339.

46. Hildebrand, 47.

47. PKT, 243.

48. PKT, 233.

49. PKT, 235-6.

50. Modern historians realize that these elderly descendents actually were quite ignorant of some of the true facts about the settlement, which is understandable, since they were not well-educated and had spent their lives wresting a living from the wilderness.

51. PKT, 645; He also reported that, before the capture, the Dutch had sent a ship loaded with trading goods for the Lenape, who had formerly been trading partners of the Swedes, and tried to bribe them to trade with the Dutch instead.

52. PKT, 18.

53. PKT, 725-6.

54. Kerkkonen, 227.

55. Spady, 25.

56. Spady, 19.

57. PKT, 180-1.

58. PKT, 714.

59. PKT, 102.

60. PKT, 711.

61. PKT, 607.

62. PKT, 47.

63. PKT, 184.

64. PKT, 163.

65. PKT, 174.

66. PKT, 285.

67. PKT, 727.

68. PKT, 295-6.

69. PKT, 312.

CHAPTER SEVEN
To Canada

1. Wilson, James, *The Earth Shall Weep: A History of Native America* (New York: Atlantic Monthly Press, 1999), 116.
2. Steele, Ian K., *Betrayals: Fort William Henry & the "Massacre"* (New York: Oxford University Press, 1990), 3.
3. Faragher, John Mack, *A Great and Noble Scheme: The Tragic Story of the Expulsion of the French Acadians from Their American Homeland* (New York: W.W. Norton, 2005), 245.
4. Wilford, John Noble, *The Mapmakers* (New York: Alfred A. Knopf, 1981),100-105.
5. PKT, n393.
6. Wilson, 114.
7. Wilson, 116-7.
8. Wilson, 114.
9. Wilson, 117.
10. PKT, 141.
11. Mann, Charles C., "The Founding Sachems," *New York Times*, July 4, 2005, sec. A, 17.
12. PKT, 138.
13. Faragher, 257-277.
14. PKT, 345.
15. PKT, 139-40.
16. Larsen, Esther Louise, "Peter Kalm, preceptor." *The Pennsylvania Magazine of History and Biography*.74 (1950): 503.
17. Larsen, Esther Louise, "Peter Kalm's America: The Benefits which England Could Derive from her Colonies in North America," *Pennsylvania History* 22 (1955), 227-8.
18. Klinefelter, Walter, "Lewis Evans and his Maps," *Transactions of the American Philosophical Society*. New Series, vol. 61, part 7 (Philadelphia: The American Philosophical Society, 1971), 5.
19. Klinefelter, 24.
20. Bridenbaugh, Carl, *Cities in Revolt: Urban Life in America, 1743-1776* (New York: Knopf, 1955), 16.
21. Cruikshank, 23-42.
22. Klinefelter, 14-15.
23. Klinefelter, 23.
24. Kalm to Bartram, August 6, 1749, in Berkeley and Berkeley, *Correspondence of John Bartram*, 304-5.
25. Kerkkonen, 100.
26. PKT, 320.
27. PKT, 322-3.
28. Hildebrand, 48.
29. PKT, 331.
30. PKT, 342-3.
31. PKT, 344.
32. PKT, 346.

33. PKT, 602.

34. PKT, 603.

35. PKT, 611.

36. PKT, 609.

37. Flexner, James Thomas, *Lord of the Mohawks* (Boston: Little, Brown & Company, 1979), xiii-xv. Johnson was made a baronet in 1755.

38. Johnson, William, *Papers of Sir William Johnson.* Prepared under the direction of James Sullivan, State Historian, and Alexander C. Flick, State Historian (Albany: University of the State of New York, 1921-280 1:228; quoted in Hamilton, Milton W., *Sir William Johnson: Colonial American, 1715-1763* (Port Washington, NY: Kennikat Press, 1976), 81.

39. *Johnson Papers,* vol. 1, 228, quoted in Pound, Arthur, *Johnson of the Mohawks* (New York: The Macmillan Company, 1930), 86.

40. Hildebrand, 48.

41. PKT, 351.

42. Hildebrand, 48.

43. PKT, 85.

44. PKT, 333.

45. PKT, 359.

46. PKT, 360.

47. Members of the genus Smilax or cat's claw.

48. No such snake exists.

49. Kalm to Linnaeus, *The Linnaean Correspondence*, http://linnaeus.c18.net/Letters/letter_list.php, #1600, 15 February 1750.

50. PKT, 363-4.

51. PKT, 368.

52. PKT, 369.

53. Somewhere between Fort Anne and the broad river mentioned above, Kalm would have crossed from the Hudson River watershed which flows south, to the Champlain watershed which flows north. Russell Bellico, in *Chronicles of Lake Champlain: Journeys in War and Peace* (Fleischchmanns, NY: Purple Mountain Press, 1999) 55, suggests that Kalm got lost on the Poultney River, which would make a good deal of sense. The area between Fort Anne and Ticonderoga was notoriously difficult to travel through prior to construction of a canal between Whitehall and Fort Anne in 1823. Personal communication, Mike Winslow, staff scientist, Lake Champlain Committee, Burlington, Vermont, November 28, 2005.

54. PKT, 372.

55. Winslow also comments that "Today this area would be considered part of Lake Champlain. In early navigation charts, the southern portion of what is now the lake was referred to as 'Wood Creek,' and Kalm makes the same reference later when describing the location of Fort St. Frédéric."

56. PKT, 373; Bellico, 56n, suggests that they spent the night on the Ticonderoga peninsula.

57. PKT, 374.

58. PKT, 378.

59. Anderson, Fred. *Crucible of War* (New York: Vintage Books, 2001), 13; Anderson, Fred and Andrew Cayton, *The Dominion of War: Empire and Liberty in North America 1500-2000* (New York: Viking, 2005), 26.
60. Bellico, 57n.
61. Steele, Ian K. *Betrayals: Fort William Henry & the "Massacre."* (New York: Oxford University Press, 1990), 8.
62. Steele, 10.
63. PKT, 366.
64. PKT, 366.

Chapter Eight
The Honored Guest in Canada

1. PKT, 392-3.
2. PKT, 205.
3. According to Bellico, "This 45-ton ship, the *St. Frédéric*, was built in 1742 by the Corbin brothers of Québec. It made regular trips between Forts St. Frédéric and St. John, 62n.
4. According to Mike Winslow, Staff Scientist, Lake Champlain Committee, this is another case of where the definition of what constitutes Lake Champlain has changed since Kalm's time. St. John is now considered to be on the Richelieu River.
5. PKT, 399.
6. PKT, 400.
7. PKT, 402.
8. PKT, 553.
9. Hildebrand, 49.
10. PKT, 407.
11. PKT, 409.
12. PKT, 251.
13. Hildebrand, 50.
14. Roy, J.-Edmond, "Voyage de Kalm au Canada." *La Revue de Notariat,* 1900, 32.
15. PKT, 504.
16. PKT, 375-6.
17. PKT, 431, 158.
18. PKT, 416.
19. PKT, 422.
20. PKT, 445.
21. PKT, 446.
22. PKT, 448.
23. Hallock, Thomas, "Narrative, Nature, and Cultural Contact in John Bartram's Observations," in *America's Curious Botanist: A Tercentennial Reappraisal of John Bartram 1699-1777.* ed. Nancy C. Hoffman and John C. Van Horne (Philadelphia: The American Philosophical Society, 2004), 112.
24. PKT, 449.
25. PKT, 450-1.
26. PKT, 535.
27. PKT, 474-5.

28. PKT, 511
29. PKT, 387-8.
30. PKT, 489, 496.
31. PKT, 510-11; Kalm may have been mistaken. It was more likely red osier dogwood, *Cornus sericea.* James Reveal, personal communication October 2006.
32. Quoted by Koerner, 117.
33. PKT, 406.
34. Berkeley and Berkeley, *Correspondence of John Bartram,* 304-5.
35. Franklin, 383-5.
36. Roy, 30-32.
37. PKT, 466.
38. PKT, 465.
39. PKT, 466
40. Kerkkonen, 107.
41. PKT, 507; at Kalm's request, Linnaeus named teaberry or wintergreen, *Gaultheria procumbens,* after the doctor. James Reveal, personal communication, October 2006.
42. PKT, 381.
43. PKT, 501.
44. PKT, 478.
45. PKT, 511.
46. PKT, 446.
47. PKT, 447.
48. PKT, 417.
49. PKT, 526.
50. PKT, 403.
51. PKT, 425.
52. PKT, 475-7.
53. PKT, 479.
54. PKT, 509-10.
55. PKT, 544-5.
56. Roy, 28.
57. PKT, 551.
58. Roy, 33.
59. Bellico, 70n.
60. PKT, 587.
61. PKT, 590.
62. PKT, 599.
63. PKT, 600-1.

CHAPTER NINE
Return to Philadelphia

1. PKT, 602.
2. PKT, 626.
3. Lockridge, Kenneth A., "Overcoming Nausea: The Brothers Hesselius and the American Mystery." *Common-Place:* www.common-place.org., vol. 4., no. 2, January 2004.

4. Shorto, 268, 272.
5. PKT, 344.
6. PKT, 619.
7. PKT, 625.
8. Franklin, n383-4.
9. PKT, 543-4.
10. PKT, 627-8
11. Kalm to Linnaeus, *The Linnaean Correspondence*, http://linnaeus.c18.net/Letters/letter_list.php, #1599, 29 November 1749.
12. Colden papers, 257.
13. PKT, 632.
14. PKT, 638.
15. PKT, 639.
16. PKT, 644.
17. Larsen, Esther Louise, "Pehr Kalm's report on the characteristics and uses of the American walnut tree which is called hickory." *Agricultural History*, 19 (1939), 64.
18. PKT, 665.
19. Franklin, vol. 4, 61.
20. PKT, 654.
21. PKT, 655.
22. Translation by Dr. Peter S. Craig, October 18, 2006, from a document in a bound book at the Landsarkivet at Uppsala, Sweden, under the title of "Uppsala domkapitel F VII:2, folios 63-64.
23. Kerkkonen, 112, 114; Acrelius, 339; unfortunately, the church records for 1750 have been lost, so we do not know the exact date.
24. PKT, 223.
25. Franklin, vol. 3, 324.
26. Franklin, vol. 3, 459.
27. Tolles, Frederick B. *James Logan and the Culture of Provincial America*. (Boston: Little, Brown and Company, 1957), 211; Franklin, vol. 3, 483.
28. Franklin, vol. 3, 469-70.
29. Anderson, 25.
30. Franklin, vol. 3, n326.
31. Franklin, vol. 3, 324.
32. Franklin, vol. 3, 467.
33. Berkeley and Berkeley, *Correspondence of John Bartram*, 216.
34. Hindle, 21, 25.
35. Hildebrand, 58-9.
36. Kerkkonen, 114; Hildebrand, 60.
37. Joel Fry, personal communication, November 2, 2006.
38. Kalm to Linnaeus, *The Linnaean Correspondence*, http://linnaeus.c18.net/Letters/letter_list.php, #1600, 15 February 1750.
39. Kerkkonen, 113-4.

Chapter Ten
Niagara Falls

1. Hildebrand, 64.
2. Flexner, 97.
3. Pound, Arthur. *Johnson of the Mohawks* (New York: The Macmillan Company, 1930), 86-89.
4. Larsen, Esther Louise, "Lobelia as a sure cure for venereal disease." *American Journal of Syphilis, Gonorrhea and Venereal Disease* XXIV (1940), 16.
5. Flexner, xiv-xv.
6. Flexner, xv.
7. Johnson papers, 1:332, quoted in Hamilton, 82.
8. Quoted in Pound, 371.
9. PKT, 695.
10. Pound, 107.
11. Pound, 370.
12. Tsubaki, Rosemary, "A Swedish Botanist in the Mohawk Valley in 1750: Pehr Kalm (1716-1779), unpublished article.
13. PKT, 695.
14. Franklin, Vol. 4, 44.
15. Berton, Pierre, *Niagara: A History of the Falls.* New York: Kodansha International, 1997, 12-18.
16. PKT, 693-709; 773.
17. Franklin, vol. 4, 53.
18. Franklin, vol. 4, 43-53.
19. PKT, 693-709; Franklin, vol. 4, 43-53;
20. PKT, 699.
21. Franklin, vol. 4, 46.
22. PKT, 705-6.
23. Franklin, vol. 4, 52.
24. Both Klinefelter (29) and Kerkkonen (117) state that Kalm returned to Philadelphia by a different route, presumably Evan's route through Ephrata and Lancaster, but Kalm's accounts (Hildebrand, 68-71) list purchases made in Schenectady, Albany, and Kingsbridge, indicating a route on horseback along the east bank of the Hudson River, with probably a stop for just one night at Coldengham, as mentioned in Colden's letter to Linnaeus. His eagerness may have been because of his desire to return to Margaretha.
25. The Colden Papers – 1748-1754, 257-8.
26. Hildebrand, 68.
27. Collinson to Bartram, 24 January 1735, Berkeley and Berkeley, Correspondence of John Bartram, 3.
28. Hildebrand, 76.

CHAPTER ELEVEN
Native Americans

1. Roger, Jacques, *Buffon: A Life in Natural History.* trans. Sarah Lucille Bonnefoi, ed. L. Pearce Williams (Ithaca: Cornell University Press, 1997), 264.
2. Roger, 263-4.
3. Jacobs, Wilbur R., "British Colonial Attitudes," in *Attitudes of Colonial Powers Toward the American Indian.* ed. Howard Peckham and Charles Gibson (Salt Lake City: University of Utah Press, 1969), 82; Anderson and Cayton, 56.
4. Saunders, Richard H. and Ellen G. Miles, *American Colonial Portraits, 1700-1776* (Washington, D.C.: National Portrait Gallery, Smithsonian Institution, 1987), 153.
5. Pencak, William A. and Daniel K. Richter, *Friends and Enemies in Penn's Woods: Indians, Colonists and the Racial Construction of Pennsylvania* (University Park, Pennsylvania: The Pennsylvania State University Press, 2004), xii.
6. Mackintosh, Michael Dean, "New Sweden, Natives and Nature," in Pencak, William A. and Daniel K. Richter, *Friends and Enemies in Penn's Woods: Indians, Colonists and the Racial Construction of Pennsylvania* (University Park, Pennsylvania: The Pennsylvania State University Press, 2004), 14.
7. Although they were nominally Christian, I suspect that they probably still retained much of their ancestral, orally-transmitted, earth-based mythology that was the basis of nineteenth-century physician Elias Lönnrot's epic poem, *The Kalevala.*
8. Mackintosh, 9.
9. PKT, 270.
10. PKT, 686.
11. Wade, Mason, "The French and the Indians." Pencak, William A. and Daniel K. Richter, *Friends and Enemies in Penn's Woods: Indians, Colonists and the Racial Construction of Pennsylvania* (University Park, Pennsylvania: The Pennsylvania State University Press, 2004), 61.
12. Wade, 64.
13. Anderson and Cayton, 41.
14. PKT, 521.
15. Wade, 67.
16. Jacobs, 85.
17. Rystad, Göran, "The Colonization of North America," in *New Sweden in the New World 1638-1655,* ed. Rune Ruhnbro (Stockholm: Wiken, 1988), 54.
18. PKT, 518-524.
19. Jacobs, 87.
20. Hoermann, 165; For Collinson's letters to Colden about the *History of the Five Indian Nations,* see Armstrong, No. 44, March 5, 1741; No. 48, March 7, 1742; No. 53, September 3, 1742; No. 60, September 4, 1743; No. 62, March 9, 1744; No. 64, August 23, 1744; No. 77, August 3, 1747. In 1741, Collinson acquired Colden's father's copy of the 1727 edition—probably as the gift mentioned in the March 5, 1741 letter—and urged Colden to revise and update the work. See the Christie's catalogue for the sale of The Jay T. Snider Collection of Historical Americana, New York, June 21, 2005, Sale 1614, Lot 37, Lot Title: COLDEN, Cadwallader (1688-1776). *The History of the Five Indian Nations Depending on the Province of New-York In America.* New York:

William Bradford, 1727. (The date of Collinson's inscription in the Christie's lot description should be 1741, not 1747; personal communication, Karen Reeds and Thomas Lecky, June 13, 2005.)

21. Hoermann, 166-7.
22. Hoermann , 167.
23. Mann, 17.
24. Cruikshank, Helen Gere, ed. *John and William Bartram's America* (New York: Doubleday Anchor, 1957), 23-42.
25. Hoermann, 168.
26. Doblin, Helga and William A. Starna, eds. "The Journals of Christian Daniel Claus and Conrad Weiser: A Journey to Onondaga, 1750." *Transactions of the American Philosophical Society.* Philadelphia: American Philosophical Society, 1994: 84, 35-6.
27. PKT, 600.
28. PKT, 56.
29. PKT, 519.
30. PKT, 53.
31. PKT, 348.
32. PKT, 119.
33. PKT, 258.
34. PKT, 268.
35. PKT, 268.
36. PKT, 268.
37. PKT, 269.
38. PKT, 190.
39. PKT, 228.
40. PKT, 172-173.
41. PKT, 231.
42. PKT, 232.
43. PKT, 277.
44. PKT, 277-278.
45. PKT, 285.
46. PKT, 229-230.
47. PKT, 233.
48. Wade, 67.
49. PKT, 551.
50. PKT, 74-5.
51. PKT, 533.
52. PKT, 533.
53. Larsen, Esther Louise, "Pehr Kalm's description of maize, how it is planted and cultivated in North America, together with the many uses of this crop plant." *Agricultural History* 9 (1935): 98-117.
54. Larsen, "Pehr Kalm's description of maize," 109.
55. Larsen, "Pehr Kalm's description of maize," 104.
56. Larsen, "Pehr Kalm's description of maize," 106.
57. Larsen, "Pehr Kalm's description of maize," 109.

58. Larsen, "Pehr Kalm's description of maize," 110.
59. Larsen, "Pehr Kalm's description of maize," 111-112.
60. Larsen, "Pehr Kalm's description of maize," 114.
61. PKT, 518.
62. Larsen, Esther Louise, "Peter Kalm's description of how sugar is made from various types of trees in North America." *Agricultural History* 13 (1939): 149-156.
63. PKT, 269.
64. PKT, 260-1.
65. PKT, 129.
66. PKT, 353-354.
67. PKT, 394.
68. PKT, 591.
69. PKT, 354.
70. PKT, 377-378.
71. PKT, 560.
72. PKT, 520-1.
73. PKT, 588.
74. PKT, 74.
75. PKT, 556-7.
76. PKT, 561.
77. PKT, 457.
78. PKT, 694.
79. PKT, 439.

CHAPTER TWELVE
The Search for Cures

1. PKT, 447.
2. PKT, 36.
3. PKT, 108-9.
4. PKT, 127.
5. PKT, 128.
6. PKT, 56.
7. PKT, 189-191.
8. Hoermann, 29.
9. PKT, 211.
10. Leighton, Ann, *American Gardens in the Eighteenth Century* (Boston: Houghton Mifflin Co., 1976), 163.
11. Personal communication, Joel T. Fry, Curator, Bartram's Garden.
12. Hobbs, Christopher, "The Medical Botany of John Bartram," http://www.healthy.net/scr/article.asp?Id=861, November 30, 2006.
13. Berkeley and Berkeley, *Correspondence of John Bartram*, 780-78; Bartram's Garden, "John Bartram's Medicinal Plants," 2004; Hobbs; with thanks to James Reveal for providing the table and current names.
14. Actually butterfly weed, *Asclepias tuberosae*, according to Joel T. Fry, curator, Bartram's Garden, personal communication.
15. Leighton, 168.

16. Larsen, "Lobelia as a Sure Cure for Venereal Disease," 16.
17. This was the title of the journal in which this paper was published. The title of the journal was later changed. Personal communication, James Reveal, October, 2006.
18. Larsen, "Lobelia as a Sure Cure for Venereal Disease," 16.
19. PKT, 105-6.
20. Kalm to Linnaeus, *The Linnaean Correspondence*, http://linnaeus.c18.net/Letters/letter_list.php, #1597, 28 May 1749.
21. Leighton, 155.
22. PKT, 435-7.
23. PKT, 438.
24. PKT, 469.
25. Lundqvist, S. and R. Moberg, "The Pehr Kalm Herbarium in UPS, a collection of North American Plants," *Thunbergia,* 19: 1993, 1-62. The first set of Kalm specimens is in the Linnaean Herbarium of the Linnean Society of London at Burlington House.

CHAPTER THIRTEEN
Kalm as a Scientist

1. Larson, James L., *Interpreting Nature: The Science of Living Form from Linnaeus to Kant* (Baltimore: The Johns Hopkins University Press, 1994), 5.
2. Ziman, John. *Reliable Knowledge: An Exploration of the Grounds for Belief in Science* (Cambridge: Cambridge University Press, 1978, 1996), 46.
3. PKT, 57-9.
4. PKT, 306-7.
5. PKT, 290-1.
6. PKT, 295.
7. Koerner, 109.
8. PKT, 44.
9. Juel, H.O. and John W. Harshberger, "New Light on the Collection of North American Plants made by Peter Kalm." *Proceedings of the Pennsylvania Academy.* 81 (1929): 297-303.
10. PKT, 34-35.
11. Koerner, 121.
12. Koerner, 123.
13. Kalm, Pehr. "Report to University of Åbo" dated July 1,1755, re: his visit to America; Philadelphia: Historical Society of Pennsylvania. Gratz Collection, Case 12, Box 9. English translation by Kristina Antoniades, MD, for the American Swedish Historical Museum, 5.
14. Dupree, A. Hunter. *Asa Gray: American Botaninst, Friend of Darwin* (Baltimore: The Johns Hopkins University Press, 1959), 235-7.
15. Larson, "Lobelia as a Sure Cure for Venereal Disease," 18.
16. Miller, Kenneth R., *Finding Darwin's God* (New York: HarperCollins, 1999), 196.
17. Slaughter, 58-9.
18. Quoted in Dewitt, 80-81.
19. Kerkkonen, 148.
20. PKT, 54.
21. PKT, 384-5.

22. PKT, 106-7.

23. PKT, 189.

24. PKT, 72.

25. PKT, 65.

26. PKT, 71.

27. PKT, 2.

28. KVtE, 48.

29. PKT, 328-330.

30. Commager, Henry Steele, *The Empire of Reason: How Europe Imagined and America Realized the Enlightenment* (Garden City, New York: Anchor Press/Doubleday, 1977), 80.

31. Ibid.

32. PKT, 33.

33. PKT, 463.

34. PKT, 37-39.

35. PKT, 75-6.

36. PKT, 104.

37. PKT, 75-6.

38. PKT, 75-76.

39. PKT, 103-4.

40. PKT, 337-8.

41. PKT, 447.

42. Dray, 77.

43. www.geocities.com/Athens/Aegean/7023/indigo.html; November 30, 2006.

44. According to James Reveal, the nomenclature for the rock chestnut oak is not yet settled; it will likely result in the rejection of *Quercus primus* and the use, instead, of *Quercus montana*. Personal communication, October 2006.

45. KT, 78.

46. PKT, 88.

47. PKT, 185.

48. PKT, 77.

49. PKT, 92-3.

50. PKT, 214.

51. Kritsky, Gene. "John Bartram and the Periodical Cicadas: A Case Study." In *America's Curious Botanist: A Tercentennial Reappraisal of John Bartram 1699-1777.* eds. Nancy E. Hoffman and John C. Van Horne (Philadelphia: The American Philosophical Society, 2004), 43-51.

52. PKT, 151.

53. Kerkkonen, 127.

54. Kerkkonen, 120-1; Lundqvist, and Moberg, 2.

55. Kerkkonen, 125.

56. PKT, xvii.

57. Kerkkonen, 126.

CHAPTER FOURTEEN
Kalm as Environmentalist

1. PKT, 308.
2. PKT, 307.
3. PKT, 307.
4. Wuorinen, *Finns on the Delaware*, 15-17.
5. Koerner, 128.
6. PKT, 97-98.
7. PKT, 279.
8. PKT, 309.
9. PKT, 308.
10. PKT, 308-9.
11. Hawke, David Freeman, *Everyday Life in Early America* (New York: Harper & Row, 1988), 33.
12. Anderson and Cayton, 84.
13.   PKT, 152.
14. PKT, 368.
15. Kalm, Pehr and John James Audubon, "The Passenger Pigeon," *Smithsonian Institution Annual Report for 1911*. Washington (1912), 422.
16. PKT, 252, 369.
17. "The Passenger Pigeon," 415.
18. "The Passenger Pigeon," 412.
19. PKT, 153.
20. PKT, 20.
21. PKT, 147.
22. PKT, 27-28.
23. Franklin, vol. 4, 480.

CHAPTER FIFTEEN
Return to Sweden

1. Hildebrand, 77.
2. Kalm to Linnaeus, *The Linnaean Correspondence*, http://linnaeus.c18.net/Letters/letter_list.php, 5 December 1750; quoted in Kerkkonen, 117.
3. Kerkkonen, 128.
4. Hildebrand, 76.
5. Hildebrand, 77.
6. Kerkkonen, 127; Mead, 143.
7. Kerkkonen, 231; Six of these are now in the library of the University of Helsinki.
8. Kalm to Linnaeus, *The Linnaean Correspondence*, http://linnaeus.c18.net/Letters/letter_list.php, #1603, 5 April 1751.
9. Kalm to Linnaeus, #1610, 12 October 1751.
10. Kerkkonen, 117-118; Mead, 143.
11. Kerkkonen, 237.
12. Kerkkonen, 218.
13. Franklin, vol. 4, 113.
14. Berkeley and Berkeley, *Correspondence of John Bartram*, 324.

15. Larsen, Esther Louise, "Peter Kalm's Short Account of the Natural Position, Use, and Care of Some Plants, of which the Seeds Were Recently Brought Home from North America for the Service of those who Take Pleasure in Experimenting with the Cultivation of the Same in Our Climate." *Agricultural History* 13 (1939):33-64.
16. Hildebrand, 14.
17. Klinefelter, 30.
18. Linnaeus to Bäck, 28 May 1751; quoted in Lindroth, 54.
19. Kalm to Linnaeus, *The Linnaean Correspondence*, http://linnaeus.c18.net/Letters/letter_list.php, #1607, 20 June 1751.
20. Koerner, 155.
21. Collander, Runar, *The History of Botany in Finland: 1828-1918* (Helsinki: Societas Scientiarum Fennica, 1965), 13.
22. Kerkkonen, 118.

CHAPTER SIXTEEN
Life as Professor at Åbo

1. Kukkonen, Ilkka, "Pietari Kalmin Viljelyskokeiden Merkkejä Hänen Vanhassa Puutarhassaan Hirvensalon Sepsalossa." *Turun Ylioppilas IV,* Turku: Turun Yliopiston Ylioppilaskunta, 1955, 184.
 2. Records of St. Maria's Church in Turku, personal communication, Seija Niemi.
 3. Kerkkonen, 219.
 4. Kalm, Pehr. Report to University of Åbo.
 5. Kerkkonen, 219.
 6. Kerkkonen, 220.
 7. Kukkonen, 185.
 8. Kalm's report to the Consistory, 3.
 9. Kerkkonen, 220.
10. Niemelä, 77.
11. Thanks to Arno Kasvi of the Botanical Garden of Turku University, who took me to Seipsalo and told stories about Kalm's time there. It is hoped that the university may be able to acquire the property and restore the garden. Part of the eighteenth century house and barn still survive.
12. Kerkkonen, 232.
13. Kerkkonen, 232-3.
14. Kerkkonen, 234.
15. Leikola, 8.
16. Kerkkonen, 235; Roy, 9.
17. Mead, 21.
18. Roy, 9.
19. Leikola, 8.
20. Eskelinen, Heikki S., "Peter Kalm 200-year Memorial Exhibition." Typescript copy of a description of the September 1979 exhibition at the University of Turku Library.
21. Larsen, "Peter Kalm, Preceptor," 502.
22. Collander, Runar, *The History of Botany in Finland: 1828-1918.* Helsinki: Scietas Scientiarum Fennica, 1965, 13.

23. Kerkkonen, 224.

24. Larsen, "Peter Kalm, Preceptor," 504.

25. Koerner, 130.

26. Mead, 150-1.

27. Kerkkonen, 228.

28. Kerkkonen, 185.

29. Kerkkonen, 242-3.

30. Niemelä, Jari, *Vain hyödynkö tähden?* (Helsinki: Suomen Historiallinen Seura, 1998), 24.

31. Niemelä, 98.

32. Niemelä, Jari. Kalm onkin Gadd! Suomen Sukututkimusseura. http://www.genealogia.fi/genos/67/67_22.htm#1#1, 29 November 2006.

33. Kerkkonen, 243.

34. Kalm, Pehr, Report to University of Åbo, dated July 1,1755, re: his visit to America; Philadelphia: Historical Society of Pennsylvania. Gratz Collection, Case 12, Box 9. English translation by Kristina Antoniades, MD, for the American Swedish Historical Museum.

35. Kerkkonen, 240.

36. Mead, 151.

37. Kerkkonen, 240.

38. Ibid.

39. Kerkkonen, 244.

40. Personal communication, Riikka Kaisti; plaque on the vicarage at St. Mary's Church.

41. Kerkkonen, 234.

42. Leikola, 3.

43. Klinefelter, 30.

44. *Pensilvaniae, Novae-Caesarae, Novi-Eboraci, Aqusanishuonigae, et Canadae, Brevis Delinieatio. Juxta Itinera P. Kalm, a Ludovico Evans, 1750.* Aeri incise a Fr. Akrel, cura S. Kreander, 1784; Klinefelter, 32; Library of Congress Geography and Map Division, LC Maps of North America, 1750, No. 705.

CHAPTER SEVENTEEN
The Outcome of Kalm's Journey

1. Koerner, 121.

2. Larsen, "Peter Kalm's Short Account, 64.

3. Kerkkonen, 221.

4. Leikola, Anto, Exhibition Pehr Kalm and his Voyage to North America 1747-1751. Arranged by Helsinki University Library. Helsinki, Government Printing Centre, 1988, 7.

5. Niemelä, *Vain hyödynkö tähden?*, 84.

6. A botanist, Mariette Manktelew, and I found a specimen at Lövsta which we believed to have been descended from seeds sent by Kalm.

7. Kerkkonen, 222.

8. Quoted in Koerner, 117.

9. According to a private communication from Mike Winslow, staff scientist, Lake Champlain Committee, Burlington, Vermont, white mulberry was actually introduced to America from Asia.

10. PKT, 67.

11. PKT, 408.

12. An American mulberry in the Botanical Garden in Uppsala is said to have been planted by Kalm.

13. Koerner, 149.

14. PKT, 67.

15. PKT, 96.

16. Koerner, 117.

17. PKT, 78.

18. PKT, 408.

19. Larsen, *Maize*, 104.

20. Linnaeus to Kalm, 1758, KBX651.

21. Raskin, N.M. and I.I. Shafranovskii, *Erik Gustavovich Laxmann: Noted Traveler and Naturalist of the 18th Century.* (New Delhi: Amerind Publishing Co. Pvt. Ltd., 1978), 9.

22. Berkeley and Berkeley, *Correspondence of John Bartram*, 346.

23. Franklin, vol. 4, 511.

24. Berkeley and Berkeley, *Correspondence of John Bartram*, 380.

25. Berkeley and Berkeley, *Correspondence of John Bartram*, 445.

26. Polis and Savage, 61-63.

27. Franklin, vol. 4, n54.

28. Colden papers, 7:185.

29. Mead, 20.

30. Personal communication, Bradley P. Dean, director, Media Center, Thoreau Institute at Walden Woods, Lincoln, Massachusetts, June 12, 2001.

Bibliography

Acrelius, Israel. Translated by William M. Reynolds. *A History of New Sweden.* Ann Arbor: University Microfilms, Inc., 1966.

Anderson, Fred and Andrew Cayton. *The Dominion of War: Empire and Liberty in North America 1500-2000.* New York: Viking, 2005.

Anderson, Fred. *Crucible of War.* New York: Vintage Books, 2001.

Armstrong, Alan W., ed. *Forget not Mee & My Garden: Selected Letters, 1725-1768 of Peter Collinson, F.R.S.* Philadelphia: American Philosophical Society, 2002.

Bailey, L. H. *How Plants Get Their Names.* 1933. New York: Dover Publications, Inc., 1963.

Bartram, William. "Some Account of the Late Mr. John Bartram, of Pennsylvania." In *Travels and Other Writings.* The Library of America, 1996, 577-81.

Bartram's Garden. "John Bartram's Medicinal Plants," brochure, Philadelphia, 2004.

Beijbom, Ulf. "Sweden's First Voyagers to America." In *New Sweden in the New World 1638-1655.* edited by Rune Ruhnbro. Stockholm:Wiken, 1988.

Bellico, Russell P. *Chronicles of Lake Champlain: Journeys in War and Peace.* Fleischmanns, NY: Purple Mountain Press, 1999.

Benson, Adolph B., ed. *Peter Kalm's Travels in North America: The English Version of 1770.* 2 vols. New York: Wilson-Erickson Inc., 1937.

_____. "Pehr Kalm's Writings on America." *Scandinavian Studies and Notes.* May 1933.

_____. "Pehr Kalm's Journey to North America." *The American-Scandinavian Review.* June 1922, 350-55.

Berkeley, Edmund and Dorothy Smith Berkeley. *Dr. John Mitchell: The Man Who Made the Map of North America.* Chapel Hill: The University of North Carolina Press, 1974.

_____. *The Life and Travels of John Bartram: From Lake Ontario to the River St. John.* Tallahassee: University Presses of Florida, 1982.

Berkeley, Edmund and Dorothy Smith Berkeley, eds. *The Correspondence of John Bartram: 1734-1777.* Gainesville: University Press of Florida, 1992.

Berton, Pierre. *Niagara: A History of the Falls.* New York: Kodansha International, 1997.

Blunt, Wilfrid. *The Compleat Naturalist: A Life of Linnaeus.* New York: The Viking Press, 1971.

Brands, H. W. *The First American: The Life and Times of Benjamin Franklin.* New York: Doubleday, 2000.

Bridenbaugh, Carl. *Cities in Revolt: Urban Life in America, 1743-1776.* New York: Knopf, 1955.

Bridenbaugh, Carl and Jessica Bridenbaugh. *Rebels & Gentlemen: Philadelphia and the Age of Franklin.* New York: Reynal & Hitchcock, 1942.

Brown, Ralph H. *Mirror for Americans: Likeness of the Eastern Seaboard, 1810.* New York: Da Capo Press, 1968.

Chaplin, Joyce E. "Mark Catesby, a Skeptical Newtonian in America." In *Empire's Nature: Mark Catesby's New World Vision.* Amy R.W. Meyers and Margaret Beck Pritchard, eds., Chapel Hill: University of North Carolina Press, 1998.

Chancellor, E. Beresford. *The XVIIIth Century in London: An Account of its Social Life and the Arts.*1920. London: B. T. Batsford Ltd., 1933.

Colden, Cadwallader. *The Letters and Papers of Cadwallader Colden.* Vols. IV and VII. Printed for the NY Historical Society, New York: AMS Press, 1973.

Collander, Runar. *The History of Botany in Finland: 1828-1918.* Helsinki: Societas Scientiarum Fennica, 1965.

Commager, Henry Steele. *The Empire of Reason: How Europe Imagined and America Realized the Enlightenment.* New York: Anchor Press/Doubleday, 1977.

Crévecoeur, J. Hector St. John de. *Letters from an American Farmer.* 1782. Reprint, London: J. M. Dent & Sons, 1926.

Cronon, William. *Changes in the Land: Indians, Colonists, and the Ecology of New England.* New York: Hill and Wang, 1983.

Crosby, Alfred W. *Germs, Seeds and Animals: Studies in Ecological History.* Armonk, NY: M.E. Sharpe, Inc., 1994.

_____. *The Columbian Exchange: Biological and Cultural Consequences of 1492.* Westport, Connecticut: Greenwood Press, 1972.

Cruikshank, Helen Gere, ed. *John and William Bartram's America.* New York: Doubleday Anchor, 1957. *Observations on the Inhabitants, Climate, Soil, Rivers, Productions, Animals, and Other Matters Worthy of Notice, Made by Mr. John Bartram, in His Travels from Pensilvania to Onondago, Oswego and the Lake Ontario, in Canada.* To which is annexed a Curious Account of the Cataracts of Niagara, by Mr. Peter Kalm, A Swedish Gentleman Who Traveled There. London: Printed for J. Whiston and B. White, in Fleet-Street, 1751. Darlington, William, *Memorials of John Bartram and Humphrey Marshall.* (facsimile of the edition of 1849) New York: Hafner Publishing Company, 1967, 23-42.

Dewitt, F. Dawtrey. *The Romance of the Apothecaries' Garden at Chelsea.* 3rd ed. London: Cambridge University Press, 1928.

Dray, Philip. *Stealing God's Thunder: Benjamin Franklin's Lightning Rod and the Invention of America.* New York: Random House, 2005.

Doblin, Helga and William A. Starna, eds. "The Journals of Christian Daniel Claus and Conrad Weiser: A Journey to Onondaga, 1750." *Transactions of the American Philosophical Society.* Philadelphia: American Philosophical Society (1994): 84, 1-64.

Dupree, A. Hunter. *Asa Gray: American Botanist, Friend of Darwin.* Baltimore: The Johns Hopkins University Press, 1959.

Eriksson, Malin. "Sten Carl Bielkes och Pehr Kalms försöksodlingasr vid Lövsta," unpublished paper, Swedish University of Agricultural Sciences, 2005, personal communication.

Eskelinen, Heikki S. "Peter Kalm 200-year Memorial Exhibition." Typescript copy of a description of the September 1979 exhibition at the University of Turku Library.

Ewan, Joseph. *A Short History of Botany in the United States.* NewYork: Hafner Publishing Co., 1969.

Fänge, Ragnar. "Introduction: Early Hagfish Research." In Jens Peter Lomholt, Roy E. Weber and Mans Malte, eds. *The Biology of Hagfishes.* London: Chapman and Hall, 1998.

Faragher, John Mack. *A Great and Noble Scheme: The Tragic Story of the Expulsion of the French Acadians from Their American Homeland.* New York: W. W. Norton, 2005.

Flexner, James Thomas. *Lord of the Mohawks.* 1959. Reprint, Boston: Little, Brown and Company, 1979.

Frick, George Frederick and Raymond Phineas Stearns. *Mark Catesby the Colonial Audubon.* Urbana: University of Illinois Press, 1961.

Gallinat, Wilton. "Maize: Gift from America's First Peoples," In Nelson Foster and Linda S. Cordell, eds., *Chilies to Chocolate: Food the Americas Gave the World.* Tucson: The University of Arizona Press, 1992.

Gleason, Henry A. and Arthur Cronquist. *Manual of Vascular Plants of Northeastern United States and Adjacent Canada.* 2nd ed., 7th printing, with corrections, Bronx, NY: New York Botanical Garden, 2001.

Goerke, Heinz. *Linnaeus.* New York: Charles Scribner's Sons, 1973.

Hamilton, Milton W. *Sir William Johnson: Colonial American, 1715-1763.* Port Washington, NY: Kennikat Press, 1976.

Harshberger, John W. *The Botanists of Philadelphia and Their Work.* Philadelphia, 1899.

Hawke, David Freeman. *Everyday Life in Early America.* New York: Harper & Row, 1988.

Hedrick, U.P. A *History of Horticulture in America to 1860.* New York: Oxford University Press, 1950.

Hildebrand, Bengt. *Pehr Kalms Amerikanska Reseräkning.* Helsinki: Svenska litter-
aturséllskapet i Finland, 1956.

Hindle, Brooke. *The Pursuit of Science in Revolutionary America, 1735-1789.* Chapel
Hill: University of North Carolina Press, 1956.

Hoermann, Alfred R. *Cadwallader Colden: A Figure of the American Enlightenment.*
Westport, Connecticut: Greenwood Press, 2002.

Hoffman, Nancy E. and John C. Van Horne, John C., eds. *America's Curious
Botanist: A Tercentennial Reappraisal of John Bartram 1699-1777.* Philadelphia:
The American Philosophical Society, 2004.

Hobbs, Christopher. "The Medical Botany of John Bartram,"
http://www.healthy.net/asp/templates/article.asp?PageType=Article&ID=
861, 3 November 2006.

Isaacson, Walter. *Benjamin Franklin: An American Life,* New York: Simon & Schuster, 2003.

Jacobs, Wilbur R. "British Colonial Attitudes and Policies toward the Indian in
the American Colonies," In Howard Peckham and Charles Gibson, eds.,
Attitudes of Colonial Powers toward the American Indian. Salt Lake City: University of Utah Press, 1969.

Jalava, Mauri A. "Pehr Kalm: First Contact (1749-1750)." *Journal of Finnish Studies,* 4 (2000), 4-16.

Jennings, Francis. *Empire of Fortune: Crowns, Colonies & Tribes in the Seven Years
War in America.* New York: W. W. Norton, 1988.

Johnson, Amandus. *The Swedes on the Delaware 1638-1664.* Philadelphia: The
Lenape Press, 1914.

Johnson, Sir William. *Papers of Sir William Johnson.* Vol. 1. Prepared under the
direction of James Sullivan, State Historian, and Alexander C. Flick, State
Historian. Albany: University of the State of New York, 1921-28, 228.

Juel, H. O. and John W. Harshberger. New Light on the Collection of North
American Plants made by Peter Kalm. *Proceedings of the Pennsylvania Academy.* Philadelphia, 1929.

Kalm, Pehr. *Kalm's Visit to England on His Way to America in 1748.* Translated by
Joseph Lucas. London, 1892.

———. Report to University of Åbo, dated July 1, 1755, re his visit to America;
Philadelphia: Historical Society of Pennsylvania. Gratz Collegection, Case
12, Box 9. English translation by Kristina Antoniades, MD, for the American
Swedish Historical Museum.

———. *The Linnaean Correspondence,*
http://linnaeus.c18.net/Letters/letter_list.php., 3 November 2006.

Kalm, Pehr and John James Audubon. "The Passenger Pigeon." *Annual Report
Smithsonian Institution for 1911.* Washington, DC: 1912, 407-417.

Kastner, Joseph. *A Species of Eternity.* New York: Alfred A Knopf, 1977.

Kelley, Joseph J., Jr. *Life and Times in Colonial Philadelphia.* Harrisburg, Pennsylvania: Stackpole Books, 1973.

Kerkkonen, Martti. *Peter Kalm's North American Journey: Its Ideological Background and Results.* Helsinki: Finnish Historical Society, 1959.

Klinefelter, Walter. "Lewis Evans and his Maps," *Transactions of the American Philosophical Society.* New Series, vol. 61, part 7, Philadelphia: The American Philosophical Society, 1971.

Koerner, Lisbet. *Linnaeus: Nature and Nation.* Cambridge: Harvard University Press, 1999.

Kukkonen, Ilkka. "Pietari Kalmin Viljelyskokeiden Merkkejä Hänen Vanhassa Puutarhassaan Hirvensalon Seipsalossa." *Turun Yliopilas IV,* Turku: Turun Yliopiston Ylioppilaskunta, 1955.

Labaree, Leonard W., Whitfield J. Bell, Jr., Helen C. Boatfield, and Helene H. Fineman eds., *The Papers of Benjamin Franklin.* Vols. 3 and 4. New Haven: Yale University Press, 1961.

Landes, David S. *The Wealth and Poverty of Nations: Why Some Are So Rich and Some So Poor.* New York: W. W. Norton & Company, 1998.

Larsen, Esther Louise. "Pehr Kalm's Description of Maize, How It Is Planted and Cultivated in North America, Together with the Many Uses of This Crop Plant." *Agricultural History* 9 (1935): 98-117.

_____. "Peter Kalm's Short Account of the Natural Position, Use, and Care of Some Plants, of which the Seeds were Recently Brought Home from North America for the Service of those who Take Pleasure in Experimenting with the Cultivation of the Same in Our Climate." *Agricultural History* 13 (1939):33-64.

_____. "Peter Kalm's Description of How Sugar is Made from Various Types of Trees in North America." *Agricultural History* 13 (1939):149-56.

_____. "Pehr Kalm's Report on the Characteristics and Uses of the American Walnut Tree which is Called Hickory." *Agricultural History* 19 (1939):58-64.

_____. "Lobelia as a Sure Cure for Venereal Disease." *American Journal of Syphilis, Gonorrhea and Venereal Disease* XXIV (1940):13-22.

_____. "List of Articles by Kalm which Have been Translated and Published by Esther Louise Larsen." *Agricultural History* 17 (1943):172.

_____. "Pehr Kalm's Observations Concerning the Usefulness of the American So-called Cockspur Hawthorn for Quickset Hedges." *Agricultural History* 19 (1945):254-55.

_____. "Pehr Kalm's Observations on the Fences of North America." *Agricultural History* 21 (1947):75-78.

Larsen, Esther Louise. "Peter Kalm, Preceptor." *The Pennsylvania Magazine of History and Biography.* 74 (1950):500-11.

_____. "Peter Kalm's America: The Benefits which England Could Derive from Her Colonies in North America." *Pennsylvania History* 22 (1955): 216-228.

Larson, James L. *Interpreting Nature: The Science of Living Form from Linnaeus to Kant.* Baltimore: The Johns Hopkins University Press: 1994.

Leighton, Ann. *American Gardens in the Eighteenth Century.* Boston: Houghton Mifflin Co., 1976.

Leikola, Anto. "Linnaeus, Kalm and the Finns," A paper delivered at the conference "Thinking through the Environment." Turku University and Abo Akademi, September 16, 2005.

_____. "Exhibition, Pehr Kalm and his Voyage to North America, 1747-1751." Arranged by Helsinki University Library. Helsinki: Government Printing Centre, 1988.

Lindroth, Sten. "The Two Faces of Linnaeus," In Tore Frängsmyr, ed., *Linnaeus: The Man and His Work.* Berkeley: University of California Press, 1983.

Linnaeus, Carl to Kungliga Svenska Vetenskapsakademien. 11 January 1746, L5267. http://linnaeus.c18.net/Letters/letter_list.php, 3 November 2006.

Lockridge, Kenneth A. "Overcoming Nausea: The Brothers Hesselius and the American Mystery." *Common-Place:* http://www.common-place.org/vol-04/no-02/lockridge/., vol. 4., no. 2, January 2004, 3 November 2006.

Lundqvist, S. and R. Moberg. "The Pehr Kalm Herbarium in UPS, a collection of North American Plants," Uppsala, Sweden: The Botanical Museum, Uppsala University, *Thumbergia,* 19 (1993):1-62.

Mackintosh, Michael Dean. "New Sweden, Natives and Nature." In William A. Pencak, and Daniel K. Richter, eds., *Friends and Enemies in Penn's Woods: Indians, Colonists and the Racial Construction of Pennsylvania.* University Park, PA: The Pennsylvania State University Press, 2004.

Mann, Charles C. "The Founding Sachems," *New York Times*, July 4, 2005, p. A17.

Mayr, Ernst. *The Growth of Biological Thought: Diversity, Evolution, and Inheritance.* Cambridge: Belknap Press, 1982.

Mead, William R. *Pehr Kalm: A Finnish Visitor to the Chilterns in 1748.* Trowbridge, Wiltshire: The Cromwell Press, 2003.

Meyers, Amy R.W. and Margaret Beck Pritchard. "Introduction: Toward an Understanding of Catesby," in Amy W. R. Meyers and Margaret Beck Pritchard, eds., *Empire's Nature: Mark Catesby's New World Vision.* Chapel Hill: University of North Carolina Press, 1998.

Miller, Kenneth R. *Finding Darwin's God.* New York: HarperCollins, 1999.

Morgan, Edmund S. *The Genuine Article: A Historian Looks at Early America.* New York: W. W. Norton & Co., 2004.

Morgan, Edmund S. *Benjamin Franklin.* New Haven: Yale University Press, 2002.

Niemelä, Jari. Kalm onkin Gadd! Suomen Sukututkimusseura.
    http://www.genealogia.fi/genos/67/67_22.htm#1#1, 29 November 2006.

_____. *Vain hyödynkö tähden?* Helsinki: Suomen Historiallinen Seura, 1998.

Norman, Hans. "A Swedish Colony in North America," In Rune Ruhnbro, ed., *New Sweden in the New World 1638-1655.* Stockholm: Wiken, 1988.

Pencak, William A. and Daniel K. Richter. *Friends and Enemies in Penn's Woods: Indians, Colonists and the Racial Construction of Pennsylvania.* University Park: The Pennsylvania State University Press, 2004.

Polis, Crystal A. and Robert E. Savage. "Calming John Bartram's Passion: Sweden's Scientific Certification of Philadelphia's Botanist," In Nancy E. Hoffman and John C. Van Horne, eds., *America's Curious Botanist: A Tercentennial Reappraisal of John Bartram 1699-1777.* Philadelphia: The American Philosophical Society, 2004.

Pound, Arthur. *Johnson of the Mohawks.* New York: The Macmillan Company, 1930.

Raskin, N. M. and I. I. Shafranovskii. *Erik Gustavovich Laxmann: Noted Traveler and Naturalist of the 18th Century.* New Delhi: Amerind Publishing Co. Pvt. Ltd., 1978.

Rhodes, Richard. *John James Audubon: The Making of an American.* New York: Alfred A. Knopf, 2004.

Ritterbush, Philip C. *Overtures to Biology: The Speculations of Eighteenth-Century Naturalists.* New Haven: Yale University Press, 1964.

Roberts, Michael. *The Age of Liberty: Sweden 1719-1772.* Cambridge: Cambridge University Press, 1986.

Roger, Jacques. *Buffon: A Life in Natural History.* Translated by Sarah Lucille Bonnefoi and edited by L. Pearce Williams. Ithaca: Cornell University Press, 1997.

Rousseau, Jacques and Guy Béthune. *Voyage de Pehr Kalm au Canada en 1749: Traduction annoté du journal de route.* Montréal: CLF, 1977.

Roy, J.-Edmond. "Voyage de Kalm au Canada." *La Revue du Notariat,* 1900.

Ruhnbro, Rune, ed. *New Sweden in the New World 1638-1655.* Stockholm: Wiken, 1988.

Rydén, Josef. "Johan Printz of New Sweden," In Rune Ruhnbro, ed. *New Sweden in the New World 1638-1655.* Stockholm: Wiken, 1988.

Rystad, Göran. "The Colonization of North America," In Rune Ruhnbro, ed. *New Sweden in the New World 1638-1655.* Stockholm: Wiken, 1988.

St. John de Crèvecoeur, J. Hector. Translated and edited by Percy G. Adams. *Crevecoeur's Eighteenth Century Travels in Pennsylvania and New York.* Lexington: University of Kentucky Press, 1961.

Saunders, Richard H. and Ellen G. Miles, *American Colonial Portraits, 1700-1776.* Washington, D.C.: National Portrait Gallery, Smithsonian Institution, 1987.

Schwartz, Richard B. *Daily Life in Johnson's London.* Madison: The University of Wisconsin Press, 1983.

Skottsberg, Carl, ed. *Pehr Kalms Brev Till Friherre Sten Carl Bielke.* Åbo: Åbo Tidnings och Tryckjeri Aktiebolag, 1960.

Shorto, Russell. *The Island at the Center of the World: The Epic Story of Dutch Manhattan and the Forgotten Colony that Shaped America.* New York: Doubleday, 2004.

Slaughter, Thomas P. *The Natures of John and William Bartram*. New York: Alfred A. Knopf, 1996.

Spady, James O'Neil. "Colonialism and the Discursive Antecedents of *Penn's Treaty with the Indians*," In William A. Pencak and Daniel Richter, eds. *Friends and Enemies in Penn's Woods: Indians, Colonists and the Racial Construction of Pennsylvania*. University Park, PA: The Pennsylvania State University Press, 2004.

Stafleu, Frans A. *Linnaeus and the Linnaeans*. Utrecht, Netherlands: International Association for Plant Taxonomy, 1971.

Starna, William A. "The Diplomatic Career of Canasatego," In William A. Pencak and Daniel Richter, eds. *Friends and Enemies in Penn's Woods: Indians, Colonists and the Racial Construction of Pennsylvania*. University Park, PA: The Pennsylvania State University Press, 2004.

Stearns, Raymond Phineas. *Science in the British Colonies of America*. Urbana: University of Illinois Press, 1970.

Steele, Ian K. *Betrayals: Fort William Henry & the "Massacre."* New York: Oxford University Press, 1990.

Tolles, Frederick B. *James Logan and the Culture of Provincial America*. Boston: Little, Brown and Company, 1957.

Tsubaki, Rosemary. "A Swedish Botanist in the Mohawk Valley in 1750: Pehr Kalm (1716-1779)." unpublished article, personal copy.

Uglow, Jenny. *The Lunar Men: Five Friends whose Curiosity Changed the World*. New York: Farrar, Straus and Giroux, 2002.

Wade, Mason. "The French and the Indians." In Howard Peckham and Charles Gibson, eds. *Attitudes of Colonial Powers toward the American Indian*. Salt Lake City: University of Utah Press, 1969.

Waldron, Richard. "New Sweden: An Interpretation," In Joyce Goodfriend, ed., *Revisiting New Netherland: Perspectives on Early Dutch America*; Leiden: Brill, 2005.

Weslager, Clinton Alfred. *The Log Cabin in America: From Pioneer Days to the Present*. New Brunswick, NJ: Rutgers University Press, 1969.

Wilford, John Noble. *The Mapmakers*. New York: Alfred A. Knopf, 1981.

Wilson, James. *The Earth Shall Weep: A History of Native America*. New York: Atlantic Monthly Press, 1999.

Wuorinen, John H. *A History of Finland*. New York: Columbia University Press, 1965.

_____. *The Finns on the Delaware 1638-1655: An Essay in American Colonial History*. New York: Columbia University Press, 1938.

Ziman, John. *Reliable Knowledge: An Exploration of the Grounds for Belief in Science*. Cambridge: Cambridge University Press (1978) 1996.

Index

Purple Mountain Press, established in 1973, publishes books of colonial history and books about New York State. Under its Harbor Hill imprint, it also publishes maritime books and distributes the maritime books of Carmania Press (London).

For a free catalog, write Purple Mountain Press, PO Box 309, Fleischmanns, NY 12430-0309, or call 800-325-2665, or fax 845-254-4476, or email purple@catskill.net.

Visit us on the web at www.catskill.net/purple.